The Feminist Challenge
to the Canadian Left, 1900-1918

In this stud_ _anadian
socialist mc_ _timate
decline of f_ _e, the
Socialist Pa_

Newton _ _sed a
radical chal_ _vomen
fought to be_ _vomen's
issues, inclu_ _y, and
women's su_ _ective
on these iss_ _in the
women's mc_

Broadenir_ _Newton
analyses the_ _– the
Canadian Le_ _d draws
conclusions_ _gender
characteristi_

JANICE NEW_ _ork
University.

The Feminist Challenge to the Canadian Left, 1900-1918

JANICE NEWTON

McGill-Queen's University Press
Montreal & Kingston • London • Buffalo

© McGill-Queen's University Press 1995
ISBN 0-7735-1262-4 (cloth)
ISBN 0-7735-1291-8 (paper)

Legal deposit first quarter 1995
Bibliothèque nationale du Québec

Printed in Canada on acid-free paper

This book has been published with the help of
grants from the Social Science Federation of Canada,
using funds provided by the Social Sciences and
Humanities Research Council of Canada, and from
the Faculty of Arts, York University.

McGill-Queen's University Press is grateful to the Canada
Council for support of its publishing program.

Canadian Cataloguing in Publication Data

Newton, Janice, 1952–
  The feminist challenge to the Canadian Left :
  1900–1918
  Includes bibliographical references and index.
  ISBN 0-7735-1262-4 (bound) –
  ISBN 0-7735-1291-8 (pbk.)
  1. Women and socialism – Canada – History –
  20th century. 2. Women in politics – Canada – History –
  20th century. 3. Feminism – Canada – History.
  I. Title.
  HQ1453.N496 1995   335'.0052   C94-900808-7

Typeset in Sabon 10.5/12
by Caractéra production graphique, Quebec City

Contents

Illustrations

Acknowledgments

My interest and enthusiasm for this subject was kindled in the late 1970s, and I am indebted to a number of people who have helped me in the intervening years. I thank Philip Cercone of McGill-Queen's University Press for the wonderful ongoing support and commitment he has offered to this project. The conscientious and able research assistance of Jennifer McRea-Logie and Samantha Arnold was invaluable. I am also indebted to my feminist writing group, including Karen Dubinsky, Ruth Frager, Franca Iacovetta, Lynne Marks, Susan Prentice, Joan Sangster, Carolyn Strange, Mariana Valverde, and Cynthia Wright. While reviewing previous versions of the manuscript, their collective support, humour, and wisdom kept me mindful of the pleasures of this work and its significance to feminist research in Canada. I am especially grateful to Ruth Frager for her generous sharing of sources and for her friendship, and to Susan Prentice for her support and insights. I have valued the sage advice, encouragement, and feedback offered by my York colleague Patricia McDermott. I also want to thank Carlotta Lemieux for the skill and grace she brought to the editing of this book. She has been a delight to work with.

Two people deserve special mention. I thank Dr Lieba Lesk for the clarity, consistency, and compassion she shared with me throughout the process. Finally, I thank my dear friend Dr Mimi Divinsky for the invaluable ways her friendship sustained me throughout my work on this book.

*The Feminist Challenge
to the Canadian Left, 1900-1918*

CHAPTER ONE

Introduction

The resurgence of feminism in the early 1970s created shock waves across Canadian society that can be felt to this day. One of its results was a growing interest in women's history, which initially focused on the struggle of women around the turn of the century to gain the right to vote. As historians explored the development of the suffrage movement, they discovered a broad range of issues that had engaged the feminists of that period. The focus on suffrage contributed to the idea that these feminists had been involved in a worthy historical cause. But their ideas for improving women's lives do not seem relevant to contemporary women. After all, we won the vote.

A different understanding of feminism emerges if one shifts attention to the women of the Canadian socialist movement. Canadian socialists criticized the growing inequities of Canadian society and the capitalist wage system, which they believed was its root cause. In addition, the women socialists challenged the havoc that capitalism wrought on women's lives. While many of them believed in the goal of women's suffrage, they also wanted broad and significant changes that would improve the position of women in Canadian society. As they struggled to articulate the distinct interests of women from a socialist perspective, they grew suspicious of the middle-class bias of the established women's movement. Like their middle-class sisters, they found themselves drawn into politics in unprecedented ways, yet their political convictions, class background, or ethnic heritage often made them unwelcome or uncomfortable within the ranks of middle-class women's organizations or mainstream political parties. Thus, instead of working through such groups, they threw their support behind Canada's newly emerging socialist movement. In exploring the challenges these women faced as they became politically active, this book contributes to our understanding of the remarkable growth of the prewar left.

Why should we care to know more about these socialist women? Some might argue that socialism has been thoroughly discredited by the demise of Communist regimes around the world. Yet these turn-of-the-century women presented a view of socialism that is distinct from today's collapsing Communist regimes. They envisaged a socialism in which the concerns of both sexes would be equal and in which democratic processes would be central. It might also be argued that the socialist women were too few in number and influence to be significant – and they were indeed a minority in socialist ranks. But an analysis of their unique views can broaden our understanding of the complexities of turn-of-the-century feminism. Another objection might be that the demands and concerns of turn-of-the-century feminists no longer speak to us.

To assess these arguments, this book will examine the three largest English-speaking socialist organizations in the years preceding World War I. While these organizations were part of a growing international socialist movement, they had distinctive roots in the economic and social realities of the Canadian context, and the aspects of them that were of significance to women will therefore be briefly discussed.[1] The first was the Canadian Socialist League (CSL), a loose federation of socialist locals, which was formed in 1898 and flourished briefly for a few years. Each local was permitted to set its own program as long as the program was consistent with "socialist principles." These principles were never sharply defined, but members embraced the ethical and social concerns reminiscent of the early British socialist movement and the American socialist movement.[2] Women's activities flourished under this flexible arrangement. Women supported local organizations, joined executive committees, and wrote for the CSL's newspaper. In turn, the CSL supported specific propaganda efforts directed at women. Most notably, it was the first political organization in Canada to nominate a woman for legislative office. By 1902, the CSL had expanded to sixty locals across Canada, but it was soon eclipsed by the success of another party in British Columbia.

From a variety of small splinter groups, the Socialist Party of Canada (SPC) was taking root in British Columbia, finding support among miners, loggers, and urban working-class communities in Vancouver and Victoria.[3] As in the CSL, women were active in a variety of roles; but unlike the CSL, the SPC was more explicitly Marxist in its program. It was dedicated to educating the working class to the need for a socialist transformation of the economic system. Its brief platform called for:

1 The transformation, as rapidly as possible, of capitalist property in the means of wealth production (natural resources, factories, mills, railways, etc.) into the collective property of the working class.
2 Thorough and democratic organization and management of industry by the workers.
3 The establishment, as speedily as possible, of production for use instead of production for profit.[4]

Eager to distinguish itself from other more moderate pro-labour parties, the SPC included no specific immediate demands that did not "advance the interests of the working class and aid the workers in their class struggle against capitalism." The party feared that focus on other reforms would deflect the working class from a socialist agenda, but working-class interests were narrowly defined as the waged-labour relationship, or the relationship between "masters and slaves."

Concurrent with this rejection of reforms, the party also abandoned women's suffrage. Yet the label "impossibilist party" did not deter the SPC from gaining in popularity over the more moderate CSL. Many of its leading supporters had a long history of working for radical and labour organizations, but they expressed disgust for traditional political parties and labour leaders, whom they felt had sold out the cause of the working class. In 1903 the socialists gained 8 per cent of the popular vote in British Columbia, electing James Hawthornthwaite to the provincial legislature.[5] Socialists across Canada viewed this achievement as affirmation of the party's political agenda. Within a year, the CSL disbanded, and many of its members joined with British Columbian socialists to form the Socialist Party of Canada.

For a time, the SPC dominated the left in Canada. The Dominion Executive Committee exercised centralized control from British Columbia, authorizing the affiliation of locals from across the country. Yet several issues engendered discontent: the demand for greater autonomy for ethnic locals; the role of the national executive over local organizations; affiliation with the Second International; and short-term electoral demands in the party's platform. Discontent festered in pockets across Canada, but it was not until 1911 that another national party was formed, the Social Democratic Party of Canada (SDPC). Its members retained a commitment to educate Canadian workers to "a consciousness of their class position in society" and to "organize them into a political party to seize the reigns of government and transform all capitalist property into the collective property of the working class." But the SDPC was also willing to consider specific electoral reforms, including the demand for women's suffrage. A mark of the party's popularity in the years before World War I is that its paper, *Cotton's Weekly*, became the largest-selling socialist newspaper in Canada and the thirtieth-largest paper in the country.[6]

Despite their differences, the three socialist organizations shared two common assumptions about women's issues. First, they firmly believed that capitalism was to blame for the problems facing women, and they struggled to articulate the devastating impact it had on the lives of women as Canada entered the twentieth century. Second, they agreed with feminists that women's political activism would be shaped by their concern for maternal and domestic duties. Despite inconsistencies and contradictions, through these two assumptions the socialist movement gave a unique perspective to debates over the "woman question."

This book contributes four important dimensions to our perception of the prewar years. First, it provides a missing link in our understanding of the growth of the early socialist movement. The birth of Canadian socialism has been chronicled elsewhere, but with the exception of the Finnish socialists in Canada, the major monographs have failed to address the role that women played in building and shaping the movement.[7] This book establishes that women played distinct and significant roles in building the early socialist movement in Canada and that women's issues were a factor in the organizational development of the movement. Second, the book challenges the common assumption that only middle-class women had the leisure to engage in politics. Despite significant constraints, a complex of social, familial, and ethnic bonds drew working-class and radical women into politics, though their political activities have often been obscured in historical records. Third, this book introduces a small but significant contingent of feminists who were active within the ranks of the socialist movement, proving that socialist feminism has a heritage that dates from the turn of the century in Canada.[8]

The fourth and final contribution is less direct but perhaps most important. These feminists did not scorn the domestic sphere; rather, they struggled to understand how socialism might transform both the private and public worlds: the home; relations between men and women; and the waged-labour relationship. Their debates about the transformation of the domestic realm are most striking.

They shared a belief in the maternal role of women, but they did not simply mimic the views of the women's movement. I believe this compels us to reassess our understanding of turn-of-the-century feminism. To explain this point, let us briefly review some of the debates on the subject, which, to date, have been dominated by analysis of the suffrage movement.

In 1950 the first major monograph on the suffrage movement in Canada was published by Catherine Cleverdon.[9] This pioneering work chronicled the political battles of the mainstream suffrage organizations. Cleverdon cast the suffrage movement in a liberal, progressive light, as part of the slow but steady evolution of democracy, though she expressed disappointment at the pace of change. Historians of the 1970s returning to the study of suffrage also were disappointed that the vote did not lead to greater change. How can one account for this "failure"? Initially, suffragists were blamed on two counts: the social character of the movement and the inherent weakness of its ideology. In social terms, the suffragists were seen as a group of middle- and upper-class women of British heritage. With leaders such as Nellie McClung and Lady Aberdeen, their aim was to win the right to vote, not to transform society or broaden political participation to include other classes and races. This emphasis on the social characteristics of suffragists cast them as narrow and inherently conservative. Carol Bacchi's *Liberation Deferred?* typifies this approach and remains the most significant monograph on the suffrage movement in Canada since Cleverdon's book. Her conclusions are emphatic. Canadian suffragists were middle class and nonradical: they could not have effected a radical challenge to the political system because "the majority never had a revolution in mind."[10]

Bacchi's research and conclusions have come under considerable criticism. No one has seriously disputed the idea that the suffrage leadership was predominantly middle class. These women were assumed to be privileged with free time to engage in social clubs and political lobbying. Whether the suffragists allowed their class interests to override the bonds of sisterhood is a matter of dispute. Forbes, for example, demonstrates that in at least one context, middle-class women of Halifax appreciated and defended the needs of working-class women. They established a women's employment bureau and initiated a campaign for technical education. Forbes also argues that the suffragists held radical beliefs about women's equality but that they strategically resorted to moderate public arguments in order to diffuse opposition and criticism.[11] Hale's research on the British Columbian suffragists supports Bacchi's argument that the middle-class suffragists initially approached working-class women in a philanthropic manner, offering social reforms *for* working-class women. Later, they came to appreciate that working-class women should decide for themselves how best to use the ballot.[12] Recent research has revealed that class loyalty was paramount for the prominent radical suffragist, Dr Emily Stowe. Bacchi characterizes her as a radical feminist, but Stowe broke the bonds of sisterhood with a patient, the domestic servant Sara Ann Lovell, when she disclosed Lovell's abortion request to her employer.[13] In the name of serving the best interests of all women, suffragists often succeeded. However, they often also served their own class and their own racial and ethnic interests. On balance, however, evidence to challenge Bacchi's characterization of the class character of the Canadian suffrage movement is fragmentary.

Other countries have been more advanced in producing detailed local studies that demonstrate the diversity of the suffrage movement and its supporters. In Britain and the United States, for example, although the initial research on suffrage presented the movement as dominated by white middle-class women, more recent research has revealed that working-class and non-white women also were involved. Fragments of evidence suggest that similar patterns may have been true in Canada, but this is only beginning to be integrated into overviews of the suffrage movement. The leading example of such an integrated history is found in *Canadian Women*, where Prentice and her co-authors mention several black women who were active in supporting women's suffrage, though they offer no analysis of the significance of ethnicity and race in the fight for suffrage. Given the importance of the abolitionist movement in the early stages of the American suffrage movement, one wonders how much it influenced suffragists in Canada.[14] Clearly, there is a need for more local and regional research into the social character of the supporters of suffrage, beyond the institutionalized national organizations, before we can make reliable generalizations. Nevertheless, the existing research does suggest that at the national institutional level the Canadian suffrage movement was dominated by white middle-class women and that there was minimal participation from other classes and ethnic groups. At best, the suffrage movement had an ambivalent legacy in relation to working-class women.[15]

Beyond the class and social character of the suffragists, the ideology of suffrage has come under careful scrutiny. Linda Kealey argues that although some suffragists used egalitarian arguments to defend women's autonomy and an increased public role for women, most suffragists believed in "maternal feminism." They shared "the conviction that woman's special role as mother gives her the duty and the right to participate in the public sphere. It is not her position as wife and mother that qualifies her for the task of reform, but the special nurturing qualities which are common to all women, married or not." This belief in women's special maternal role (not women's autonomy) explained their nonradicalism: "Women were the group touted as the social group capable of initiating social change, while at the same time their biological rationale doomed them to a restrictive social role based on home and family. Any element of radical criticism in their social thought disappeared under the very weight of 'maternal feminism.'"[16] Wayne Roberts agrees that the radicalism inherent in the suffrage movement's ideal of "self-fulfilment and equality" was ultimately undermined. His evidence points to the pivotal role of the emerging middle-class women's professions, which failed to carve out autonomous roles for women and instead relegated them to a subordinate status within male-dominated hierarchies. Like Kealey and Bacchi, Roberts sees the radical potential of the suffrage movement crushed under "stultifying definitions of motherhood."[17]

Valverde's study of the social purity reformers sheds further critical light on the racist underpinnings of the ideology of maternal feminism. Although she does not focus on suffragists, she convincingly demonstrates that the rhetoric of the social purity reformers to "mother the race" implied specific and hierarchical relationships for different racial and ethnic groups.[18] This mode of analysis might fruitfully be applied to the suffragists. Certainly, there has so far been little secondary evidence that the suffragists consistently challenged the racist implications of the maternal feminism espoused by social purity reformers. This would have implications for class as well, because many racist ideas were directed at the new immigrants who occupied the bottom rungs of the class hierarchy.

More recently, scholars have tempered the critical scrutiny of suffragists. *Canadian Women* emphasizes the radicalism inherent in the feminist stand against patriarchy.[19] Despite the dominance of middle-class women, suffragists represented a radical challenge to Canadian society because they challenged man's domination of women. Strong-Boag argues that the suffragists claimed the vote on two grounds: their maternal role and the natural justice of extending the franchise. By claiming the full rights of citizenship and challenging men's dominance in the public sphere, they also undermined men's domination of women in the private sphere.[20] In contrast to the preceding arguments, Strong-Boag acknowledges the class-bound limitations of the movement while emphasizing the radicalism inherent in the suffragists' gendered critique of society and their focus on domestic issues.

At the core of these different versions of the suffrage movement is the controversy over the ideological basis of turn-of-the-century feminism, which was dominated by a concern with woman's domestic and maternal role and was limited by its specific assumptions about both class and race. Some argue that maternal feminism was inherently limited because it did not oppose the restriction of women to the domestic sphere. Others describe it as radical because it expanded woman's sphere into the political realm. Still others argue that a focus on domestic issues allowed women to resist men's domination in the domestic realm. These polarizations of egalitarian feminism and maternal feminism have outlived their usefulness. Although this book cannot resolve these controversies over the class or feminist character of the suffrage movement, it can explore feminist views in a decidedly different class context. The results will compel us to reconceptualize the meaning of feminism in the pre-suffrage years.

The simultaneous idealization and denigration of women's work – and mothering is often seen as a central component of women's work – has been a striking and pervasive development in twentieth-century culture which we must view with scepticism. From the outset, I reject the notion that a concern for maternal or domestic issues is inherently nonradical. Just as the working class shapes its own existence in a specific context, socialist women framed their own political mobilization in a way that reflected the realities and experiences of their lives. Their activism was built on their pride and concern for women's work within the home. There is nothing inherently nonradical about that concern for, as we shall see, a small core of feminist women within the socialist movement accepted maternal feminism and turned it to radical ends, making the home a primary site for radical socialist transformation to enhance the autonomy of women. Not only did they use it to claim their rightful place in politics, as did the suffragists, but they challenged their comrades to advocate a socialist restructuring of domestic work and mothering, just as socialists advocated a socialist restructuring of the factory. Their radicalism was not liberal, even though they sometimes espoused the values of equal citizenship, autonomy, and self-fulfilment, and they never confronted the racism that pervaded this era of nation building. They focused on domestic and maternal roles, as did other feminists, but their vision was distinct from the feminism of their liberal and middle-class contemporaries. They wanted nothing less than the socialist transformation of women's domestic and maternal roles.

This radical feminist voice did not prevail within the socialist movement. To account for this failure, we need not turn exclusively to idealist arguments about the inherent weaknesses of the ideal of the family wage or maternal feminism, for the struggle for ideological pre-eminence was contested in an arena that was already heavily weighted in favour of men. Men dominated politics in general; they dominated the party executives and the editorial positions, and they infused masculine dominance into the social atmosphere of the left. This is about the exercise of power over real structures as much as it is about power embedded in ideology and discourse. Thus, a factor of major importance is that the processes by which women raised their voices were stifled in the nascent stages of building the socialist movement. This process of struggle, accommodation, and suppression of socialist women will deepen our understanding of turn-of-the-century feminism and the challenges women faced as they became politically active.

In the following chapter, we look at the lives of several women who made significant contributions to the early left. This exploration of their lives will reveal how diverse class, ethnic, and political commitments shaped women's activities. Chapter 3 examines the gendered nature of the political and social setting that framed the participation of women. As noted above, the political culture of the left was profoundly male-dominated, and this posed significant constraints for women. Sometimes they successfully challenged these constraints, but more often they carved out legitimate space for themselves within them.

The succeeding four chapters focus on the different themes that animated socialist debates on the "woman question": the home, paid work, sexuality, and politics. Chapter 4 discusses the debates on the socialist transformation of woman's workplace, the home. These debates provide crucial insights into socialist views on some related issues. Some people saw the factory as the prime site for socialist transformation. Others regarded the home as an equally important site: they contended that socialism would do as much to transform the home as the factory, through collectivized and socialized labour.

Chapter 5 looks at the attention given by the socialists to the plight of the wage-earning woman who could not afford the luxury of working in her own home and was forced to enter the labour market to support herself and her family. Chapter 6 explores the socialists' considerable concern about problems related to sexuality, the foremost among these being prostitution and the threat of "white slavery." Socialist views on suffrage and on woman's role in political life are examined in chapter 7. Finally, chapter 8 chronicles the left's fragmentation during World War I and looks at the impact the war had on women's issues within the left. Although a number of important contradictions run through the socialist debates during these years, one point is clear: these issues cannot be understood in isolation from one another. If we are to hope to understand the socialists' views on suffrage, we must see them in the context of socialist views on women in the home and in the labour force, and in relation to sexuality.

While recognizing the connection between social issues, the early socialist women were not exclusively concerned with the destructive impact that capitalism had on women's lives. They had the optimism and breadth of vision to believe that a different kind of world was possible through a socialist agenda. This is not to suggest that heroines or magical solutions will be found in these pages. Socialist women did not speak with one voice, and they often reflected the prejudices of the era. They were divided by class, ethnicity, and political conviction, and like many of their contemporaries, they often used these distinctions to advance their own interests at the expense of others. Some used the privileges and distinctions of class to challenge one another, for not all socialists were working class. Some used the conventions of masculinity and femininity to carve out legitimate space in the socialist arena. Others used ethnicity or race to defend or attack particular positions. Within such a context, socialist women were vastly outnumbered and sometimes silenced by their male comrades. All of this reduced the feminist vision within the socialist movement.

Yet this book is not simply a tale of the loss of a feminist voice within the early socialist movement. Throughout, I have emphasized the importance of the *process* of continual struggle and accommodation embedded in the forging of a political movement. The feminists of the left who appear in these pages are neither anachronistic nor a mere historical fluke; their views sprang from an effort to understand the world in which they found themselves. They were among the many contenders in the political arena competing for pre-eminence in the minds of voters at the turn of the century. What concerns us is the process by which their views either survived or languished. There is nothing inevitable or foregone about that process, however weighted the odds may have been against feminist views being seriously considered. It was a process of struggle on the part of women and men who used the tools at hand to advance their particular vision of what a better world would look like. This book is intended to deepen our understanding of that process.

Socialist women vied with others for the right to define the socialist agenda, and in their voices we find an impressive breadth of vision. With courage and foresight they confronted many of the social forces that were transforming Canadian life. They were critical of the privileges of class, but they also wanted to forge a political movement that spoke directly to the concerns of women. They believed that socialism could challenge capitalism and at the same time help to build a new world for men and women, a world free of domination and exploitation – in the bedroom, in the kitchen, in the factory, in Parliament, and in their own movement.

This vision kindles our imagination, for today's feminists struggle with the same issues. In the home, feminists challenge the division of domestic labour and the brutality of wife assault; in the labour force, they challenge sexual harassment and job discrimination; in sexual relations, they confront the realities of pornography, prostitution, and sexual assault; and in the political arena, they struggle to make their voices heard. Like their historical predecessors, today's feminists grapple with the connections between these problems. The plight of the battered woman is related to economic dependence; economic dependence is rooted in the injustices of the labour market; these injustices are reinforced by sexual harassment on the job; and the lack of political will to change all this reveals the absence of women's voices in the halls of power. Far from our having won the battle, the issues raised by these turn-of-the-century feminists are still with us. Their vision of a better world still has the power to capture our imagination.

CHAPTER TWO

The Political Roots
of Women's Radicalism

In a 1909 article, "For Plain Women," Mary Cotton Wisdom described a political meeting of four women from the Eastern Townships of Quebec; two were writers, one was a society woman and one a home body. Hinting at the tension they felt on becoming involved in political matters for the first time, Wisdom began with a vehement disclaimer, stating that they were not meeting to discuss styles, gossip, men, or each other's clothes. As a measure of their serious-mindedness, Wisdom assured her readers, the ladies wore simple shirt waists, plain hats, and short skirts because of the rain. They earnestly discussed matters in which "all women" should be interested: "signs of the times, the economic questions of the day, the old age pensions, the poverty and crime around us," and they left with plans to establish a group "to study ways and means, to help remedy if we can by our united or single efforts the appalling conditions with which we are surrounded."[1] In this brief description, we catch a glimpse of the compelling sense of urgency that drew these women into political action, an urgency arising from their perception of the "appalling" social problems they saw around them. We are also alerted to their sense of discomfort at venturing into a man's terrain – politics. Political action, even in such a mild form, required them to affirm both their sense of femininity and their serious intent. In the overt need to describe themselves as feminine but not frivolous, one can appreciate the challenges some women must have faced in their efforts to recast and legitimize women's identity and concerns in the political arena.

Were these four typical of the kind of women who helped shape the Canadian left? Unfortunately, the historical record provides scant and sometimes conflicting information about women socialists. Estimates about the numbers of women active on the left varied widely. Even within different parties, local branches reported varying levels of participation; some reported 50 per cent female membership, while others announced the exceptional presence of women at meetings or the first women to join a local. In the context of the debates over the role of women within socialism, disparate estimates were embellished for political gain. For example, the editor of the *Western Clarion*, the official SPC paper, stated that women were few and that they joined merely because certain men did. A more specific estimate claimed that not one in ten members of the Socialist Party was a woman. Some women may have participated in socialist events but never bothered to pay dues or actually join a party. The Canadian evidence, including photographs of these early events, suggests that women did participate in significant numbers.[2]

Some of these different estimates are related to the ethnic composition of the locals, since the numbers of women varied widely within different ethnic groups. Finnish socialists, for example, not only encouraged them to join and provided separate branches for women and children, but evidence suggests that they had higher participation rates of women than any other local socialist organizations.[3] One account of Toronto locals described the Finnish branch as the largest branch, with many women participating; the Jewish branch as having "a number of earnest women who take an active part in the branch affairs"; and the English branch as too exclusive, lazy, and the worst of all: "The English speaking branch has some [women] but they are all so retiring, you know. They attend meetings fairly well, but there is only one that ever says anything, yet when she does it is well worth hearing." Brief mention was also made of women participating in the Italian local.[4] Despite these estimates, further research is needed in the foreign-language socialist press and archives for a generalization to be made with greater certainty. One can estimate, however, that women probably never exceeded 10 per cent of the membership of the left. Their small numbers doubtless inhibited their ability to influence a male-dominated movement.

Male English-speaking socialists predominated in the leadership of key left-wing organizations such as the Canadian Socialist League (CSL), the Socialist Party of Canada (SPC), and the Social Democratic Party of Canada (SDPC). Members distributed English-language party papers, such as the *Western Clarion* and *Cotton's Weekly*, across Canada. Most women socialists identified in this press were married.[5] Of the few wage-earning women mentioned, Jewish garment workers were prominent, especially in such large cities as Montreal, Toronto, Winnipeg, and Edmonton.[6] Although a high percentage of Finnish women participated in the labour force and in Finnish socialist organizations, they were seldom acknowledged in the English left-wing press, though they were vocal in the Finnish left-wing press. The dual demands of employment and domestic responsibilities, compounded by barriers of language and ethnicity, no doubt helped to mute wage-earning socialist women; in the national English-language socialist press, their voices were rarely heard or their presence noted. Most of the women who were active and vocal were homemakers primarily engaged in unpaid domestic labour. In this, they reflected the pattern of the general population, for although higher percentages of women worked in the larger urban centres, the majority of women at this time did not work for wages. Those who did so were usually young and single.[7] This profile of woman as homemaker, not wage earner, is important to keep in mind while examining the concerns that women expressed as they became politically active.

It is difficult to make extensive generalizations about the other "plain women" who joined socialist organizations. If men were the subject under consideration, the task would be easier, for the left-wing press often published biographies of socialist men, describing their political and social backgrounds. In the case of Roscoe Fillmore, a man active in the Socialist Party of Canada, there is a full biography written by his grandson. Unfortunately, no similar biographies were published on women socialists, and even recent biographies of male socialists seldom cast light on the activities or concerns of the women.[8] However, by combing the available sources, we can piece together brief biographical sketches of some of the more prominent women whose names recurred in the pages of the English left-wing press and at socialist gatherings, executive meetings, and party conventions. As others have observed, issues of life-cycle, familial, and social relationships, and social norms and conventions have often shaped women's lives; this is true of these socialist women, too.[9] However, as their lives begin to take shape and form, we can discern several key issues that animated their political activism at the turn of the century. Through the details of their lives, we can also begin to appreciate the profound challenges they faced in becoming politically active and in consolidating women's presence and interests within the left.

Several women distinguished themselves in the earliest socialist organization, the Canadian Socialist League. Edith Wrigley, wife of George Wrigley,[10] edited the women's column in *Citizen and Country*, a Toronto newspaper that supported the CSL. She was also the

Ontario superintendent for temperance in Sunday schools in the Woman's Christian Temperance Union (WCTU).[11] Her column, "The Kingdom of the Home," appeared only briefly, but in it she raised issues that echoed the concerns of the women's organizations of the time: suffrage, charity, prohibition, intemperance, war, the servant problem, prostitution, and immorality.[12] She specifically urged the members of the WCTU to subscribe to the paper, and she headlined a theme that was characteristic of maternal feminism – that the values of the home sphere (love and purity) should become the guiding principles in the political realm.

Then there was Margaret Haile, who was propelled into the spotlight when the CSL nominated her as its candidate for North Toronto in the provincial election of 1902. Her campaign met with opposition from various quarters. When her opponents at one meeting failed to prevent her from speaking, some of the audience walked out. The labour paper, the *Toiler*, refused to endorse her candidacy, and some politicians challenged her right as a woman to contest the election, but they were unable to prevent her name from appearing on the ballot. According to the *Citizen and Country*, Haile became the first woman in the British Empire to run for elected office, garnering eighty-one votes for the CSL in her riding. Weston Wrigley credited women who helped in the campaign with contributing to this socialist "success."[13]

According to the *Citizen and Country*, Margaret Haile was born in Canada and had been a socialist for many years. She spent time in the New England states working for the Connecticut Socialist Labor Party and for the Massachusetts Socialist Party, and she acted as delegate to the 1902 Socialist Party convention that nominated Eugene Debs for president. As well, Haile edited the first women's column in an English-language socialist publication in the United States.[14] Her commitment to socialism stemmed from her experience in the WCTU. Mari Jo Buhle describes her as one of those socialist women who "still clung to the notion of the home as a traditional source of woman's power [and to] domesticity as a special feminine preserve."[15] Some evidence of these attitudes emerged during her Ontario election campaign. She held several public meetings in which she raised the issue of sex equality in the political and economic spheres while stressing woman's unique qualities. The threat of sexual exploitation and prostitution gave women far greater reasons than men for needing socialism, for "when a man is unemployed ... in desperation he commits suicide. Woman out of employment too frequently stands upon a precipice far more dreadful than that of suicide."[16] In her Canadian writings,

Socialist
Candidates For the
Ontario Legislature.

Toronto Branches Ontario Socialist League.

To the Electors of Toronto :

JAMES SIMPSON,
Socialist Candidate For East Toronto.

THE Socialists of Toronto have nominated candidates to contest the constituencies of East, West, North and South Toronto, in recognition of the fact that no matter how many issues may be raised by capitalist politicians to confuse unthinking minds, there is but one real fundamental issue before the workers of Canada to-day—that of SOCIALISM vs. CAPITALISM.

Socialists recognize that two classes exist in society to-day, the class that produces the wealth and the class that appropriates it —the working class and the capitalist class. On the side of Capitalism are arrayed both Liberal and Conservative parties, representing all those whose interest it is to maintain and perpetuate the present system which enables them to live upon the labor of others ; together with a lot of well-meaning people who vainly imagine that the present industrial system can be patched up a little and made to answer the purpose. On the side of Socialism stands the Socialist Party, representing the organized demand of the wage-working class for a socialist system of industry, in which the principle of co-operation shall take the place of the present competitive warfare.

The Liberal and Conservative parties are but the two wings of the Capitalist party, which stands for competition The Socialist party stands for co-operation. The Liberal and Conservative party organizations receive large donations from wealthy corporations and individuals who desire special privileges from the Government. The Socialist party is supported by the wage-workers themselves. Some honest and independent men may be nominated and elected by the old parties to give an air of respectability, but when the party whip cracks they must fall into line or be hounded to political death. R. L. Richardson's career illustrates this fact.

So long as the workers continue to send their employers to Parliament to legislate for them, they need not be surprised if Factory Acts are unenforced, sweat-shops multiply, women and children are allowed to work long hours in unsanitary conditions, and if such acts as old age pensions, adopted in other countries, are unheard of here. Nor is it surprising that laws are enacted requiring certain property qualifications in aldermen and mayors, which practically bar out working people from participating in the government of our municipalities.

The Socialist candidates are the only advocates of woman suffrage ; and in order to emphasize their belief in the right of women to take part in the making of the laws under which they have to live, they have nominated a woman as candidate for North Toronto. We trust that no advocate of woman suffrage in this district will fail to record his vote in favor of the first woman candidate for the legislature in Canada.

The Socialist Party is the only one which has a clearly-defined policy regarding the liquor traffic, viz., that so long as this traffic exists it should be under public ownership and control, and that at any time, the people can, through the system of direct legislation, which is also one of the planks of their platform, decide whether or not it shall continue.

The Socialist Party is fighting the political battle of organized labor. At the last meeting of the Canadian Trades and Labor Congress the Canadian Socialist League was commended for its co-operation with the labor movement. It recognizes that trades unionism can be made a power in the movement for the emancipation of labor if its members will strike at the ballot box.

Read our platform carefully, compare it with the Liberal or Conservative literature, and ask your-selves whether this is not the party which deserves your votes and your support.

S. A. CORNER,
Socialist Candidate For South Toronto. | MARGARET HAILE,
Socialist Candidate For North Toronto. | JOHN A. KELLY,
Socialist Candidate For West Toronto.

Ontario Socialist League's election platform

she often used the differences between men and women, rather than equality-based arguments, to argue for radical social change.

Is it surprising that such women as Haile and Wrigley could have both an affiliation with women's organizations and a commitment to socialism? Women's organizations such as the WCTU, the missionary societies, the YWCA, and the National Council of Women provided a growing venue for women's participation in social and political reform in the late nineteenth and early twentieth centuries.[17] On several counts, they would have attracted some women with socialist leanings; but on other counts, some socialist women might have been uncomfortable in their ranks.

What made women establish these organizations and what caused other women to join them? Religious and evangelical convictions, or a concern that the churches were not living up to Christian ideals, was often foremost. Christian beliefs had prominent roots in many women's organizations and in radical organizations and working-class movements. Towards the end of the nineteenth century, theological controversy and concern over social and economic conditions in Canada led to the increasing secularization of religious thought and the growth of demands for social reform. Several prominent individuals active in the British and Canadian left had their intellectual roots in this Christian tradition.[18] So, too, did many women's groups. The main tenet of Christian reform was the belief that Christians ought to apply Christian values to existing social conditions in order to realize the "Kingdom of Heaven here on earth." Some church-based reformers endorsed activism on women's issues such as women's suffrage, equal pay for women, access to education, and improved factory laws. Although women's missionary societies afforded women greater autonomy than the male-dominated churches did, overall women were constrained by traditional roles. Bacchi argues that the "radical feminists who challenged sex stereotyping usually moved outside the traditional churches."[19]

Religious or evangelical convictions did not prevent women's organizations from taking up secular issues such as reform of social conditions. The YWCA, for example, blended evangelical Christianity with attempts to house working-class young women in urban centres and to institute domestic science in the school curriculum. The WCTU, though widely associated with the campaign to abolish drinking, also became involved in women's suffrage, anti-smoking, and social purity.[20] Religious or evangelical conviction was often crucial in its own right, even as it legitimized women's activities in these more public spheres. While it may not have been their primary agenda at the outset, these women's organizations played an important role in fostering women's radicalization. They challenged the restriction of women to domestic life, educated women in social issues, eased their transition into politics, and provided training in basic political skills such as public speaking and parliamentary procedures. Women who might otherwise have shunned political or reform activities could exercise autonomy from male control and could enjoy the comfort of female companionship and organization while receiving practical training in the political process. These skills could readily be transferred to radical organizations.

Women's organizations also publicized the "woman question": Was woman's place within the home, or did women have a rightful role to exercise in the public sphere? As articulated at the time, there were two dimensions to this question. The first was the focus on a range of social and political issues that affected women in particular (for example, temperance, prostitution, urban reform, regulation of working conditions for women, and education for women). The presence of women speaking out on these matters raised a more fundamental question concerning women's place in the modern world, and thus women's political activity became the second dimension to the woman question. Women's organizations used equal-rights arguments as well as maternal feminism to legitimize woman's place in the public sphere, though the latter prevailed. They believed that "women were endowed with special qualities and virtues; that they were, in general, morally superior to men; and that as a result of their nurturing and mothering roles, they had the qualities which now needed to be applied to the public life of the nation."[21] Rooted in the experiences of women within the home, maternal feminism was a persuasive form of argument in the context of the times, overshadowing more egalitarian claims for the expansion of women's rights and more radical claims for the transformation of women's role in the home and in society at large. Domestic concerns shaped women's lives, even the lives of working-class women and those who worked for pay. The development of a more radical, socialist-feminist voice would require the ability to transcend middle-class biases, but this would not necessarily entail a rejection of women's concerns about their domestic and maternal roles. These were concerns that working-class women also shared. Rather than being seen as merely a pragmatic tool to avoid confrontation or divisiveness, maternal feminism was an integral component of the belief system that drew women into social and political activism.

What of the social character of these women's organizations? The organizations did not speak for all women equally. Their agendas often placed the women reformers and women recipients of assistance in relationships that reflected class, gender, and racial barriers.[22] The food, shelter, and medical aid offered by women's organizations was directed at the less-fortunate "deserving" others

– usually immigrant and working-class women. However, the same aid could also serve the middle-class interests of its members. In short, while evangelical and charitable goals may have assisted working-class women as clients, at the same time they created barriers that prevented working-class and immigrant women from participating as equals within women's organizations.

Several examples will serve to illustrate this point. The promotion of domestic science by the National Council of Women and the YWCA reflected their middle-class concern about the decline in the number of servants willing to work in middle- and upper-class homes. Initially, it was not their own daughters they sought to teach; it was the daughters of the working-class, who had been turning away from domestic service in droves.[23] Working-class women using the YWCA's homes in urban centres did not always share the organization's fervour for Bible classes, preferring instead to make use of the gymnasiums and swimming pools.[24] One woman explicitly resented her treatment at the YWCA: "I was never treated by servants as I am by those who call themselves ladies."[25] Even the more radical WCTU has been charged with imposing the middle-class values of thrift and morality on the working class (though one wonders why we should accept the view that these traits were the preserve of the middle class).[26] Material aid – food, shelter, medicine – was often welcomed by working-class women, but there is some evidence that they were less welcoming of the reformers' enthusiasm for moral uplifting.[27] Certainly, racist and imperialist ideas, which were often directed at non-British immigrants, were embedded in the social agendas of such groups as the WCTU and YWCA.[28] Whether as clients or as members, it is unlikely that working-class or immigrant women would have been received as equals in women's organizations. Further, given the class and diverse ethnic origins of many socialists, it is not surprising to discover evidence that some working-class and radical women felt discomfort within the ranks of these women's clubs. Nonetheless, some women drawn to the left brought with them values they shared with the middle-class women's movement. Prominent among these was maternal feminism and the desire to improve woman's place in the modern world.[29] The presence of women such as Haile and Wrigley in the early Canadian socialist movement confirms that Canada experienced a trend similar to one in the United States, in which many women came to socialism from the women's movement, especially the temperance movement.[30]

Less conventional religious beliefs, which sprang from the religious controversy of the late nineteenth century, influenced some early radicals. One small nontraditional religious sect that had some popularity among radicals was theosophy. Founded in England by Madame Helena Blavatsky, it wedded Christian and oriental thought to assert the pre-eminence of spiritual over empirical knowledge – the immanence of God in the material world. Theosophy came to have particular appeal for women because of its belief in a woman-centred divinity. Canadian feminists, radicals, and Fabian socialists, including Phillips Thompson, Helena Gutteridge, Dr Emily Stowe, and Flora MacDonald Denison, were among the supporters of theosophy in Canada.[31] Thus, in both conventional and nonconventional forms, religious beliefs were an important part of the social controversy that fostered radicalism and the turn-of-the-century woman question.

Although some women rose to prominence within the CSL, their commitment to issues such as prohibition and Christianity did not fit comfortably within the socialist movement after the SPC eclipsed the CSL in 1904. The SPC had locals across Canada, but much of its political leadership came from British Columbia, where the party's support relied predominantly on male trade unionists in the mining and logging towns and in Vancouver and Victoria. The SPC relied on a Marxian brand of socialism, stressing the class struggle between workers and bosses, the need to educate the workers to their class interests, and demands for collective ownership of the means of production. Its brand of Marxism was to the left of Fabian and labourite elements in the European socialist movement.[32] It opposed any cooperation with traditional political parties and disparaged the wisdom of supporting reform measures that merely deflected from the need for socialism. While emphasizing the need for education, its conception of the working class focused narrowly on male workers. This change in the character of the socialist movement had dramatic implications for the women who were drawn to it. Socialist women were now compelled to make tactical choices when reconciling their interest in women's suffrage, Christian socialism, or prohibition with their own integration within the SPC.

As the decade evolved, ideological, ethnic, and class differences divided members over the issue of temperance. At times, the SPC emphasized an explicitly class-conscious mistrust of the middle-class bias of the WCTU: the goals of the WCTU were viewed with suspicion, as satisfying the bosses' need for "sober slaves." The party press also opposed local option and prohibition campaigns for being reformist and for failing to attack the cause of the liquor problem. At other times, the party defended the individual right of

PLATFORM
Socialist Party of Canada

We, the Socialist Party of Canada, in convention assembled, affirm our allegiance to, and support of the principles and programme of the revolutionary working class.

Labor produces all wealth, and to the producers it should belong. The present economic system is based upon capitalist ownership of the means of production, consequently all the products of labor belong to the capitalist class. The capitalist is therefore master; the worker a slave.

So long as the capitalist class remains in possession of the reins of government all the powers of the State will be used to protect and defend their property rights in the means of wealth production and their control of the product of labor.

The capitalist system gives to the capitalist an ever-swelling stream of profits, and to the worker an ever increasing measure of misery and degradation.

The interest of the working class lies in the direction of setting itself free from capitalist exploitation by the abolition of the wage system, under which is cloaked the robbery of the working-class at the point of production. To accomplish this necessitates the transformation of capitalist property in the means of wealth production into collective or working-class property.

The irrepressible conflict of interests between the capitalist and the worker is rapidly culminating in a struggle for possession of the power of government—the capitalist to hold, the worker to secure it by political action. This is the class struggle.

Therefore, we call upon all workers to organize under the banner of the Socialist Party of Canada with the object of conquering the public powers for the purpose of setting up and enforcing the economic programme of the working class, as follows:

1. The transformation, as rapidly as possible, of capitalist property in the means of wealth production (natural resources, factories, mills, railroads etc.,) into the collective property of the working class.

2. The democratic organization and management of industry by the workers.

3. The establishment, as speedily as possible, of production for use instead of production for profit.

The Socialist Party, when in office, shall always and everywhere until the present system is abolished, make the answer to this question its guiding rule of conduct: Will this legislation advance the interests of the working class and aid the workers in their class struggle against capitalism? If it will the Socialist Party is for it; if it will not, the Socialist Party is absolutely opposed to it.

In accordance with this principle the Socialist Party pledges itself to conduct all the public affairs placed in its hands in such a manner as to promote the interests of the working class alone.

Socialist Party of Canada's platform

workers to indulge in alcohol without interference from the state.[33] While such verbal criticism of prohibition might be expected, the party went even further. The socialist MLA Hawthornthwaite was against miners being forbidden to buy alcohol; liquor was served at some party events; the party paper carried advertisements for it; and some party members were expelled for joining a local option league. In one instance, there were complaints that a party organizer appeared drunk on stage.[34] Such activities would have outraged and alienated any socialists who had strong prohibitionist convictions, including women with links to the WCTU.

Aside from resisting the reformist or middle-class elements associated with prohibition, the party had other grounds for opposing it. The consumption of alcohol was predominantly a male activity; "respectable" women did not drink, for the most part, and men tended to drink in exclusively male environments.[35] Since drinking was thus implicitly associated with masculinity, prohibition was one means by which women could exert influence over masculine behaviour. This connection, well understood and exploited by the WCTU, helps to account for the tremendous appeal this organization had among women and for the hostility it provoked in some men. The SPC actively fostered the association of masculinity with socialism in order to strengthen its appeal among male trade unionists. Prohibition directly threatened this masculine image. Not surprisingly, some male socialists opposed prohibition with the same vigour they unleashed in opposing women's issues and women's presence within the party.[36] Prohibition also had significance for some ethnic groups. It was an important issue for Finnish socialist organizations, many of which had evolved from temperance societies.[37] Tolerance of alcohol may have added one more barrier to cooperation between the SPC and the Finnish socialists, who had the highest participation rate of women.

Reflecting a similar trend in British socialism,[38] the SPC criticized Christian socialism and sometimes expressed overt hostility to specific religious groups, notably, Roman Catholics, Methodists, and the Salvation Army.[39] In its most extreme form, it argued that a Christian who believed in individual salvation could never be a socialist, and a socialist who believed in the collective power of the working class could never be a Christian.[40] This attitude exposed the efforts of the SPC to distinguish itself as much as possible from the intellectual heritage of Christian socialism by rejecting any Christian justification for social change, including the evangelical emphasis on individual redemption. The SPC ridiculed the reform efforts of the Salvation Army, the Roman Catholic Church, and the

Methodists. Some of this antagonism can be attributed to the direct competition that organizations such as the Salvation Army posed in their propaganda efforts directed towards the working class.[41] Other SPC members argued that religious convictions were of no consequence to socialism and that the party should refrain from attacking Christian socialists.[42] As one woman put it, "If men and women are to be free, they should be free to practise any religion they see fit."[43] While the attack on Christian socialism may have alienated many Christians, this distancing of socialism from Christianity may have made the party even more attractive to non-Christians, especially Jewish and Finnish socialists.

The hostility to Christian socialism went beyond rejection of Christianity. It also embodied an attack on women. The party identified religious devotion with political conservatism, and it deemed women to be more religious than men. The SPC's paper described women as particularly subject to religious dogma and less able to think "clearly" for themselves.[44] Although the background of many socialist women in churches and in Christian-based organizations such as the WCTU helped to shape their political radicalism, the SPC's attack on Christian socialism denigrated their socialist credentials.

Despite these unwelcoming conditions, several women socialists rose to prominence within the SPC. Ruth Lestor fully embraced the party platform.[45] Originally from Manchester, England, she and her husband gained prominence in Canada in 1909–11 during a speaking tour for the SPC.[46] Touted as the first lady socialist lecturer in Canada, Lestor claimed to speak "naturally from the standpoint of the woman's interest in social conditions." Despite this claim, an analysis of her speeches and writings reveals that, like the SPC, she often considered women's issues relevant only when construed from a class perspective that put the male worker at the centre of the class struggle.

Drawing on her experience of women workers in England, Lestor often focused on women workers in capitalist society. She assumed that only women who worked like men – in the paid labour force – would have a serious interest in socialism. But this assumption ignored, among other things, the reality that most women in Canada, even working-class women, were not in the paid labour force. Her emphasis on paid labour reflected the tendency of the SPC to focus on those areas in which women's interests corresponded to men's, without allowing women's concerns legitimacy in their own right. Characteristically, Lestor concluded one article by stating that women were going to "march alongside the men ...

Charles and Ruth Lestor

Companions and Comrades, marching for the conquest of the world, for the workers."[47] Despite her emphasis on the woman as worker, Lestor sometimes employed the rhetoric of maternal feminism to urge women to become socialists. However, she insisted that the SPC's line on women was correct: "The true revolutionist loses all sight of sex ... A woman is a man – that's all."[48]

Lestor shared the SPC's contempt for the views of the Christian reformers who blamed social problems on alcoholism or sin. Drawing on her years of experience as a nurse in mental institutions in England, she argued that madness was caused not by sin or alcohol but by the monotony of the factory girl's life. In contradiction to her claims about the advantages of women working, she blamed working mothers for the problem of lunacy because they could not care properly for their infants. She concluded that capitalism bred lunacy and that ridding the world of capitalism would make it sane.[49] Thus, despite her focus on working women, the contradictions of her arguments provided a tenuous defence for woman's place in the labour force.

Some of Lestor's remarks about women were more misogynous than the views expressed by her male comrades. Initially, Lestor thought that the SPC tried to keep women out of its ranks, and she made every effort to encourage women to join. But on reflection, she decided that this had been the wrong course of action – the party needed not just women, but women who were "mentally equipped with knowledge sufficient to understand what they are doing." She observed that woman "is so ignorant that she does not yet possess that knowledge that entitles her to membership in our ranks." Echoing assumptions commonly held in the international socialist community, she described women as conventional, ignorant, cruel, and bound by religion and fashion: "Religion seems to cling to a woman longer than it does to a man; perhaps it is that woman goes to church, more especially when she has anything new to go in." Her views would have been alien, if not antithetical, to those women who were drawn into the socialist movement from the tradition of maternal feminism reflected by the WCTU or from the conviction that socialism would make a Christian life possible.

Lestor acknowledged the price she paid for her strict adherence to the SPC line. She lamented going for years without female companionship because she rarely found, she said, "one of my own sex worth talking to." Although she claimed that the comradeship of men was adequate compensation, she also stated that truly revolutionary women, such as she, had a difficult time because they were ostracized by other women in the movement.[50] Her isolation from other women would have set her well apart from those women activists of this era who enjoyed the close friendship and support of other women.[51] Despite her prominence as a woman socialist, Lestor did not identify with women or with women's issues, and consequently she was isolated from the women who were trying to recast domestic labour from a socialist perspective. Her experience demonstrates the difficulty that a woman socialist could face in supporting the SPC line while at the same time trying to advance women's interests within the left.

Another notable woman socialist who supported the SPC was Sophie Mushkat. Although she was from a different background than Lestor, she too agreed with the SPC's rejection of suffrage and religion, but she broke with the party in her support of prohibition.[52] A Russian Jewish immigrant of Polish descent, Mushkat had come to Canada with her father William in 1905 and settled in the Maritimes. She had not been a member of a socialist organization in Russia but had been a sympathizer for many years. She joined the SPC around 1908,[53] and both she and her father became vigorous party supporters. Mushkat was first noted for her activities in organizing and speaking. According to the SPC organizer in the Maritimes, Roscoe Fillmore,[54] she spoke on several occasions, sometimes drawing crowds of 1,200. She even faced violence, as hostile crowds or police tried to disrupt socialist meetings. Fillmore commended Mushkat for her courage: "She persisted in attending the meeting and speaking even when we were all sure we would be 'pulled in.'" The topics of her speeches ranged from poverty, "The Class Struggle," and "Socialism and Trade Unionism" to "The Materialist Conception of History," but she also spoke on women's issues, as in her talk "On Woman's Place in the Socialist Movement." Fillmore emphasized that her speeches were not frivolous; he commended her for talking "plain straight socialism without ever once mentioning ice-cream, bon-bons, directoire gowns or peach basket hats."[55]

Since Mushkat's soap-boxing would have been an unusual activity for a woman, reports of her speaking style are of interest. Alleged to be the only lady socialist speaker, she was labelled the "Mother Jones of Canada." In some sense this was apt, for she was not described as a genteel speaker: "Miss Mushkat, her sleeves rolled up to the elbows, vigorously pummelled the various bogeys created ... by the capitalist papers to frighten people from taking part [in socialism]."[56] Her speaking style poses a striking contrast to the timidity exhibited by the "four plain women" described at the opening of this chapter.

One soap-box speech in Moncton, New Brunswick, led to a disturbance that involved the police, and Mushkat later appeared in court as a witness. Her testimony at the trial confirmed her commitment to socialism. On taking the witness stand, she refused to swear on the Bible. Without revealing that she was Jewish, she explained that she did not believe in the afterlife but believed that she would be punished by her conscience for misdeeds. When asked by the lawyer the aim of the SPC, she replied that she was proud to be a member of a party whose aim was to give "the workers the full value of their labour." Her answers drew applause from the audience and a reprimand from the judge, who dismissed her testimony because she had not sworn on the Bible. In other public speeches, she pragmatically employed the argument that only socialism would abolish all evils and make a Christian life possible.[57]

In late 1910, Mushkat travelled west to Calgary. There she continued her speaking tours under the auspices of the SPC and hustled subscriptions for the party paper. While on tour, she made good use of her language skills in English, Russian, and Polish, even providing a translation for the party press of the experiences of a Russian serf who had moved from Russia to Canada and tried to establish himself as a farmer. She was also active in organizing the campaign to elect socialist T. Edwin Smith, from Taber, Alberta.[58] Mushkat's speaking ability and her facility in languages were clearly an asset. But the SPC did not organize fund-raising drives for its women organizers as it did for the men, so despite Mushkat's popularity, the expenses of her tours often amounted to more than the money she raised. On one tour, for example, she reported expenses of $200, which exceeded the $108 she raised. When she finally collected a surplus on another tour, she was criticized for the mishandling of funds.[59] The last report of her activities is a brief mention in the minutes of the Dominion Executive Committee in 1915. She became involved in the prohibition campaign in Alberta, despite the SPC's rule forbidding members from participating in reform causes or sharing the platform with other parties. The dominion executive reviewed her activities and endorsed the action of the Alberta executive to expel her from the party. No further mention is made of her actions during this campaign or of the party's reasons for expelling her.[60]

Mushkat's life is fascinating for several reasons. Judging from the evidence, she was clearly an exceptional woman. Her speaking style was doubtless influenced by her class, ethnic background, and character. That such an indefatigable party worker should have been expelled is a reflection of the sectarian spirit that dominated the SPC during these years. While Mushkat was popular among working-class and mining communities, her agnostic and antireligious sentiments would have antagonized those socialists who had strong Christian convictions, and her speaking style would not have appealed to all socialist women. The sectarian climate of the SPC and the differences in class, ethnic, and religious background, as well as varying commitments to social issues, made it difficult for many prominent socialist women to identify with the voices of women within the SPC.

On the other hand, there were some socialist women who, though disagreeing with the SPC platform, worked within the party to make it more receptive and supportive of women's issues. Such a woman was Bertha Merrill Burns.[61] Unlike Ruth Lestor, Merrill Burns was committed to feminism and prohibition as well as socialism, and she strove to integrate these causes in her political activities whenever possible. Arriving in British Columbia in 1900, she soon became active in the socialist movement in Nelson. She was the first woman executive member of the Socialist Party of

British Columbia, and she took part in local activities both by writing and by giving speeches. In July 1903 she moved to Vancouver, where she took a position on the editorial board of the *Western Clarion* as editor of the women's column. She was a signatory to the establishment of the Western Socialist Publishing Company. She was also involved in the founding convention of the Socialist Party of Canada and was an executive member of the party. These activities made her a leading figure in the development of the early socialist movement in British Columbia. In addition, she had the distinction of being the most widely published female writer in the Canadian socialist press.

Merrill Burns's column, "We Women," which appeared regularly in the party press of 1902 and 1903, covered a range of issues designed to interest women in the cause of socialism. As well as writing about women's suffrage, she discussed religion, morality, temperance, free love, prostitution, women in paid labour, child care, and women in the home. An astute propagandist, she used these popular issues to help make socialism appeal to women in the home and in the paid labour force. Her column also printed letters from readers, covered the activities of both Canadian and international socialist women, carried poems and articles by leading socialist women, and provided suggested readings for women who were interested in socialism. Among her recommendations were works by Engels and Bebel as well as books by the sex radicals Edward Carpenter and Moses Harman. Her column did much to keep the readers informed of the importance of the "woman question" in socialism.[62]

In December 1903, Bertha Merrill (as she then was) married Ernest Burns, treasurer of the Socialist Party. Thereafter, she referred to herself as Bertha Merrill Burns (like many feminists of her day, retaining her maiden name as a middle name). Ernest's socialist politics were marked by a considerable amount of tolerance and by an abhorrence of sectarianism.[63] In contrast to the leadership of the Socialist Party, he endorsed reforms and criticized party members for treating Marxism as a dogma that could not be questioned. He endorsed women's suffrage and was one of the few male socialists to give speeches on women's issues – for example, "Women and the Labour Problem."[64] In 1907 he was suspended from membership of the party until "he could conscientiously support the platform and programme of the SPC." In later years, Ernest claimed that the party's stance on women's suffrage was one of the grounds for his discontent. Although Merrill Burns was not included in the suspension, she claimed to be proud that Ernest held the distinction of being the only member expelled for his convictions.[65]

By all accounts, Merrill Burns shared many of her husband's political convictions. In correspondence with Mrs Ramsay Mac-Donald, wife of the British Labour leader, she credited her awakening to socialism to her concern for working women: "My indignation over the treatment of certain young girls employed in the mechanical department of the paper where I worked first caused me to investigate the general conditions of women's work in that city and from that investigation sprung my first interest in socialism."[66] From her articles and correspondence, it is clear that Merrill Burns was well read in the socialist classics as well as in the works of thinkers such as Charles Darwin and Edward Carpenter. She demonstrated a sound grasp of socialist principles and a commitment to the working class, and did not shy away from talking about collective ownership of property and class struggle. This did not prevent her from exploring the social position of women. Unlike Ruth Lestor and Sophie Mushkat, Merrill Burns did not focus exclusively on wage-earning women, and she acknowledged that women from different walks of life were important and welcome in the socialist movement. While she analysed the position of working women, she insisted that socialists had to appeal to housewives. Consequently, her women's column often discussed the socialist transformation of domestic labour. Her lack of religious conviction was never overt in her columns or articles, but she acknowledged in her private correspondence that she considered herself unaffiliated with any church, preferring the label socialist, agnostic, or freethinker (and she complained that the census takers would not accommodate her in this respect).[67] Nevertheless, she evaded the ire of Christian socialists by not publicizing her views.

Merrill Burns did, however, publicly dispute the party line on several issues: she favoured reforms such as prohibition and women's suffrage; she challenged the SPC's lack of internal democracy; and she endorsed local plebiscites on prohibition and "the social evil" – prostitution. While sharing political views that clashed with the SPC, she and her husband initially worked within the party to persuade members to change the party platform; but at the same time, they actively supported other causes. For example, Merrill Burns organized a "pink tea" for Mrs MacDonald, to discuss the idea of establishing an alternate party, and in private correspondence she acknowledged that the Socialist Party of Canada was fully controlled by the "Impossibilists." In the summer of 1906, Merrill Burns wrote to Mrs MacDonald to report the formation of their new protest party, the Social Democratic Party of Canada (SDPC).[68] Half the members of the new party were drawn from the disenchanted ranks of the SPC, including many Finns. While Merrill Burns acknowledged that the party was still small, she looked forward to its developing into a provincial party. She also reported that there was a "good percentage of women in our new party and we mean to so conduct ourselves that we shall keep them here."[69] She and her husband were active in promoting the SDPC in British Columbia. She publicized its presence through her correspondence with radicals across Canada,[70] and although the SDPC remained small in the province, the Burnses continued to support it vigorously.

Unlike some of their contemporaries, the Burnses managed to integrate their commitment to socialism and women's issues, though not without cost. Although they were charter members of the SPC, they were unable to persuade that party to support women's suffrage or prohibition. While there is no record that Merrill Burns was expelled from the SPC, it is clear that the party disapproved of her commitment to these causes, and thus she and her husband worked to build an alternative socialist party that would be more amenable to such concerns.[71]

Other socialists across Canada who were similarly disenchanted also joined the SDPC, which consolidated its national presence in 1911. Although the SPC and SDPC platforms were similar, the SDPC avoided the impossibilism label by including some reforms in its political platform. It was also more receptive to ethnic locals within its ranks than the SPC was. Some members who shifted their allegiance to the new party had been outspoken critics of the SPC for its crude attacks on Christian socialists.[72] The SDPC proved more accepting of the compatibility of socialism and Christianity, and it officially cooperated with the Toronto Christian Fellowship.[73] Thus, it provided continuity for socialists who remained committed to the intellectual heritage of Christian reformism.

The SDPC was also more flexible on prohibition and did not go as far out of its way to offend prohibitionists. *Cotton's Weekly*, which was to become the official paper of the SDPC, had a temperance column for the first year, reflecting the strong prohibitionist convictions of its editor, William Cotton. He moderated his support of temperance over the years but continued to refuse to print liquor advertisements and even appealed to members of the WCTU to vote for socialism. He also rebutted some of the more strident claims of the SPC on prohibition. To those who argued that prohibition would cause unemployment, he retorted that the demise of prostitution

William Cotton, 1904

would do the same, yet this was not an adequate reason to refrain from working for its abolition. Rather than ridiculing the prohibitionists, *Cotton's Weekly* tended to present them in a positive light.[74] Because of its stance on temperance and Christianity, the SDPC attracted many who were alienated from the SPC.

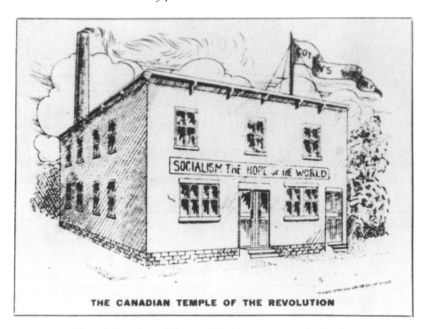

THE CANADIAN TEMPLE OF THE REVOLUTION

The printing plant of *Cotton's Weekly* in Cowansville, Quebec

Mary Cotton Wisdom, the sister of William Cotton, shared her brother's prohibitionist convictions. She was born in 1878, the oldest child of Charles Cotton, member of a prominent family in the Eastern Townships of Quebec.[75] Her mother, Alice MacKay, was a direct descendant of the United Empire Loyalists. The death of Alice when Mary was only fourteen, thrust upon her the responsibility of raising her three younger siblings: Alice, Charles, and William. The brothers were well educated, each spending a year in France on a scholarship and earning a law degree in Canada; Mary received singing lessons in New York. By all accounts, the entire family was keenly interested in politics and economics, often debating the issues of the day.

After her marriage to the engineer Stuart Wisdom, Mary accompanied her husband on his trips to remote mining camps where, by her own account, she was often the only "white woman" in the area. Between trips they lived in a house in Sweetsburg, Quebec, called the "Anchorage," which her father had bought for her. While completing his education to become an engineer and metallurgist, her husband had worked as a labourer in mines and smelting plants in Sydney, Nova Scotia, on the eastern seaboard, and in northern Ontario. He worked twelve-hour shifts, and every two weeks, when

Mary Cotton Wisdom, 1898

the shift changed, he worked twenty-four hours straight. These working conditions caused Mary and her husband to come to favour labour unions, even though they themselves were middle class.

In 1908, when her youngest brother William bought a newspaper called the *Observer* and transformed it into the socialist *Cotton's Weekly*, Mary Cotton Wisdom began editing the women's column. Fortunately, she provided her readers with some insight into her initial impressions of socialism.

A few months ago I looked upon socialism with horror. To-day, I honour it above all other movements working for the betterment of mankind … A friend of mine who lives a domestic, secluded life on a farm, held up her hands in surprise, when she learned that I actually attended socialist meetings. She asked me in real earnest if I was not afraid "that some of those foreigners would stick a knife in me." She seemed to think that socialists were a set of men who went around with bombs in their pockets and knives in their belts, ready and anxious to commit murder. Alas, how we are maligned … Socialists are bound together in a great cause. They are trying to help the weak, to rise the fallen, to lift the burden of oppression, to overthrow crime and bind up the broken hearts, trying to fulfil the teachings of Christ in truth.[76]

The picture of socialists as knife-wielding, bomb-throwing foreigners was by then well publicized in films and newspapers,[77] and it would have struck fear in the hearts of many white, English-speaking, middle-class Canadians. Even Wisdom clearly felt a need to calm her readers' apprehensions about foreigners. The identification of socialism with familiar Christian ideals was probably crucial in her overcoming her initial fears of socialism.

Wisdom's columns never exhibited an extensive interest in a Marxian economic analysis of capitalism, though she did have a wide-ranging interest in current social issues, empathizing with the poor and deprived. Her commitment to socialism, however, was not paramount. In one article, entitled "My View of Socialism," she disputed the argument that socialism would result in a perfect world. Although she acknowledged that we "will be better off when we cease to eat each other financially," she insisted that no form of government by men would ever be perfect. Only when the "Messiah Himself shall come and take the reins of government into his own hands, will the perfect government be ushered in," she stated.[78] Wisdom was, however, eager to highlight the problems of male domination and woman's role in society: "I will confess just among ourselves that though I believe earnestly in socialism, I have not the energy to keep keyed up to the high pitch of pulling my hair in desperation over the evils of capitalism … This is a free country in which every man has the vote. (I just wish every woman had) and if the men want socialism they can have it simply by casting their vote at the next general election that way."[79] In this she had a point. Despite the SPC's class analysis, the party's early vision of the transition to socialism was never clearly spelled out, except insofar as it urged the working class to vote the socialist ticket.

In many respects, Wisdom typified the women of her generation, class, and ethnic background who were involved in the Canadian women's movement and were also drawn to the left. Her early affiliation with socialism reflected her understanding that it could complement Christianity and foster improved, equitable social conditions. She also believed that socialism needed to address suffrage and prohibition. Her views on Christianity and "women's" issues thus conflicted with the SPC's platform – a fact that doubtless contributed to her growing disenchantment with socialism.[80]

Of less prominence but strong commitment was Mary Norton, who joined the Social Democratic Party in 1912 and became secretary for her local.[81] Like many socialist women of her era, she cited Edward Bellamy's work as an early influence on her thinking. During the same decade, she maintained involvement in the women's movement: joined the Pioneer Political Equality League, campaigned for the suffrage referendum in British Columbia, and joined the Women's International League, an organization that sent a peace mission to Europe during World War I. She became involved in the fight for workmen's compensation after her husband died as a result of an industrial accident. Until her death in the 1970s, she maintained her interest in socialism, women's issues, and trade unionism.

In contrast to the other women socialists discussed in this chapter, Norton's family did not share her enthusiasm for socialism. She was already married and had children when she joined the SDPC, and later in life she reflected that her activities had probably meant that her husband had suffered at home, though he did not interfere with her political activities. But even though Norton's husband and children were not interested in socialism, they must have provided passive support for her political activities, at the very least by not opposing her or by taking over some household responsibilities while she attended meetings or campaigned; and the children must have continued to do so after Norton was widowed. Without family support, it would have been difficult for a married woman to be politically active.

Norton did not think there was sex discrimination in the SDPC. She insisted that the party did not ban separate meetings for women, that women accumulated "aggressive spirits," and that they learned a lot from the various speakers who addressed them. At the same time, she did observe that men had advantages in not being housebound – alluding not only to the constraints of domestic work but also to the social conventions that kept unescorted "respectable" women out of public spaces (except, of course, the newly emerging department stores).[82] This was an era in which women were just beginning to claim an independent presence in city streets. As one worker put it, "There were no girls. They were just starting to work in the offices, they operated the telephones, worked in cafes and in some of the stores. But they disappeared out of circulation at 6 o'clock and you never saw them again until the next day. Talk about a man's world!"[83] Women socialists had to accommodate these constraints. In forming a socialist women's

committee of suffragists, Norton stressed the convenience of afternoon meeting times because women usually wanted to stay home
in the evenings. While the regular party meetings were held at a
time convenient for the male members, Norton took it for granted
that the party would not make a similar accommodation for
women; she considered it "non-discriminatory" because it allowed
women to organize their own afternoon meetings. This reflects the
extent to which some assumptions about gender-distinct roles
remained unrecognized within the party, even by a woman who
fought for women's rights.

Norton confirmed that the SDPC was much more supportive of
women's suffrage than the SPC was. After she joined the SDPC, she
campaigned for the suffrage referendum by speaking to farmers on
their way to market. Although she did not have to hide her suffrage
sympathies from her socialist comrades in the SDPC, she tried to
keep her socialist activities from the suffrage women for fear that
they would discriminate against her. Norton admired Helena
Gutteridge, a local activist for women's rights and trade unionism,
but she judged her too conservative and never joined Gutteridge's
suffrage organization. Gutteridge was in fact a radical, working-
class campaigner who was deeply involved in British Columbia's
suffrage and labour movements. Norton's perception of her as
conservative perhaps reflects a socialist criticism of her work within
the labour movement.[84] When Norton held a tea for her suffrage
colleagues, she refused to invite Gutteridge for fear that the suffragists would discriminate against people holding street meetings.
She recounted: "Mrs MacGill once saw in the newspaper the
election of the officers of the socialists and I happened to be on
the list for some office. To her eternal credit she said to me 'If I
couldn't have a good standard of life under this government I'd be
a socialist too.' But all the others [suffragists] that I met thought
that [socialism] was the last association they wanted to [be associated with]."[85] Norton's life testifies to the support that socialist
women in the SDPC gave to suffrage, but it also reveals the difficulty
they had in forming alliances with suffragists.

Common threads emerge from these profiles of women socialists.
While their class backgrounds varied, several had an identifiably
middle-class background. We can only speculate how class may
have shaped their politicization or their political views. Judging by
the contrast between Mary Cotton Wisdom and Sophie Mushkat,
there were probably dramatic differences in their styles of organizing and their knowledge of working-class realities. But the prominence of middle-class women is not unusual, for a number of

middle-class men also rose to prominence in the early socialist movement. Perhaps more significant for women was the fact that their activism was sustained in the company of family members – notably, husbands, fathers, and brothers – who shared their political views. By contrast, there is less evidence that family members supported men's political activism (though this may be because biographers have shown less interest in the familial context of male activism). Men likely had greater autonomy within the family to pursue political activities.[86] Religion, prohibition, and the "woman question" figured largely in the women's political activities, but their commitment to socialism sometimes alienated them from their allies in nonsocialist organizations. Carrying these concerns with them into the socialist movement, women did not always fit comfortably with the politics of the male-dominated left, especially with the SPC. They were far from being a cohesive group, and their differences in ethnicity, religion, and class sometimes aided (but sometimes fragmented) the coherence of their interests within the left. Vastly outnumbered by male comrades in a movement that did not value women's interests, socialist women faced considerable odds in sustaining a presence within the left and in articulating interests common to women in the socialist movement.

CHAPTER THREE

Reckoning with the Gentler Sex: The Left's Reception of Women in Its Ranks

A record of the political activities of leading socialist women, as described in the preceding chapter, is far easier to trace than the experiences of those who did not live in the limelight. Previous generations of scholars have thought it either unimportant or impossible to piece together an understanding of women's activities from a historical record in which the women seldom spoke for themselves. But the task is neither impossible nor unimportant. As this chapter sketches a picture of socialist women's activities, it draws on the same sources that other historians have used, at times reading against the grain and looking for traces of women's experience in evidence that seems far removed from gender. Although the historical record has left us more abundant information about men, it can still shed considerable light on women's experiences at socialist meeting halls and picnics.

Women drawn into politics were deterred or encouraged by the extent of hospitality with which the parties welcomed them. Socialists often proudly claimed that they treated women as equals. One socialist accused the average politician of welcoming "the ladies" at the outset of his speech and then ignoring them, and he asserted that socialists addressed their "audience irrespective of sex distinction as 'Comrades'; and generally devote[d] quite a lot of time to the woman question."[1] Another stated that socialism would not make women equal, because it recognized that men and women were already equal.[2] Each of the socialist parties organized many events to attract women members. Vancouver's first annual socialist picnic in 1902 was given in an effort to "encourage lady comrades to greater efforts." Although a relatively small number of women attended, it was hoped that many more would join the movement: "The socialist movement in Vancouver has been a men's movement in the past but the gentler sex will have to be reckoned with in future – a socialism which does not attract the women cannot live."[3]

Nevertheless, not all socialists agreed with this ideal or what it might entail. One meeting to discuss "Why Women Should Be Socialists" provoked the antagonism of some of the men. They opposed enfranchising women in the Socialist Party of British Columbia because women did not have a parliamentary vote, and they feared that women would simply vote as their husbands did. The women's column in the *Western Clarion* provided a stiff rejoinder to such an argument: "Who on earth should they vote with if not with their own husbands? If the husbands vote wrong that isn't because their wives are fools. But it is fact that a woman cannot cast a vote in either one way or the other unless she is accused of voting to please some man. She is supposed to be incapable of forming convictions of her own on any subject under the sun, or of exercising the right of decision for herself on any matter."[4] Merrill Burns contended that in recording membership, a male secretary "numbered the male members whole numbers and their wives fractions. For instance: John Jones, 1; Peter Smith, 2; Mrs. Peter Smith, $2\frac{1}{2}$; and if Peter Smith had a daughter old enough to belong to the local she, I doubt not, would have been numbered $2\frac{3}{4}$."[5] In view of such practices, one has to be sceptical about socialist claims that women were treated equally. In these early years, they had to fight to gain equality in the movement.

Strict emphasis on the equal treatment of men and women sometimes reinforced existing inequities. Since women either had no independent income or earned wages significantly lower than those of men, equal dues for membership could impede them from joining. In order to have equity or fairness, family dues were sometimes accepted, or smaller dues based on a person's ability to pay; but this accommodation did not always meet with success. Reduced rates for women were criticized by Merrill Burns because "after having come into the Party at reduced rates ... we are grudged the right to a voice in the councils of that party by the men in general who compose it."[6] Given women's social circumstances, this is but one example of an accommodation that would have been necessary to encourage the participation of women.

Other subtle problems arose from the gender-distinct social conventions among different classes and ethnic groups. Smoking was not only a male activity, but men who smoked were often excluded from women's company. According to middle-class convention, men retired to a separate room after dinner to talk and smoke. A smoking environment could thus keep women away from meetings.[7] Women protested this masculinization of the movement. In the early years of the socialist press, while the CSL was trying to gain the support of the WCTU, some members of the temperance society wrote to the *Citizen and Country* to complain about the tobacco advertisements, but with no effect: the tobacco ads continued. In later years, a Toronto SPC local voted to ban smoking at its meetings, as did the Ontario socialist convention of 1907.[8] Nevertheless, members of the Toronto local continued to smoke, with the encouragement of the executive members – much to the chagrin of G. Weston Wrigley, who claimed that the "vile odour of smoke of cheap tobacco" made it difficult for refined women to attend: "Not long ago an Italian lady comrade was criticized for not attending the Italian Branch meetings, the critic being one who had attended these meetings and probably helped to fill the hall with clouds of tobacco smoke ... The average smoker is about as selfish as a hog in a trough of hot swill." Wrigley approvingly noted that the Finnish locals discouraged both smoking and drinking at their gatherings in an effort to make women and children welcome. Although himself a smoker, he recognized that the habit posed a class and gender barrier for women, who were concerned for their "respectability" when attending mixed public gatherings.[9] Like drinking, smoking was a social custom that declared socialist meetings to be male terrain. Not surprisingly, some women expressed reluctance to trespass on that terrain.

Vulgarity, often directed at women, also lent a distinctively male aura to the meetings and the party papers. For example, an article attacking Goldwin Smith's criticisms of socialism was couched in language that would have been highly embarrassing to women: "There is a periodicity about his [Smith's] outbreaks that would suggest that the moon has something to do with them. His last menstrual period was July the 29th when he was delivered of the usual mess."[10] While such coarse language may not have been part of the usual discourse of working-class men, its use at meetings and in the party papers reinforced the message that socialism was a man's movement in which women were not welcome.

Insults towards women, particularly elderly women, were another cause of offence and alienation: "Gribble [a socialist organizer] is going to frighten away from our meetings all the old ladies of both sexes." At times, racism was an element in the insult, as when a writer criticized the Finns for their endorsement of a broader platform that included immediate demands for women's suffrage and autonomous ethnic locals: "The majority of the Finns

I know to be feminine enough to insist on being something more than revolutionary socialists."[11] To be a womanly socialist was an insult; to be a manly socialist was a compliment. Since socialism was so clearly a man's movement, a woman had to become manly to be considered a good socialist – an impossible and offensive expectation. The vulgar language also disparaged the customary ways women organized themselves, at socials or teas. When women complained about the language, they were not taken seriously. The *Western Clarion* responded to one complainant by stating that such objections "are invariably made by mentally lazy or insincere people."[12] The paper did not noticeably alter its language in response to women's complaints.

The language in the SDPC's paper was less vulgar, but at times it echoed the same themes. Some articles paternally addressed socialist men, urging them to vote for socialism to protect their wives and children. Other articles urged women to encourage their husbands to fight for socialism and not to complain when the men went to meetings.[13] Rather than women fighting alongside men, men would bring socialism to women, for this was depicted as a man's struggle. Despite the number of women who sold the paper, the column listing the names and sales of subscription hustlers was changed from "The Firing Line" to "The Boys Who Battle for Freedom" in 1913. One article implied that those who did not fight for socialism were not men:

Are you a man? Or are you just so much flesh, blood and bone in an existing condition? Is your thinking apparatus your own? Or is it molded into shape by others to suit their requirements? Do you think for yourself? ... Can you look a person in the eyes and say "I am your equal"? Or do you bend your knees and say "Sir" or "My Lord"? ... You are either a man or a fool. To which class do you belong? ... A man has a broad intellect, free thoughts, and absolute command of mind and body. A man stands for equal justice for all and no halfway compromise.[14]

By appealing to the male worker's sense of masculinity, such rhetoric was undoubtedly an effective way to promote men's rebellion against a sense of powerlessness and subordination. But not only did it fail to address women; it also implied that women were unable or had no reason to mount a similar challenge.

As noted earlier, ethnicity may have played a role in whether women felt comfortable speaking at public meetings. English women were thought to find it more uncomfortable than others, but this may have been the result of male behaviour. One woman fumed that "men show less consideration for women after becoming Socialists" and they "take a pride in their roughness of speech, and altogether strike the stranger as being as grumpy and discourteous a bunch as could well be." Another insisted that "discouraging comments of men often deter them [women] from voicing their convictions."[15] Both of these complainants urged men to be more encouraging, respectful, and courteous towards women. G.W. Wrigley once again chided men for their behaviour towards women members:

I can hear Comrade McKenzie say that "most women are Socialists because some man is," and Comrade Lehaney saying that "women have no place in the revolutionary movement," and Comrade Drury and Shier making their weak objections to women becoming voters. And I'm aware that many men comrades who are earnestly working for Socialism, boss their wives as their employers boss them, and will hesitate to lift the chains which keep women in sex bondage as well as class bondage.[16]

A woman echoed these concerns, saying that socialist men played the socialist on the street corner but were petty tyrants at home. While men, she noted, complained that women and children prevented them from working for socialism, at the same time they refused to stay home with the children so that their wives could go to meetings.[17] These comments underscore how male reluctance to shoulder some of the endless obligations of domestic labour posed concrete limitations on the full participation of women in politics.

The discontent with male behaviour that found expression in the party papers reveals some capacity for self-criticism, but not all women agreed that these problems were serious. One woman concluded that if women socialists were to fight capitalism, they "must be prepared to meet greater obstacles than tobacco smoke or coarse talk."[18] Her statement emphasizes the extent to which the social conventions of the left were male-defined. Tobacco and coarse speech were not the only issue, but they contributed to a masculine social atmosphere. Although she was prepared to accept these male conventions, other women found the discomfort of trespassing on male terrain too severe. Doubtless, socialist women would have been prepared to fight obstacles from their class enemies. This is quite different from fighting obstacles that have been created by one's allies.

In spite of the sometimes hostile reception of women, the parties did make some efforts to encourage their participation, though there were important differences in the extent to which each party

was officially willing to accommodate women. With its more centralized structure, the SPC was the least willing to recognize a
distinct status for women within the party. It rejected the idea of
a women's column in the belief that special women's interests did
not exist. The executive was against having separate women's
branches within the party, just as it opposed the idea of having
separate ethnic locals.[19] Despite the dominion executive's position,
ethnic locals and women's organizations were in fact organized. In
Toronto, a Socialist Women's Study Club met weekly in 1908 to
study Engels's *Origin of the Family*, *Looking Forward* by Rappaport, and *Marxian Economics* by Unterman. With striking parallels
to contemporary feminist pedagogy, the meetings had no leader.
This was thought to be an advantage: "We could possibly have
worked to better advantage with an experienced leader, but we
think the deficiency had been the means of more individual expression of opinion." The dues collected were put towards buying
books for a library.[20]

Achieving recognition of women's concerns within the SPC was
an uphill battle. Proposals that the SPC address the particular needs
of women had to be carefully worded to conform to the party
platform. The English branch in Toronto debated a proposal to
educate women within the party, and in September 1908 it put the
following resolution before the Ontario Socialist Convention:

Whereas the Socialist Party is the political expression of the working class,
and Whereas one-half the workers (the women) are disenfranchised, and
Whereas the Socialist Party of Canada in its printed matter and its political
propaganda has almost exclusively confined its efforts to that part of the
working class which has votes, and Whereas, judging by the limited
number of women in the party membership, the male members are making
no effort to interest their wives in the party work, and educate them to
women's historical status in society, and Whereas an independent movement is arising in all parts of the world aiming to secure the franchise for
women, making it necessary that the women of the working class know
how to use the ballot when it is secured, be it therefore Resolved that this
Convention instructs all speakers and Local organizations to make a more
direct appeal to the workers for universal suffrage; to arrange for meetings
to be addressed by women lecturers; and recommends the Dominion
Executive to supply Locals with literature dealing with woman's position,
as a worker in capitalist society.[21]

Although the resolution carefully avoided endorsing women's
suffrage, it was opposed by those who saw the proposal as an

immediate demand for the vote. Mrs Wrigley, one of the three women who were among the thirty-three delegates at the convention, defended the resolution, explaining that "the sole object was to educate the women and secure assistance for that purpose." In the end, the convention unanimously adopted the resolution.[22]

The SPC provincial executive in Ontario was selective in choosing women socialists to do speaking tours in the province. Several women were asked, including Miss Nellie Leh, Mrs Triller, and three members of the National Woman's Committee of the Socialist Party in the United States: Meta Stern, Ann Maley, and Margaret Prevy. Of these, only Meta Stern favoured the autonomy of women's branches; the others staunchly opposed organizational autonomy for women. While there is no evidence that the provincial executive was successful in securing these speakers, May Wood Simons, a member of the National Woman's Committee, toured Canada in 1911. Her reception in Berlin, Ontario (today's Kitchener), was overshadowed by the hockey game, which drew a large crowd. As well as arranging speaking tours for women, the provincial executive appointed Miss Sana Kallion, delegate of the Finnish local in Port Arthur, to be the first woman organizer for the Socialist Party of Canada.[23]

In early 1911, dissenting members of the SPC held a convention that led to the formation of the Canadian Socialist Federation. Among the issues raised was the concern that power should no longer be concentrated in the hands of a dominion executive but should be decentralized to the membership at the local level. This would leave the central body to act as a federation with power delegated to it from the affiliated locals.[24] The concern with decentralization proved to be of importance in relation to the establishment of autonomous women's branches, because the Canadian Socialist Federation soon became the Social Democratic Party of Canada.

As noted in the previous chapter, the SDPC was much more flexible in accommodating the special interests and needs of women. It had women's columns, encouraged women to write for its paper, established separate women's branches, and devoted special propaganda efforts to women. In British Columbia, a resolution proposed by the Burnaby local called for the creation of a women's organization committee in every local, to be headed by men in the absence of any women members. In addition, the local called for the appointment of a woman secretary for the women's committees who would be elected by the provincial executive. The resolution passed unanimously and Merrill Burns was elected.[25] Unfortunately, little else is known about these autonomous branches that might shed light on the uniqueness of the women's organizing efforts.

In addition to the new women's branches, the SDPC employed various strategies to encourage the participation of women. A women's club met once a week in Montreal, suggestions were made in the party press to improve propaganda efforts directed at women, and men were encouraged to bring their wives to party meetings. In Hamilton, the local organized a "social" to interest women in joining the party. In a rare departure from the norm, one man attending did his part to make the evening a success: "Comrade Bert Taylor is also worthy of praise for the heroic way he stuck to his post of dish washer, proving himself a socialist in spirit as well as belief." The evening was deemed a success for attracting the first two women to enrol in the local.[26]

Women experienced other gender-specific constraints as they became active in the left. Unlike many of the men, whose political activism spanned several decades, few women are known for their ongoing activities throughout this period. The birth of children, sickness in the family, and other domestic matters curtailed their political activities.[27] Limited as they were by their domestic responsibilities and constrained by the masculine character of the movement, most women probably took on tasks that minimized the discomfort they felt within such a male-defined movement. For example, women were most frequently mentioned for their participation in local party events. Early socialist gatherings were often organized like church services. Singing and entertainment, often provided by women, preceded the main speaker. As one account noted, their performance provided "a much appreciated relief from the ponderous flow of eloquence of the speakers."[28] Women were also mentioned in the press for preparing and organizing the food for party socials, picnics, and conventions. It is clear from many of these accounts that this was presumed to be a woman's task: "While arrangements this year call for a 'Basket Picnic' (i.e. where each attending party is expected to have its lady member prepare and bring with it eatables equivalent for its own needs) any stray Reds of a bachelor variety who may be running loose in those parts will please accept this invitation to join in the fun."[29] The food not only fed the comrades; it raised money for the movement. At box socials, for example, women were expected to bring a picnic basket of food, which would be auctioned off to the highest bidder. The women also raised money in a less gender-distinct fashion by organizing lectures and selling party papers.

Social Democratic Party picnic, Capilano Canyon, British Columbia, 1907.
A handwritten list attached to the photo identifies the participants as, left to right, front row: Mr Wilkinson, Victor Midgley, H. Norton Jr; second row: H. Sibble, unknown, Sara Menzies, Dessis Rogers; third row: Mary Rogers, Fred Faulkner, E. Burns; fourth row: unknown, Young, M. Wilkinson, Wilkinson (brother), F. Parr, Mrs Burns, Parr, Johnson, Lang; fifth row: J. Work, V. Hamilton, S. Norton, unknown, unknown, Botting, S. Work, unknown, Wilkinson, Miss Wilkinson, Harvey Norton Sr

The social importance of these activities should not be over-looked. Picnics, socials, parades, and dances helped to maintain the solidarity and appeal of the left. The women cared for the travelling speakers and organizers, and this hospitality virtually sustained the propaganda efforts of the movement. Speakers depended on the generosity of local members to billet them. At times, the hospitality extended beyond the provision of bed and board. One organizer who fell ill while on tour was nursed back to health by several "she Comrades."[30] J.B. Osborne, a blind socialist lecturer of twenty-five years' standing, described how a "lady comrade" cared for him when he toured in her area. She "always sees to it that there are no spots on my clothes, presses my pants, washes and irons all my neckties, handkerchiefs and underclothes, as well as mends the same, knits me woollen socks and gives them to me when I return here."[31] One wonders, in the midst of all her caring, if she had time to attend Osborne's lectures! These examples illustrate the gender-distinct ways in which women made important contributions to the movement. Their efforts supported its financial and propaganda activities and contributed a vital ambience. In this way, the women created a more humane and sociable movement, sustained solidarity, and extended the appeal of socialism.

Women were also noted for activities that were not as gender-distinct. As mentioned earlier, the names of the people who sold and distributed the party paper were printed in its columns. Although men's names outnumber the women's, the list alone may not accurately reflect the women's efforts. One woman said she avidly read her husband's paper and then passed it around among their friends; but only her husband's name was recorded in the subscription column. In another instance, a husband said that his wife would save a dollar from her "household fund" to keep *Cotton's Weekly* out of debt. Some women even won "hustler" awards for selling the largest number of papers.[32] By these accounts, selling a party paper was a propaganda activity that women easily combined with their domestic obligations.

Although women's letters were often published in the socialist press, remarkably few of the articles were written by women, let alone by women in Canada.[33] Indeed, only a small handful of articles by Canadian women found their way into the socialist press; even fewer women had their work published over an extended period of time. In contrast, the written contributions of several notable male socialists continued to appear in the press year after year. Besides Bertha Merrill Burns and Mary Cotton Wisdom, there were two other women, Margaret Allen and Bertha Smithers, who had editorial responsibilities for a brief period.[34] But it should be remembered that women were not always fully credited for their activities. Mrs Stechishin and her husband edited the Ukrainian socialist paper *Robutchyj Narod*, and according to the *Western Clarion*, the two together were "the editors, managers and whole staff" for the paper. However, secondary sources on the Ukrainian socialists in Canada focus exclusively on the husband and fail to acknowledge the wife's role.[35] Despite such examples of women being written out of history, the fact remains that few Canadian women wrote for the socialist press in a sustained way. Only one woman, Merrill Burns, had her work published and distributed as an English-language party pamphlet.[36]

Some women worked behind the scenes in an organizing capacity; they arranged tours of speakers, propaganda meetings, demonstrations, and election campaigns. They laid on unusual events to raise money or attract support for the party: a socialist theatre, a socialist newsstand, a socialist Sunday school, a children's red flag drill troupe for demonstrations. One successful effort was the 1911 May Day demonstration in Montreal at which women pinned red tags to all the demonstrators.

While there were few women who organized these events, there were even fewer who became public speakers. Some did give speeches at their locals – an occasion that was usually advertised as a unique or exceptional event in order to draw women to the audience. A woman speaking to her own local often received support and commendation, but public speaking was another matter. At the turn of the century, it was still very remarkable to have a woman speak on a public platform. As the decade rolled on and women activists became more vocal, the novelty of female public speakers began to wear off. Still, within the left, one gets a sense that female socialists who took to the podium were considered unusual. Several prominent women speakers from elsewhere, mostly the United States, toured in Canada, and this helped soften the environment for the few Canadian women who took up public speaking. The left did not offer notable support for the women who toured. Speakers were expected to charge a fee to cover their expenses. While many of the male organizers made claims on the central funds of the party to support a speaking tour, there is no comparable record in the English socialist press of women speakers being supported in such a fashion. Grace Silver, for example, covered well over 3,000 kilometres in thirty-seven days during her speaking tour in 1914, and she raised the money to cover all her expenses.[37]

While any socialist speaker was likely to engender a certain amount of antagonism, women socialists experienced a particularly hostile response when speaking in a public forum. A typical example is a heckler's description of his behaviour towards Emma Goldman: "One night, Jimmy Simpson, myself and King [William Lyon Mackenzie King] walked into a socialist party meeting on 76th Adelaide – a small hall they had on Adelaide Street West – the first time that Emma Goldman came to Canada to speak on Anarchism, and remarkable as it may seem, I kept such a running fire on Emma Goldman for the silly philosophy that she was preaching that they threw us all out."[38] Even for a practised speaker, it would require considerable skill and determination to remain undaunted by such behaviour. The attacks were even worse when one was "soapboxing." Because this form of speaking was so public and the audience was not restricted to those who had bought tickets, the speaker was subject to verbal harassment and even violence from passers-by. Only a few women were noted for having mastered this difficult skill.[39]

Hostility to women on a public platform and the denial of suffrage undoubtedly limited women's ability to campaign for public office. While the left nominated men for municipal, provincial, and federal office, women were rarely advanced as candidates unless at the municipal level, the one exception being Margaret Haile.[40] The creation of public space as a legitimate arena for women was an important prerequisite for their equal participation in the left. This legitimacy was still in its infancy during this time, born of the efforts of the women's movement.

The overall pattern of women's political activism on the left seems to have been governed by several factors: the reluctance of women to participate in political activity that was socially constructed as masculine; the hostility of men towards the political activism of women; and the exclusive responsibility for domestic obligations which fell to women and diverted them from political activities. Some socialists who recognized these limitations called for "special" measures to bring women into the socialist movement. In a sense, special measures were already in place for the comfort of men; the timing and location of meetings, the habitual smoking and vulgarity, and the disparagement of and hostility towards women all contributed to the masculine atmosphere of the socialist movement. With socialists organized in such gender-specific ways, the integration of women within the left would have required, at a minimum, the creation of autonomous organizations in which they could establish, in a positive way, what it meant to be a "womanly" socialist. In the absence of this, we are left with a clearer sense of men's political culture. Nevertheless, some women did organize in separate locals, and they used the speaker's podium, the soap box, and the party press to articulate key issues which they considered crucial to the socialist agenda. Not the least of these was the socialist transformation of the domestic sphere.

CHAPTER FOUR

Left to Rot "Amongst Her Stew Pots and Kettles": The Kingdom of the Home

Household labour at the turn of the century was all in the woman's domain. Bearing, feeding, clothing, nursing, and comforting children was often described as the central feature of this work. Without the benefits of modern inventions such as washing machines and vacuum cleaners, housekeeping was physically arduous and time-consuming. Although electricity and indoor plumbing were coming into use, many women in working-class and rural households laboured without these innovations until well into the twentieth century. Since domestic labour dominated women's lives, it is understandable that images of household and maternal duties permeated socialist discourse as it permeated the feminist movement more generally. It was the ground on which women stood when they assessed the world and considered political change.

Much of the research emerging on the transformation of mothering and domestic labour in twentieth-century Canada focuses on the decades after World War I.[1] Several issues emerge that are crucial to our understanding of the prewar era. First, although changes in domestic labour occurred slowly and unevenly, especially between rural and urban settings and between working-class and middle-class households, the ideological and material groundwork for these changes was laid well before the 1920s. Changes in household technology and the introduction of consumer goods were crucial for the transformation of domestic labour. The use of washing machines and vacuum cleaners did not only depend on disposable income and the gendered distribution of decision-making power within households (which priorized men's work); it also depended on the availability of electric power.

While Ontario began its campaign to extend electric power to rural districts in the 1920s, in rural Saskatchewan many households did not have access to the power networks until the 1950s. However, the focus on large consumer items, such as washing machines and vacuum cleaners, leads one to see the changes happening much later in the century. If we consider the smaller, more common items, such as soap, candles, cloth, and sewing machines, we can see that the transition to the consumer-based household was well underway by the turn of the century. To create a market for these consumer goods, advertisers often denigrated women's traditional household skills, offering instead the "benefits" of machine-produced, scientifically developed goods. The combined impact of public schooling and technological change meant that women laboured in greater isolation within the home.

Women's work within the home was also being systematically transformed and devalued from other quarters. By 1900, political and economic theories had effectively undermined the concept of the housewife as someone productive; the census recorded housewives and children as dependants.[2] Meanwhile, male-dominated professions such as medicine attacked women's skills in childbirth, child rearing, and care of the sick, and thereby undermined the traditional female support network of mothers, sisters, and midwives, often to the detriment of women's health.[3] Thus, the transformation of woman's domestic labour occurred unevenly across Canada, and a wide range of social forces undermined the reliance on woman's household skills and the goods she produced.

Second, current research often distinguishes between different kinds of household labour: reproduction and care of children, care of working adults, care of dependent adults, and paid work within the home.[4] These distinctions were usually blurred in turn-of-the-century discussions of the woman question. This blurring is significant. When writers moved from the topic of child bearing to talk about other household tasks, the reverence, idealization, and gender-specificity attached to child bearing also infused the other aspects of women's work. This blurring served different ends. In the hands of maternal feminists, it enhanced the status and prestige of a woman's role in the home and justified participation in public life. In the hands of more conservative thinkers, it reinforced woman's place in the home and her responsibility for all domestic labour. Among socialists, this blurring served different ends.

How are we to understand the left's embrace of maternal and domestic images? While socialists held widely varying views on the subject, many did accept the prevailing belief in woman's special maternal qualities and her domestic role. Did these views mean that there was no potential for radical thought? Despite Carol

MRS. CANADA—"Don't you think the baby grows, Doctor?"
DR. GRAFT—"Yes, but look at the Cat!"

Redrawn from sketch by Geo. Toseland. Dauphin, Man.

Bacchi's claims, these ideas were not unique to the middle class: the left strenuously debated the significance and relevance of woman's domestic and maternal roles in the development of social-ism. Left-wing feminists echoed the idea that women would "mother the race," without challenging the racist implications of these images. Many working-class women were not engaged in paid labour outside the home; and even those who were, by and large believed themselves to be destined for a life as wife and homemaker. It is therefore essential to consider the views about women's domes-tic role without taking it for granted that these concerns were inherently middle class. Some socialist feminists did indeed have a revolution in mind, a revolution that went beyond the industrial realm – a revolution of domestic labour itself.

Linda Kealey argues that the ideal of the "family wage" (the belief that men should earn enough to support a family)[5] so dominated the left's thinking that it became impossible for feminism to survive. She contends that the ideal of the family wage not only undermined woman's claim to equality and independence, but it "operated very powerfully to support existing inequalities in trade union and particularly socialist organizations. This ideology helped to perpetuate attitudes and policies on the 'woman question' which limited the appeal of those organizations to women. It also defined the contributions women could make to the socialist movement."[6] In short, belief in the family wage retarded the development of feminism in the left. This chapter will challenge that contention, insofar as the acceptance of the importance of women's role in the home sphere did not enfeeble some socialist feminists but, rather, that it provided a powerful ideological ground on which to mobilize women to fight for increased power and autonomy.[7] The failure of the socialist movement to advance feminism rested partly on its ultimate rejection of the significance of the domestic realm for the socialist agenda.

Two distinct ideological traditions informed socialist debates on the domestic role of women. Communitarians grappled with the problem of women's dependence on men. They saw women's oppression as being rooted in the domestic sphere, where women suffered isolation and economic dependence. The socialist transformation of women's domestic labour was as central to their agenda as was the socialist transformation of waged labour. Several communitarian socialist communities were established briefly in Canada. Collectivizing and socializing domestic tasks such as cooking, child care, and washing was expected to emancipate women from the oppression of their role as isolated, dependent housewives.[8]

Some popular American feminists advanced the communitarian socialists' view. In *The Grand Domestic Revolution*, Dolores Hayden calls these women "material feminists" because their commitment to the transformation of the domestic sphere was not exclusively moral or philosophical but was based on economic and material grounds. Material feminists were committed to transforming the material conditions within the home; they advocated socializing domestic labour and establishing women's control over it.[9] Their objectives were feminist: women should have autonomy and control over their own labour.

Marxian socialists emphatically rejected such schemes as utopian. Accepting political economy's growing denigration of women's household labour as "unproductive,"[10] they insisted that scientific socialism's prime requirement was the transformation of industrial waged labour; women's emancipation would follow. Limited proposals such as communal child care and food services were endorsed only because they permitted the equal participation of women in the industrial labour force. In contrast to the communitarian socialists, who saw the feminist transformation of domestic labour as a primary goal of socialism, the Marxian socialists endorsed the transformation of domestic labour only to the extent that it contributed to the full socialization of industrial labour. Thus, the international socialist tradition offered two conflicting views of domestic labour in the socialist agenda.[11] The tension between these positions was evident among the Canadian left. An important measure of each party's attitude towards women's domestic role was whether and to what extent the party press encouraged and sustained a women's column. The controversy over whether to have a women's page revealed important differences in the socialists' understanding of the relevance of domestic labour.

Before 1905, the socialist press touted several different women's columns. The first, edited by Mrs Wrigley, was the product of requests from readers of the *Citizen and Country* to provide a regular column of general interest to women. Titled "The Kingdom of the Home," it was headed by a four-part statement defending the ideals of maternal feminism. Although Mrs Wrigley's column appeared in only a few issues, it revealed important assumptions about subjects that were deemed to be of particular interest to women. One article explained that since questions "affecting our homes and happiness have not been considered so fully as they should be ... we have established a Woman's Department in these columns." It further promised to provide a "weekly budget of home literature that should be a help to those who realize that the character of the people is dependent on the purity of their homes."[12] Fulfilling this promise, both in the women's column and elsewhere, the paper discussed scientific improvements and labour-saving devices for the household; the hardships faced by farm women and women who ran boarding houses; and the problem of poverty, which prevented people from making a decent home. The emphasis on women's interest in the home and their maternal duties created a potential conflict. An argument linking women exclusively to the home could undermine the legitimacy of their presence in politics, and therefore in the socialist movement. Yet failure to address domestic issues that were of concern to women could make socialism less appealing to them. Arguments presented in the women's columns "Woman Is Man's Social Equal" and "We Women" tried to reconcile these conflicting positions.[13]

The pre-1905 women's columns recognized that domestic and maternal duties were the particular responsibility of women and emphasized that these duties fell within the purview of socialism. Women could not afford the luxury of confining themselves to home matters, because capitalism's reach contaminated even the private recesses of home life. Bertha Merrill Burns argued that a woman should turn to socialism to save her family from the ravages of capitalism:

A woman buys sugar and finds it half sand; she buys milk made of half chalk and water ... she buys coffee grown on a bean plant in Canada and tea gathered from willow trees. How, then, is woman to provide pure food for her family? She can never do it so long as the present profit system prevails in our mercantile world, for all these adulterations are made for profit – that some man or corporation of men may make money. When the Nation produces all these things for USE and not for profit, then, and then only, may the housekeeper expect to obtain pure and wholesome food for her family.[14]

Because capitalism touched on every aspect of the woman's home duties, Merrill Burns concluded that women should owe their allegiance to "the redemptive doctrines of Socialism." Women were not, however, to confine themselves to the home: "Should the home not recognize that it is but one part of the whole and that we have no right to live alone for our homes, our families, and neglect public and social duties?"[15] Woman's natural concern for the home thus became the rationale for political involvement.

In a similar vein, the early women's columns defended socialism from the criticism that it would destroy the home. Capitalism, not socialism, was the villain. In a socialist world, men would be able to afford to marry, and mothers would not be forced to work to support themselves. This argument was thought to appeal directly to mothers:

What will socialism do for a woman with four children – or more? ... Socialism will give to every mother the right to bear her children in love, not loathing; to welcome them to her arms with joy, not fear. It will give her likewise, all good things with which to surround them; it will remove anxiety as to their future, and enable her love to shield and bulwark their lives until they are grown to years of strength. It will not relieve her from the thousand and one calls for service that are made upon mothers always, for baby faces must be washed and baby wails must be attended to, even under the wise sway of socialism. But what mother considers it a hardship to do for her children? It is because she cannot do what she will that she is unhappy.[16]

Such an argument does not imply any socialization of the domestic relations within the home; under socialism, women would continue to bear full responsibility for domestic labour. It was thought that socialism would increase male wages sufficiently so that mothers could remain at home. The socialist promise lay in the possibility of a decent home life and the fulfilment of motherhood.

Other articles expanded this vision. As socialism would transform the workplace of men – both the relationship between worker and boss, and work itself – so it would transform the home, the workplace of women. The analogy between woman's relationship to man and the worker's relationship to his boss permitted socialist women to challenge men's domination. They applied workers' control to both sexes. Emphasis on the maternal duties of women formed an essential part of this argument.

How would this come to pass? The most articulate and coherent explanation came from Bertha Merrill Burns. First, socialism would abolish profit: no one would live off the labour of others. With no idle rich to support, the burden of labour would be distributed equitably among the entire population. Under capitalism all working-class women laboured in their own homes, but some laboured twice: they worked as well in the households of the idle rich. Socialism meant that every woman would have to do her share, and this would reduce the domestic labour of each. Woman, stated Merrill Burns, "will work in these co-operative establishments, and as there will be no idlers to live off her labour, she will have the full value of what she produces. A few hours' labour each day will provide an ample income for all her living." With the abolition of profit, the benefits of socialized labour would accrue directly to women, rather than indirectly through husbands and fathers.

Second, socialism would abolish the isolated housewife and would socialize domestic labour.[17] Existing methods of domestic labour such as cooking, washing clothes, and sewing were viewed as outdated because women worked in isolation. Socialism would take these tasks out of the home, just as capitalism had appropriated such domestic tasks as the baking of bread. Under socialism, the work would be managed collectively and scientifically, not for profit. "Washing and cooking and sewing may all be done far better in co-operative establishments, where skill and art and science are applied for the purpose of doing the best possible work, and where cheap labour and shoddy appliances are not used in order to pile up profits."

Third, socialists echoed the era's enthusiasm for scientific innovation in the home. Women were being criticized for their failure to apply these new methods. To sell consumer products, commercial interests actively undermined household reliance on women's

THE RICH WIDOW AND THE POOR ONE.

THE TWO WIDOWS.

MR. MONEYBAGS—"What! abolish Rent and Interest, and take away the revenue from which our widows and orphans derive their living!"

MR. WORKMAN—"You do not think about the widows and orphans who have no Rent and interest to live upon. Abolish our unjust system, which perpetuates inequalities, as pictured above, and establish Socialism. Then all women will be economically independent, and there will be equal opportunities for all."

skills.[18] For example, *The Physiology of Motherhood*, produced by the British Chemists Company in 1900, provided advice to mothers on child care, discouraging home remedies and traditional customs. Rocking a baby was denigrated as analogous to giving it opiates, yet the book encouraged and even advertised the use of sundry "scientifically produced" medicines, tablets, and pills for infants. One feminist response to this assault was the domestic science campaign designed to train women in scientific techniques for application in the home.[19] Socialists similarly aspired to introduce scientific inventions and methods to eliminate the "almost totally unnecessary" drudgery of housework – but not in private households. The advantages of "co-operative-social-labour" would be immediately apparent "in food laboratories, where chemical and hygienic knowledge is applied to the preparation of wholesome, nutritive and attractive food; in scientific laundries, where clothes may be instantly cleansed by the application of electrified water; in departments of drapery and clothing, where the principles of art and utility are brought to bear upon the problem of clothing the people." Scientific methods would include the design of kindergartens for working mothers, and socialized medicine.

Finally, socialized domestic labour would emancipate women from their dependence on men. Women would control their labour. The abolition of dependence and isolation within the home would allow for the development of social skills reputed to complement, not contradict, woman's maternal role. Woman's work in co-operative institutions "would be educative and social; it would develop her both mentally and physically and make her fit for the exercise of the maternal function when prompted by nature thereto." For Merrill Burns, the socialization of domestic labour and women's control of their labour were essential components in the development of socialism. This expanded the argument, supported by some socialists and certainly by trade unionists, that women should be driven out of the labour force and relegated to their proper sphere, the home. Through her influence as editor of the women's column, Merrill Burns was able to present an image of socialism that integrated discussions of domestic matters while at the same time opposing the restriction of women to that sphere alone. As she put it, "Motherhood means more than fatherhood and costs more to achieve. Socialism recognizes this fact and must provide opportunity for the mother wit to express itself in the affairs of the state."[20] Merrill Burns and other women socialists challenged the assumption that women belonged only in the home. The home was viewed as being torn asunder by capitalism. Woman's duty was to continue to meet the needs of her family through the transformation of domestic work and through her participation in the public realms of work and politics.

Thus, the women's columns before 1905 espoused a view of socialism that corresponded with that of the communitarian socialists; transformation of the domestic realm was an essential component of this socialist agenda. A host of issues pertinent to the domestic lives of women were discussed in the paper's columns, thus broadening the appeal of socialism to women, but there was no real consensus of opinion. R.P. Pettipiece, the editor of the *Western Socialist*, thought such matters had little to do with socialism:

The aims of the Socialist are clear and definite viz. the collective possession and democratic administration of all the material means necessary to a full and free human life. Growing out of this there are of course boundless implications touching the sexual relations, mental culture, religion, etc., but these are *no essential part of scientific socialism. Economic justice between man and his fellows*, adjusts him, and establishes that normal, true and natural relationship from which may flow the limitless possibilities of human nature. When the necessity arises for a concrete plan or application of Socialism, be assured it will be found. (emphasis added)[21]

Indeed, the early women's column did not have a secure position. In July 1903, in the face of an upcoming election, the column was dropped – as Merrill Burns, under her pen name Dorothy Drew, explained: "'We Women' are told to 'go back and sit down' this week, in order to make room for the field discussion re: matters political. When we get a ballot of our own we'll be an equally important factor with man at election time."[22] The disenfranchised were bound to suffer dubious status in a party that placed such high emphasis on political action.

Merrill Burns's column ended in 1903, just as socialists such as Pettipiece were gaining ascendancy in the SPC in British Columbia. While there was no real debate in the party paper about its demise, the decision reflected a judgment about the relevance of the woman question, at least among those who controlled the party press. But the issue did not die. In 1908, when pressed by his female readers, the editor of the *Western Clarion* sparked renewed controversy by refusing to provide a women's column in the paper. Not only did he say he would not "cater" to women, but he further rankled them by questioning their commitment to the cause: "As a general rule, a woman who is a Socialist is a Socialist because some man is."[23] He conceded that some of the letters he received from women demonstrated their ability to write, but he questioned their ability to "keep up the pace." He further explained: "If the Clarion's 'Woman's Column' ever becomes like the 'woman's columns' in some other Socialist papers, which seem to be written for human dressmakers and cooks, the poor Scotchman [the editor himself] will be turned loose with a meat-axe."[24] Clearly, he did not consider either sewing or cooking – domestic labour – an appropriate subject for a socialist paper.

Several party members agreed. One described the push for the women's page as a capitalist tactic designed to detract from the class struggle.[25] More common was the argument that the woman question was simply irrelevant to socialism: "We have had enough – in point of fact, too much – of that woman question. There aren't any women in the Socialist movement. There may be members of the party who, incidentally, happen to be of the female sex, but that is no concern of ours. This movement of ours is an economic movement not directly concerned with biology or physiology and is above all a working class movement worthy of the interests of all the members of that class, men, women and children. Cut it out."[26] One man stated that women would no longer ask for special columns once they understood the class struggle, for then they would understand "that which will emancipate their fathers and husbands, will also emancipate them."[27] The clear assumption was that socialism's only concern was men and their waged-labour relationship with employers.

Despite the editor's objection to having a women's column, he did publish letters from party members who disagreed with him. Several urged the importance of interesting the housewife and women workers in the cause of socialism. Ada Clayton criticized the SPC's propaganda strategy that focused on waged labour: "Pointing out wage-slavery will appeal to women wage-workers as well as men, but what about that large class who get no pay at all? It is said they get food, clothing and shelter, which is about all any of the workers receive; but there is a satisfaction in having even paltry wages first-hand ... Woman is not content to be much longer supported in this way. There is as great unrest here, as there is among industrial workers; so point out the cause and remedy here as in the other case." Clayton stressed that it was important for women to write about "local affairs and how the capitalist system effects them," just as men did, and she concluded that no socialist women's column was written for human dressmakers and cooks, nor did women "devote as much time beyond what is necessary to feed and clothe our families as the men waste on whiskey and tobacco."[28]

Another woman wrote that socialist propaganda did not appeal to women because "Socialist addresses and literature are chiefly directed to men and their particular position in the system of production. Women cannot and should not recognize themselves under the name of men, and it is just as ridiculous to ignore their position as it would be, say that of miners or any one particular line of industry."[29] Another queried whether the party ignored women because they did not have the vote or the price for a subscription. She urged the paper not to ignore the female wage earner or the woman in the home: "Let us have more equality and democracy in our work and see to it that the workingman's wife is not left to mentally rot amongst her stew pans and kettles."[30]

Support for a women's page also came from men. G.W. Wrigley responded on two separate occasions to the editor's remarks, in both cases emphasizing the need for propaganda directed at women. He refused to blame women's disinterest in socialism on their "conservative nature." Rather, he blamed the men, who were so busy talking to male wage workers that they neglected women in the home:

What effort has been made to show the women who cook our grub, darn our socks and mind our kids, that they are slaves of the wage system equally with us – that they help us to produce an existence wage for ourselves and a surplus value for the boss ... Are women any less likely to become revolutionary than men? Is it not true that women have less to hope for from palliative legislation than men? Does the eight hour day appeal to the women workers – the majority of whom are in the home working long after the men throw down their tools, and even those who work in factories, shops or offices have to, on account of their lower wages, do their laundry work and make their clothes after work hours.[31]

While the *Western Clarion* did not accede to their requests for a women's column, the controversy continued – and not only because women complained. Critics of socialism added fuel to the fire by accusing socialists of destroying the home. The *Western Clarion*'s response to these charges differed from that of the earlier socialist press. Placing primary importance on the waged-labour relationship, it regarded the problem of domestic labour as simply irrelevant, or at best as a secondary matter that would be solved once men received full value for their labour.

The *Western Clarion* reiterated that it was capitalism that destroyed the home. The growing trend of women to enter the paid labour force was cited as one means by which it did so: "Capitalism has torn woman from the home, thrust her into the economic field in competition with the opposite sex, grinds her life into profits and ultimately forces her to sell her body in order to live. Capitalism today is fast destroying the home, the palace, that we are told woman should exclusively occupy as her position in society." She must "fight side by side with her proletarian male partner, under the Socialist banner in the modern world for the *restoration of that which she lost* in primitive times, 'liberty and equality'; also for the establishment of the home where peace, happiness and plenty will be the rule" (emphasis added).[32] This argument is essentially nostalgic: capitalism forced women out of the home; socialism would restore them.

The possibility of men sharing in domestic labour was never seriously entertained; but as mothers were torn from their babies and men were put out of work by competition from women, unemployed husbands might be expected to perform domestic labour while their wives worked in the factories. "In many cases full grown men remained at home caring for the babies or mending stockings while the women were engaged at the wearing work of the mill."

Men doing housework was a calamity, for it "crushed out any movement on the part of workers to assert their manhood."[33]

To the charge that socialists would destroy the home came the countercharge that capitalism was destroying the home by preventing workers from marrying. Readers were assured that a man's first impulse was to establish a home, but low wages prevented him from doing so. One article even listed the typical workingman's expenses to demonstrate that he could not afford even the luxury of falling in love and taking his girl to the theatre. Capitalism thwarted the decent impulses of workers, whereas socialism promised that the worker could marry his loved one: "It is only under socialism that he can look his fellow workers in the face and say: 'Now I'm a man.' When he can look 'that girl' in the face and say, 'Now I am free and no man can deny me the right to make a living. I am able and willing to make a living for two, are you willing to be my partner and chum for the rest of my life?'"[34] Echoing socialist films of this era, the true socialist was promised his just reward: a woman.[35]

Capitalism was further blamed for preventing workers from marrying because of its distortion of male and female demographics. In mining and logging towns, employers preferred to hire single men and sometimes prevented workers from establishing homes for their wives and families. These towns often harboured a community of prostitutes to "service" the male workers. On the other hand, in some mill towns, employers preferred to hire women, thereby making it difficult for men to find employment.[36] "It may readily be seen that such distribution of the sexes is not particularly conducive to the development of home and family ties, and the purity of sex relations ... He-towns in one place and she-towns in another."[37]

Capitalism did more than prevent marriages; it turned marriage into an economic arrangement, devoid of true affection. A woman who, for economic reasons, was forced into a marriage of convenience became a kind of prostitute, obliged to sell herself to the highest bidder in order to survive. This line of reasoning is well illustrated in the poem "For Sale":

Women? The price has never been lower
For a "light of love" or one for a wife;
A dollar bill buys the first for an hour,
The hope of a home gets the second for life.
Fine girls, too, and pleasant to see,
Mistress or wife they will play their parts –

Caught in the meshes of slavery,
Beaten, and hopeless of breaking free,
Selling their bodies, if not their hearts ...
Join in the game on a wise man's advice,
Coin is the force by which all are swayed,
From a packet of pins to a virgin maid,
It's only a matter of having the price.[38]

Marriages of economic convenience were blamed for a host of problems, such as the high divorce rate, wife desertion, infidelity, separations, wife beating, and child beating.[39]

As further proof that it was capitalism, not socialism, that was destroying homes, the *Western Clarion* discussed the impoverished living conditions of the working class. Indeed, some articles claimed that working-class homes under capitalism were not worth preserving. "What sort of 'homes' have the workers? Crowded, ill-lit, ill-ventilated, disease-breeding tenements where the gracious sun seldom shines; miserable make-believes of shacks and shanties on the foreshore; tumble-down aggregations of boat-houses and barges on the rivers; pestiverous, musty, foetid bunkhouses in the mining, logging and railroad camps; box-cars when the watchful 'brakey' isn't around; – or on the lee of a straw stack. Home! Millions of workers have lost the meaning of the word. These structures can surely stand destroying."[40] With such homes, why should the "homethrust" appeal to the impoverished working-class housewife?

What is her home but her workshop? In the country, a shelter wherein she may cook and feed and wash, when she is not in the stable or the field, by day, by night, but a rude stall for sleep. In the city, when not in a full-blown boarding house, with roomers inhabiting all rentable corners to help pay the rent. While she lives in the kitchen and sleeps in the dining-room with her lord and their brood ... Married she has a steady job – for her board and clothes. Her job is steady enough, if that is any recommendation. To cook and wash dishes, sweep and scrub, wash and iron, mend and darn, day in and day out, except while the Lord is delivering her one of his "blessings" ... She is free only when she sleeps, and is free then only to store up energy enough for the next day's slavery. Destroy the Home? Cheerfully, if Capitalism leaves us any to destroy. And the wife-slaves will owe us a hearty vote of thanks.[41]

To the charge that socialism would destroy the home, the *Western Clarion* consistently responded that capitalism was a greater threat.

By abolishing poverty, socialism would therefore make home life possible, but the precise form it would take remained vague. Some articles seemed to suggest that socialism would restore home life by removing the economic need for women to work, thereby enabling them to return to their proper place as mothers within the home.[42] Often there was a blurring between the idealization of women's role in childbirth (including the real fear of maternal mortality)[43] and the more mundane domestic labours that women faced. Certainly, socialists did not want to lose women's services on either count:

We want a system of society so organized that when any mother goes down into the valley of death to bring forth a new life she will be surrounded with every comfort, luxury and convenience possible in this civilization. There shall be in attendance the most scientific physicians and the most skilled surgery that human anatomical philosophy has been able to produce, to the end a child may be perfectly born ... She shall be in a position to give her young a constant and tender mother's care, *not until, but long after, they have arrived at the age of entry into the great institutions of learning*, which shall be the most exhaustive known to educational science, to the end that the boy or girl may become the most useful factors possible in a future generation. (emphasis added)[44]

With its idealization of motherhood, this passage blurs the distinctions between child bearing and child care and other routine domestic tasks. That a mother might provide constant and tender care to children who were at school seems to us a curious assertion, unless one assumes that the "tender care" includes the labour of washing, cleaning, and food preparation. The SPC would have women continue to perform labour in the home: isolated, unsocialized, and unpaid.

This view of socialism's effect on domestic labour becomes clearer in the discussions about its impact on rich women. Capitalist wealth, it was argued, led to marriages rife with infidelity and divorce. The idle and useless rich woman was viewed as neglectful of her children and home. With the abolition of the servant class, rich women would be forced to return to their homes to take up domestic labour – a vision that delighted some: "Picture to yourselves our near-blue-blooded dames, servant-less in their ornate and expensive homes, returning perforce to the wash tubs and slop-pails of their mothers. Imagine hubby's uncomplaining efforts to masticate and assimilate their cookery."[45] With almost punitive intent, socialism would not welcome these women into a socialized utopia.

What would be the role of the state in the socialist transformation of domestic life? Echoing Fabian arguments in Britain, some suggested that the property element in marriage would dissolve with the advent of public ownership, and the state would "suitably compensate" mothers so that they would no longer need to rely on husbands for economic survival:

Not until woman is fully compensated economically, under socialist auspices, and *motherhood is recognized as the grand normal occupation of womankind* – to be suitably recompensed by the community at large instead of being as hitherto practically left to the caprice of each individual male employer of this particular species of "female labour" – will it be possible to lay down any true basis of sexual morality ... Her and her little ones' maintenance will be a first charge on the product of the entire community.

The state's role in supporting motherhood would permit a new kind of woman to emerge. This new woman, "emancipated economically and mentally spiritualized, will be able to rise to the full measure of the inexpressibly solemn responsibilities of conception and maternity under the Collectivist regime."[46] The emphasis on the state support of motherhood neatly side-stepped feminist concerns for the socialist transformation of domestic labour, though it did liberate women from male domination within the home.[47]

The SPC's lack of detailed discussion about the transformation of domestic labour is most striking when one considers that the issue was in fact being addressed by several prominent feminists of the time. The *Progressive Woman*, an American socialist feminist paper, debated these matters, but it was scorned by the *Western Clarion* for being bourgeois.[48] Charlotte Perkins Gilman, a vocal proponent of the feminist transformation of domestic labour, lectured in Vancouver in 1905. The *Western Clarion* delayed publication so that it could cover her talk but concluded that she "gave no evidence to show that she possessed the slightest knowledge of Socialism."[49] In short, the SPC did not consider such ideas socialist.

Why did the party reject socialist-feminist arguments for the transformation of domestic labour? Barbara Taylor argues that in the British context the rise of "scientific socialism" brought with it the end of feminist concerns about domestic work (though the Fabians clearly continued to address this issue after 1900). The Canadian context suggests a different dynamic. While scientific socialism certainly played a part in the Canadian debate, the discussions were overshadowed by a defensive response to the charge that socialism would destroy the home or family. While the SPC was prepared to consider the destruction of impoverished homes, it was not prepared even to debate the possible alternative ways of organizing domestic labour under socialism.

Overtly, the SPC argued that such debates led to accusations that socialism destroyed the home; but what was really being "destroyed" by these feminist ideas? As noted in the previous chapter, the male socialists' experience as waged labourers and as privileged members of the household permeated the SPC's image of socialism. Men's waged labour was relevant; women's work within the home was not. This masculine view provided the framework that justified dismissing women's issues, including domestic labour; few male socialists were willing to reflect on their privileged reliance on woman's labour within the home.

Feminists directly challenged this male privilege on two counts. First, if domestic labour was collectivized and taken out of the household, the personal service that men could expect from their wives would be lost. Although socialists were quick to criticize a boss's privileges, the men failed to acknowledge that privilege also existed within the family, between a man and his wife. The assumption that domestic labour was mothering, and that mothering was a woman's highest and almost sacred duty, effectively camouflaged the personal service that women rendered their husbands. Few male socialists were eager to examine this aspect of capitalist development. It threatened their male privileges within the home. Second, if domestic labour was collectivized, housewives would no longer be isolated but would congregate for paid labour. In that event, the grounds for allocating domestic labour to women would no longer seem fair or reasonable. The possibility that men might some day share in domestic labour was emphatically rejected by the *Western Clarion*. If wives worked, socialist men might lose the services they took for granted; they might have to wash their own shirts, cook their own meals, or care for their own children. Hence, the insistence that socialism would return women to the home.

Such arguments narrowed the SPC's view of socialism. In typical SPC style, Alf Budden maintained that the woman question had nothing to do with socialism. In his view, the Socialist Party had few women because women lacked the "necessary knowledge of their true position" as wage-earners or as people dependent on wages. Budden claimed that he would welcome any women who had this knowledge: "For the she worker there is one issue, the destruction of the wage system ... Remember that those who talk of the woman question, of woman's rights and her place at home, who prate of social reform, and the power of the 'better sex' to overcome evil conditions by tactful means, are working against your interests. There is no 'woman question.' There is only one question for you to solve, the slave question and it galls men and women alike."[50] Issues seen to arise from woman's "true position" as the isolated worker within the home were trivialized if not scorned.

The emerging SDPC relied on the communitarian socialist tradition, and this was reflected in discussions of the presence and value of a women's page in *Cotton's Weekly*. It will be remembered that when William Cotton took over the *Observer* and turned it into a socialist paper, Mary Cotton Wisdom edited a women's page that appeared with each issue from 1908 until November 1909. Initially, the page retained the subtitle of the *Observer*'s women's page, "Household Hints, Well-tried Recipes and Useful Hints to Home-keepers," but this was shortly changed to read, "Devoted to Ways and Means for Bettering Woman's Lot in Life – Good Recipes." Later issues dropped the "good recipes" part of the subtitle and simply stated, "Devoted to Ways and Means for Bettering Her Lot in the Various Walks of Life." These revisions of the subtitle reflected a growing concern that the women's page should contain socialist content that would appeal to and educate women. As the subtitle changed, so did the content. At first, it provided readers with a range of household hints as well as advice on grooming, fashion, and child rearing, along with advertisements, quotations from the Bible, recipes, and poetry. Gradually, alongside these columns, other articles appeared that were designed to interest women in political matters and socialism. They had titles such as "To the Wives of Workingmen," "Women and Socialism," "The Ballot for Women," "Women and the Socialist Party," and "Woman's Rights," and they included a reprint of Bertha Merrill Burns's article on women and socialism.

It was no accident that this women's page presented articles about socialism and women alongside seemingly apolitical material. As capitalism destroyed the home, women rose to defend their terrain. The women's page accepted that women's labour within the home, as mothers and as housewives, qualified them to contribute their skills to the public realm and to socialism. Thus, alongside recipes for "Cocoanut Cake" and "A Good Cup Cake" appeared an article "To the Wives of Workingmen," which emphasized that working-class women should take an interest in matters that could affect them. For example: "The conditions under which the father of the family labors do very vitally interest the wife, because dangerous conditions – and they are many – may render her children fatherless and herself a widow with no means of feeding her hungry family ... It is time for the wife to realize that she needs now to bring her mind, trained in domestic economy and grown adept in expedients, to bear upon the situation."[51] Even the household hints, which were usually straightforward practical advice, at times included the message of socialism: "It is an excellent plan if you live in a house to have a 'house purse' downstairs in a convenient place so that when a little change is needed for something, you are not obliged to run upstairs for it. If you have neither home nor purse, make your husband vote for both by voting the Socialist ticket."[52] Thus, like the socialist press before 1905, the women's page of *Cotton's Weekly* linked women's domestic duties to the cause of socialism.

Like the early left-wing press, this women's column expected that socialism would modernize domestic labour. Since capitalism had failed to bring housework into the modern age, socialism would use modern science, innovation, and technology to minimize the drudgery and inefficiency of household chores. The electric iron, automatic dusters, paints, and the fireless cooker were new scientific inventions that could dramatically reduce domestic labour within the home. Sometimes this modernization was envisaged as taking place in private homes, where "much of the dirty work ... will be done by simply pressing a button."[53] This view of scientific innovation paralleled the views expressed in the campaign to introduce domestic science into school curricula.[54] What made the socialists' contribution distinctive was that it aimed to socialize this work. The socialists envisaged scientific innovations developed for cooperative ventures, such as the one in Bradford, England: "Motor vans take the food to various centres, and bring back the soiled plates. Two thousand plates can be washed, with the proper apparatus, in one hour, by two men. The plates are placed on racks and wheeled into the drying room. Washing dishes this way is not the greasy, unpleasant process with which we are so familiar. Plenty of hot water, and no greasy sink afterwards."[55] Socialized domestic labour would make obsolete the housewife labouring alone at home.

There were abundant descriptions of the advantages of socialized domestic labour:

If fifty families in a neighbourhood were to unite in buying, preparing and serving their food, there would be a saving in expense, a greater variety and better food could be bought and served for less money, and there would be an immense saving in work as well as in worry. No doubt one person could do all the buying; six cooks would be able to do all the cooking ... Ten or twelve would be a modest estimate. And they would do no more or harder work – nor as hard, because they have every convenience – than does the housewife who works six hours a day preparing food for her family of five or eight... Another benefit would be the selection and preparation of our food by specialists, which would certainly mean better and more wholesome food for us.[56]

The elimination of laundry day was welcomed with particular delight. It was an especially onerous task when few homes had hot water or even running water. "Instead of women standing all day in steamy wash-houses while their children are crying, the public van will come from the public wash-house and bring back the linen in snowy piles, washed, ironed, and aired, all ready to put on. No drying of clothes then in dirty little back yards or general upset of the house which washing-day involves. This burden alone lifted off women's backs is enough to make them to cry Hallelujah for Socialism." Similarly, house cleaning would be eliminated, because experts would take over cleaning "as regularly as we get our drains flushed by the local authorities now, and a good deal oftener."[57]

If this work was to be done by public agencies, who was to work in these establishments? Childless women and sometimes men were expected to become trained specialists in the domestic industries, thus contributing their share to the social welfare. Unlike domestic service under capitalism, none of this labour would be considered menial. Each person would be expected to do his or her share. No one would be a servant to another. In this respect, the socialists were much more class-conscious in their proposals for collectivized domestic labour than some of their contemporaries, who advocated domestic reform unmindful of class inequalities.[58]

Would mothers be compelled to work outside the home in these collective enterprises? Certainly not. Socialized domestic labour would be so efficient that mothers would be able to devote more time to the important duty of child rearing: "Socialism hopes to take slavery out of the home and to make home the place in which to rest, to learn and be happy. Socialism hopes to give the mother back to her child and also to permit the mother to give some share of herself to the larger family – the community – where her care and guidance, advice and genius, are so badly needed today." Modern devices and collectivized domestic labour were expected to be so cost-efficient that mothers could be supported by the state. "The State will make allowances for women and children, holding the just view that if a woman bears children she does her duty without earning wages as well and should receive her reward."[59] The mother was not to be restricted to child care, however, but was freed to contribute to political life.

These arguments could imply that women were prohibited from participating in the paid labour force,[60] but this was explicitly challenged by Dora F. Kerr. She insisted that if women were "idle during the many capable years of their lives when they are not engaged in maternal duties, men will have to work the more to counterbalance this idleness, which does not appeal to me to be fair towards men." She also questioned what this would mean for women's autonomy: "Total dependence of women on men would almost certainly mean that women should submit to have their thinking done for them as well as their work, in fact it is the old heaven ideal of woman's position, and surely we have had enough of exclusive masculine thinking and masculine ideas prevailing in the world."[61]

Common to these varying schemes was the insistence on the radical transformation of domestic labour as an essential part of the development of socialism. Sometimes, however, articles from the other pages of *Cotton's* seemed oblivious of the issue as they envisaged a future under socialism: "We husky comrades, when we finish our days work of about four hours, and discard our overalls may take a Turkish bath and groom ourselves as those who are made in the image of God ought to do. We will then jump into our automobiles and take a spin of a hundred or so miles 'down the pike' and return in time for our six o'clock dinner, after which we will take in the opera or any other amusement that we may wish to enjoy."[62] The women's page reminded these enthusiastic male visionaries not to lose sight of the women who would prepare the dinner and wash up after the "husky comrades." Moreover, Mary Cotton Wisdom boldly suggested that male comrades should do their share of domestic labour:

Does anyone rise and demand an eight hour day's work for the mothers of the land? Did they do so, I can truthfully say that many husbands would have to be content with a cold bite on the pantry shelf, wear undarned socks and unwashed linen. An eight hour working day for men is all very well, but instead of spending so much time discussing their own woes, they should pitch in after their day's work and help their wives ... If, instead of going to his lodge, or his club or his union, or wherever it is that he goes, to berate his employers, he should help his wife finish the weeks wash or scrub the kitchen floor or put the children to bed, his time would be spent to far better use.[63]

This article caused a furore. Wisdom defended the woman who would leave her husband a meal on the pantry shelf, preferring to "reserve her strength for ... more important things in life ... for the upbringing of those children who became among the great ones." Her maternalism challenged woman's subordination in the household by placing maternal duty above wifely duty.[64] One woman claimed that her husband threatened divorce if she followed this advice. Wisdom snapped, "I am devoutly grateful that little man with his peanut brain and soul does not belong to me ... I don't know but [that] divorce, bad and all as it is, would be preferable to living in the cramped intellectual quarters of such a husband's companionship." However, she assured her readers that they had no cause to feel sorry for her husband, for she did not follow such a practice herself, but she said that her husband would not object if she did: "Anyway, the great unselfish heart of him wouldn't care if I gave him all his meals on the pantry shelf, and what is more, if I were delicate and needed help, he would willingly prepare the meals himself and feel it a pleasure to serve his wife. That is the best sort of husband to have and the sort I love."[65]

This affair provides considerable insight into how some socialists perceived woman's role. Wisdom's assault on women's domestic servitude struck too close to home (or to the stomach) for some readers. Several months later, in the face of financial difficulties, the paper was cut from eight pages to four and the women's page disappeared. Wisdom's final column addressed the merits of having a women's page. She said that when she was criticized by a man for not writing about socialism, she was shocked to realize that men read the women's page. "I felt as if I had caught him peeking through the key hole, listening to something he had no business to hear." On the other hand, another man gave the impression that men did not read that part of the paper: "Imagine my surprise, on referring to our woman's page to have him say positively that no intelligent men ever read any woman's page, that they skipped it as uninteresting, the same as he did the patent medicine ads. The idea gave me sort of a mental slap."[66] Wisdom declared that she was heartened by this attitude: "If all the intelligent men skip this page, we can discuss exactly what we like whether it is cooking or mending or housecleaning, our neighbor's bonnets, or the general affairs of the nation, as seen from our feminine standpoint ... In the meantime, we women must do our housekeeping, the dishes have to be washed and the floor swept and the children put to bed, despite all the political agitators around us."[67] In the next issue the editor explained that the cost was too great to put out an eight-page paper and that the staff needed "more time to devote to getting out a good paper." The women's page and the patent medicine ads disappeared with no specific explanation except the general laconic comment, "More brains, less pulp."

Although there was no longer a women's page, the paper continued to carry a women's column for a brief time, followed by occasional articles with similar titles.[68] In 1911 *Cotton's* hired a woman editor, Margaret Allen, who briefly edited a women's column. While little else is known about the decision of the paper to maintain these columns, these efforts nonetheless suggest that the SDPC was considerably more tolerant of a women's page than the SPC was. The SDPC paper continued to reflect the kinds of concern that were expressed through the women's page, although the Bible passages, household advice, and recipes disappeared.

The paper also continued to speak out against the criticism that socialism was a home wrecker. One article, taken from a Roman Catholic paper, described the horrors that a socialist future might hold, including the rotation of women to different husbands once a month, the taking of all children from their natural parents, and the numbering (instead of naming) of children.[69] Such arguments were always refuted on two distinct grounds. First, it was pointed out that capitalism, not socialism, was destroying the home: capitalism made it impossible for working men to buy a home, thus forcing them to risk eviction from tenements and rented homes. Under socialism, no one would be allowed to profit from rent, and since workers would retain the surplus of their labour, they would be able to afford to own their own homes. Second, capitalism forced women out of the home into factories and unhappy marriages, whereas socialism promised women economic independence and freedom to marry for love.[70]

Economic independence for women was crucial. Bertha Merrill Burns, in an address to the SDPC, explicitly challenged those socialists (doubtless, members of the SPC) who refused to address this issue:

There are those among socialists who claim that there is no sex war – that when the working class shall have acquired possession of the means of production, and attained economic freedom, that nothing else is necessary. Each working man (and all the men will be working men in those days) will be able by his economic security to undertake the support of one or more women and everything then will be lovely. In fact, I have heard some socialists talk as though the entire aim of socialism was to secure this privilege. The supported creature is never a free creature and the man who bases the class struggle on the fact that a certain set of men are dependent upon another set of men for their means of life is a very inconsistent creature if he does not at the same time grant that women, being dependent upon men for their means of life, there must also be a sex struggle ... To end it women must be free to earn their own living.[71]

Articles in *Cotton's* were vague about how women could gain economic independence. Equal pay was endorsed by some, but it was not considered directly relevant to the woman in the home. The solution therefore had to be twofold. On the one hand, by ending waged labour, socialism would end the exploitation of women and men as waged labourers. It was presumed that the end of waged labour would make social wealth available to workers to create homes. If women worked, they would not be exploited as they were under capitalism and would therefore be in a position to choose their marriage partners.[72]

On the other hand, the paper sometimes echoed the Fabian call for "state support of motherhood" or "mothers' pensions," which would ensure that women could remain at home and care for children.[73] The key here is the belief that under socialism women would not have to work for wages while caring for children. "The lot of the woman under Socialism will be far different. She will be free. Her equality with man will be recognized. The workers will own and run industry for themselves. Plenty for all will be assured. There will be no slavery. Woman will be economically free. She will not be robbed if she is a producer of wealth. And she will be provided for liberally as a mother ... We must recognize her right to comfort and freedom from worry while she is about to become a mother and during the infancy of her children."[74] Another article similarly urged, "Let motherhood be state paid ... If she desires to remain unmarried or childless, let her have an assured income. Let woman get the same reward for equal work with men."[75]

Whatever the problems inherent in proposals for the state support of motherhood (most notably, the naive belief in the benevolence of state intervention), some articles insisted on the fundamental interconnection between economic dependence and the social subordination of women to men. Under socialism:

The woman will have the necessities of life provided for her. Maternity will be the care of the state. The mothers will have the best that science and attention and medical care can give. For the industrial organization will see to it that the future citizens will not be stunted and starved and twisted before ever they come to be born. Under Socialism THE WOMAN

WILL NO LONGER LOOK TO THE MAN FOR HER FOOD, CLOTHING AND SHELTER. Do you grasp what a revolution that will work in society? Do you comprehend what a change there will be in the relation between the sexes?[76]

Finally, like the earlier women's page, some articles in the later SDPC press discussed the socialization and modernization of domestic labour. Homes and cities would be designed differently; machinery, inventions, and public services would lighten the work within and around the home.[77] "The woman's place would be in the home, and her work would be as little and light as the combined inventive capacity of both sexes could possibly make it."[78] One article reported on the speech of "comrade Miss Brennan" at a meeting sponsored by the SDPC in Vancouver, where Brennan argued that if we can accept the idea that a machine-made suit is made better than a hand-made one, we should "see equally well, that scientific cooking, done by people trained for that trade, with the least amount of energy and the greatest economy will be equally successful." Socialism, she argued, would free women from housework and give them back "their share of the world's work, that share which the introduction of machinery has taken away from them."[79]

Lest we assume more coherence among Social Democrats than is warranted, we must keep in mind that *Cotton's Weekly* also printed articles that presented the more conservative version of this argument – that socialism would simply return women to their proper place in the home. One article argued that socialists differed on the issue of care of children because it was "no essential part of socialism." Men who did domestic labour, even if they were unemployed while their wives were at work, were ridiculed as "squaw men."[80] These views were similar to those being put forward by the SPC. Nonetheless, the SDPC's greater tolerance of women's issues and a women's page permitted a more wide-ranging discussion of the socialist transformation of domestic labour.

It is crucial to keep in mind that debates over other aspects of the woman question, which will be examined in subsequent chapters, were cast in terms of socialists' acceptance of woman's domestic and maternal roles. This remains remarkably consistent throughout the socialist press. The early socialist movement was reluctant to challenge woman's role within the home, but in the seeming decline of the home, socialists claimed important ground from which to fight capitalism. Capitalism was destroying the home; socialism, in one form or another, would redress the distortions that capitalism had wreaked upon it. More striking, however, are the contrasting feminist arguments put forward by socialist women about the socialization of domestic labour. The SPC did not endorse the socialization of domestic labour, nor was this considered a legitimate part of its agenda. Except insofar as economic need was satisfied, woman's domestic labour would remain isolated and unpaid. In contrast, the pre-1905 socialist movement and the SDPC discussed in some detail the transformation of domestic labour, looking at how it would be both socialized and placed under women's control. It is by no means clear that all socialist women adhered to these views, but a distinct feminist perspective within the left challenged the male socialists' view of the class struggle and the transition to socialism. These women believed that socialism could revolutionize their domestic lives.

CHAPTER FIVE

The Plight
of the Working Girl

Although socialists were reluctant to place domestic labour on their agenda, they were eager to wrestle with one of the more startling social changes of the century – the increasing number of women entering the paid labour force.[1] A larger proportion of women were visible working in urban centres and industry, and the mounting concern about the impact of industrialization and urbanization often coalesced around images of women "taking men's jobs" and abandoning their traditional place in the home.

In this context, it is important to remember that the vast majority of women were not engaged in paid labour outside the home. Across the country, roughly one in six women worked for wages and roughly one in seven workers were women. The women who worked tended to be employed in jobs that were thought suitable for their sex. The largest percentage were in the service sector (42 per cent), most as domestic servants. A significant number (31 per cent) did manual work, mainly in light manufacturing. Some 24 per cent of women in the paid labour force had white-collar jobs, more than half of which were in low-paying and racially segregated professions such as teaching and nursing. Only 4 per cent of wage-earning women were employed in the primary sector. These proportions had shifted somewhat by 1921. The number of women in domestic service and manufacturing had declined to 26 per cent and 18 per cent, respectively, while the number in the professions had risen to 19 per cent. Whereas in 1901 the clerical and commercial sectors had employed few women, by 1921 an increasing number had found work in these sectors. Thus, women who entered the paid labour force were predominantly employed in a limited range of occupations: domestic service, teaching, nursing, clerical work, and light manufacturing.[2]

Even within the different occupations, gender was a significant factor in organizing work and segregating women into the lowest-paying jobs. As Joy Parr compellingly demonstrates in *The Gender of Breadwinners*, sex segregation pervaded the local workplace, though the gendered definition of specific jobs could vary from one locale to another. In light manufacturing, women performed work that was judged to be comparatively unskilled, and they received wages that were dramatically lower than men's.[3] In women's professions, women occupied the lower ranks of the occupational hierarchy. In teaching, the majority of women worked at the poorly paid elementary level; the higher-paid upper levels were usually reserved for male teachers.[4] Thus, although women were entering the labour force in increasing numbers, sex segregation meant that their work, even within a given occupation, was low-paying and often differed significantly from men's. Even where both sexes did identical work, women still earned less.[5]

Immigrant women often occupied the lowest-paid sector of the female labour market, for race and ethnicity further divided the workforce.[6] Governments and private agencies actively encouraged women's immigration to fill jobs that Canadian women shunned, such as domestic service.[7] The female presence in the labour force was further characterized by its youth. In 1921 almost 70 per cent of wage-earning women were under twenty-five years of age and few women older than thirty-five worked for wages.[8] Women typically worked when they were young and single, often while they were still living at home, and most quit their jobs when they married. This pattern was imposed by employers, who refused to hire married women, and it was also expected by the wage-earning women, for they anticipated a life of unpaid domestic work once they married and had a family to raise. Both the inexperience and expectations of women hampered their ability to organize and fight for better working conditions. However, some wage-earning women defied these generalities, did not live with their parents, and had dependants to support. These women struggled to make ends meet in the face of employer discrimination, low wages, significant increases in the cost of living, and widespread discrimination against women as tenants.[9]

There remain significant gaps in our knowledge of wage-earning women during this period. The census omitted the war years, when increasing numbers of women entered the paid labour force. Census collectors did not consider a farmer's wife to be "employed," yet her labour was crucial to the economic viability of farming and provided essential income to support the growth of a staples-based farm economy.[10] Census figures also ignored the paid work that women and children did within the home: caring for children, taking in boarders, doing laundry for pay, or selling domestically produced goods such as garden produce and clothing.[11] This work may have been especially important for working-class and minority women who were struggling at the margins of survival. These gaps in our knowledge remind us that production at the turn of the century was not fully converted to a waged-labour system. All but the most privileged women worked without pay, doing domestic labour inside the home.

All workers at this time faced enormous difficulties maintaining acceptable working conditions and wages. The trade union movement was beleaguered by uncertain business cycles, dramatic increases in the cost of living, hostile employers, and pro-management governments. By 1911, only 5 per cent of the entire Canadian labour force was unionized, and by 1921 this had increased to only 10 per cent.[12] Women workers faced additional barriers. Since they assumed that their employment in the labour force was temporary, and since they received low wages and had to endure long, arduous hours of labour both at work and at home, few women had the resources, energy, or will to devote to the improvement of their wages and working conditions. Yet women workers did unionize in a variety of sectors. Garment workers, textile workers, telephone operators, domestics, nurses, retail clerks, waitresses, laundry workers, and teachers tried to organize in a number of communities across Canada between 1900 and 1920, though some jobs, such as domestic labour, proved exceedingly difficult to unionize because of the isolated nature of the work.

In most sectors, women faced the concerted hostility of employers towards unionization and demands for improved working-conditions. The trade union movement and male workers had an ambivalent response to the presence of women. The Knights of Labour supported women's strike actions, set up day nurseries for wage-earning women, and advocated equal pay for men and women in the 1880s and 1890s.[13] On the other hand, the Socialist Labour Party called for equal pay for men and women while at the same time advocating that women be prohibited from "occupations detrimental to health or safety."[14] In 1889 the Trades and Labor Congress (TLC) voted to include in its platform the "abolition of child labour" and "female labour in all branches of industrial life such as mines, workshops, factories, etc." The clause was not removed until 1914.[15] While some trade unions supported wage-earning women's right to equal pay or minimum wages, they seldom had the inclination or power to enforce these claims consistently. Furthermore, the issue of equal pay was double-edged; many of the male trade unionists assumed that if employers were forced to pay equal wages, they would preferentially hire men. Even union support for a minimum wage for women was attenuated and was given far less support than wages for men. Some unions even fought to increase the differential in women's wages; rather than supporting the woman worker's rights, they strove to preserve male privilege in the workplace.[16]

The issue was complicated by a common turn-of-the-century myth that women displaced male workers and drove down the overall wage rates of both sexes.[17] Given the segregated nature of the labour market, women rarely competed directly for men's jobs. Yet it was argued that women and children ought to be excluded from the workplace in order to maintain reasonable wage levels. This view was held by both the trade union movement and the early left.[18] Competition between workers struck at the heart of the union movement. The unions of the day were typically craft unions, organized by skilled workers in order to limit the numbers in their trade and thus increase their bargaining power with employers. Their answer to low wages was to close ranks, exclude the competition of other workers, and challenge the employers' use of non-union labour. The demand to exclude women from the workplace was consistent with the logic of craft unionism and was analogous to union arguments that opposed immigration.[19] Both women and immigrant workers were blamed for low wages.

Whatever their disagreements, unions, women workers, and middle-class reformers all pushed for reforms to protect wage-earning women. Their demands included minimum wages, the exclusion of women from dangerous foundry work, and the provision of separate washrooms for women.[20] As with equal pay, protective legislation was double-edged, for it could undermine the position of women in the labour force. Trade unionists were willing to support it because it served their own interest to do so. For although the legislation was designed to help women, the male trade unionists believed that employers would hire men in order to avoid the extra costs of the "protective" measures. Similarly, while the women's movement pushed for protective legislation, its concerns did not always reflect the interests of working-class women. Middle-class white women, in particular, were anxious about the harmful effects of waged labour on women's reproductive capacity; laws requiring seats for shop girls were defended on the belief that standing all day harmed their reproductive organs. Yet significant tensions existed between middle-class reformers and working-class women.

The National Council of Women (NCW) was hesitant in supporting minimum wages for women and put little effort into examining the grievances of wage-earning women. Like male trade unionists, its members supported measures that conveniently served their own self-interest, such as the training and immigration of domestics. Even as late as the 1930s the NCW was against married women working.[21] While the reform-minded middle class focused on issues of separate toilets and morality, wage-earning women demanded job security, better wages, and shorter working hours – demands that often went unheeded by the women's movement. No incident better illustrates this class tension than a dispute over prohibition in Winnipeg. Viewing prohibition as the imposition of middle-class standards on the working class, "the Winnipeg Women's Labour League publicly endorsed the sale of light beer and wine as a deliberate affront to the prohibitionist suffragists. In the same year, the suffragists revealed their true colours by giving support to a group of local Council women acting as scabs during a Winnipeg strike."[22] Despite seemingly good intentions, the women's movement at times proved a poor ally to the employed woman.

In short, women confronted powerful forces, both ideological and structural, in their efforts to defend their interests as workers. Representing less than 20 per cent of women, the female labour force was young, inexperienced, segregated into low-paying jobs, and often isolated in the workplace. All this served to inhibit these workers' ability to act collectively. The trade union movement, which might have offered some help, was in itself small and beleaguered, and when not actively hostile to employed women, it was at best ambivalent. The other potential ally of the employed woman, the women's movement, consistently failed to support employed women's interests, often speaking *for* working-class women rather than letting them represent their own interests. In this context, socialists were eager to claim the "problem" of wage-earning women for the socialist agenda, but much of the structural and ideological ambivalence of the era was echoed by the Canadian left.

The left and the labour movement both drew upon the myth of the family wage. They harked back to an idealized bygone era when a man earned enough wages to support a wife and family.[23] This ideal of a family wage in fact obscured the reality of working-class life, for women (and children too, in many cases) had always worked and contributed to the economic survival of the working class, though much of their labour was unpaid. How did socialists reconcile the family-wage ideal with women's fight for rights as workers? And what of the women who worked without wages within the home? They may have wanted women to have very little participation in the paid labour force, believing that this would increase their husband's or father's wage. Wherein did the interests of working-class women lie? Linda Kealey and others have argued that belief in the family wage significantly weakened women's fight for paid work and decent wages. We should approach such generalizations cautiously.

The socialist movement offered different theoretical analyses of women in the labour force, but none resolved the contradictory interests of working-class women. The ideal of the family wage was used by some to attack women's presence in the labour force. One of these critics was the German Marxist, Karl Kautsky,[24] who pointed out that the economic development of capitalism, through the introduction of machinery, enabled employers to use weaker and unskilled workers, especially women and children. "But if the wife," stated Kautsky, "and, from early childhood, also the children of the worker *are in a position to provide for themselves*, the wages of the male worker can almost entirely be reduced to the cost of maintenance of his own person" (emphasis added).[25] Kautsky's main concern was not the plight of the weaker workers – the women and children – but the impact of their employment on the male workers' wages. The woman worker was important only insofar as she contributed to the debasement of working-class family life.[26] Women's economic independence was viewed as the problem. It was, of course, assumed that socialism would somehow solve this problem, but since the ability of women to support themselves was deemed to be part of the problem, how could socialism respond to the needs of women workers?

The demand for the family wage did not necessarily prevent socialist women from demanding their rights as waged labourers. If one accepts that a man ought to earn a family wage, it follows that his wife and children should not be compelled to work because of economic necessity. If men are paid a family wage, their daughters, sons, and wives will not need to work. But the argument that women and children should not be forced to work is not the same as the argument that they ought not to work. This subtle but important distinction is too often overlooked in family-wage discussions. Some socialists of the period argued that men ought to earn a family wage but that if they did not (or if a woman was not supported by a father or husband), women ought to have the right to work and have equal pay so that they could support themselves and their families.

The German socialist August Bebel was frequently cited for his study of women in Germany, where 30 per cent of women worked for pay.[27] Unlike some trade unionists and socialists, Bebel spoke out against the working-class antipathy to women in the labour force. The solution to the problem, he argued, lay in recognizing capitalism as the source of women's oppression. In seeking liberation, women must join male comrades, and socialists should accept women as fellow workers, fight for their rights, and educate them to the need for socialism.[28] While Bebel's ideas were progressive, he was encouraging women to integrate themselves into a struggle that was essentially defined by the experience of men.

Socialist women took an interest in theoretical works that offered an analysis of their position. In 1908 members of the SPC in Toronto started a women's study club and urged other women to follow suit. The group studied Engels's *Origin of the Family, Private Property and the State*, Rappaport's *Looking Forward*, Morgan's *Ancient Society*, and Bebel's *Woman in the Past, Present and Future*.[29] American socialists and feminists, including several of the leading women socialists in the American left, further articulated and developed ideas on women and work, drawing on American experience and moulding socialist theory to the North American context. Their ideas were popularized through pamphlets, lecture tours, and party papers, especially on the women's pages. Reprinted articles from several American socialist papers that specialized in the woman question – for example, *Socialist Woman* and the *Progressive Woman* – often appeared in the Canadian left-wing press.[30]

This literature provided Canadian socialists with a third perspective on working women, one that more closely focused on the problem of woman's dependence in the home and in the labour force. Charlotte Perkins Gilman was one such American feminist whose ideas gained currency in the Canadian socialist press, mainly through the women's columns.[31] Gilman acknowledged that women had unique natural and moral virtues, and argued that these had been stultified in modern society because of woman's economic dependence. She articulated the positive side of women taking part in waged labour – that work beyond the home had the potential to develop woman's independence and maturity to the full in areas other than the maternal and feminine realms. As we shall see, socialist women in Canada echoed her lament for women's dependence, a concern that was often lost amid the theoretical discussions of capitalism.

More revealing than this abstract theorizing were themes that emerged in specific discussions regarding different kinds of work. First, the left's astonishing ignorance about the actual nature of women's waged labour in Canada crippled its ability to develop a coherent response to the needs of women in the labour force. Second, different voices spoke to women's issues within the left, and those of wage-earning women were rarely publicized and were not well represented. Third, colouring discussions about different types of work were implicit assumptions about the kind of paid work that was appropriate to men and women; socialists did not universally endorse the family-wage ideal, but they consistently argued that certain kinds of paid work "naturally" belonged to women.

Nowhere are these themes more evident than in the discussions of domestic service, the largest sector of employment for women in Canada at this time. While some well-off nineteenth-century working-class households kept a servant (often a neighbour's child), servants were increasingly becoming a luxury that few could afford. The wealthy saw the shortage of domestics as a crisis and used their influence to lobby for a solution to the "servant problem." In response, government and private agencies encouraged the immigration of potential domestic servants, preferably from the British Isles, and established training programs in domestic science. In spite of these efforts, women abandoned domestic service for factory work, and the servant problem persisted.[32]

Socialists were sensitive to this issue and offered a refreshing challenge to the class-biased construction of the servant problem: "Let every lazy wench in the country do her own work, including the emptying of slops, and the [servant] problem would be solved."[33] One writer, Spartacus, sarcastically chided working-class women: "We must at once see to it that our sisters stop the inconvenience and disgrace of the 'ladies' of Winnipeg having to empty their own slops and attend to the wants of their own bodies."[34] The comments of these men reflect working-class resentment of rich women on behalf of working-class women for their low-status occupation – but they saw no disgrace in men not emptying their own slops.

All women did not share these negative perceptions of domestic service. Finnish women, for example, viewed it as "reputable, well-paid and even independent work."[35] Nonetheless, socialists tended to stress its unpleasant aspects. Lack of control over the hours of labour, excessive demands, and ill-treatment by employers were cited as reasons women disliked domestic service.[36] Unlike factory workers, domestics were obliged to be on call at all hours. One poignant illustration is found in the short story "Katie Goes to a Ball," which recounts the dismay of a domestic servant whose plans for a night out are ruined by the thoughtless demands of her mistress.[37] Even the working man, who fought so hard for the eight-hour day and union wage, is asked to reflect on his own treatment of the hired girl: "You keep a servant girl to help your wife? Does she work eight hours a day? No, she works about fourteen, and hears a good deal of grumbling because she does not do better. Does she get union wages? No, she gets about 30 cents a day. Does she get double pay on holidays? ... The woman who works to make your life comfortable works just as many hours as you can make her work, and she gets just as little pay as you can get her to take. Is that all right?"[38]

We must view socialist men's concern for the domestic servant with some scepticism. Domestic service, after all, is housework. If one begins to stress the harsh and debilitating effects of domestic service, one could do the same with respect to housework. Indeed, middle-class women complained that the absence of servants placed undue hardship on their health and well-being, forcing mothers to neglect their maternal duties. Such an argument was expressed by "Gwen" in a Vancouver paper. She complained that the average woman could no longer afford a servant and had become a "slave" in her own home: "From early morning till late at night she must cook, housemaid and nurse; she must wash and bake, scrub and sew, sweep and dust, and look after the children ... Women are sinking into apathy and ill-health, home life is disorganized, or exchanged for hotel life, children are neglected – and why? Because the Dominion Government neither assists servant girls to come here from Europe, nor lifts the tax temporarily on Chinese domestics."[39]

The SPC had no sympathy for the hardships this "lazy" woman faced: "If to do her own work causes the bourgeois dame to 'sink into apathy and ill-health' the sinking would certainly be accelerated in the case of the servant girl who would be called upon to do that work and her own besides. It would indeed be a foolis [sic] girl that would rush in where a bourgeois madam couldn't travel without going kerflop ... Down with the slavery of doing your own work. Up with the freedom of saddling it off onto somebody else. All honour to 'Gwen,' the valiant champion of the enslaved women of the West End."[40] Ironically, in the same breath as it chided Gwen for not doing her own work, this article implicitly championed saddling women with all responsibility for domestic labour.

Some socialists stressed the moral dangers of domestic service. Gustav Prager, a frequent contributor to *Cotton's Weekly*, spoke of two English girls adopted as servants into Christian homes. One was "worked to the limit of her capacity, treated distinctly as an inferior, had to eat her meals at odd times in the kitchen, shed many a tear from loneliness." Her sister fared even worse. She was eleven years old when adopted into a home to act as a servant, and "at the tender age of thirteen she became a mother, outraged by the scoundrel who had promised to protect her and the good woman discarded her and thrust her out into the world, and spoke of her as a depraved, sinful creature." The vulnerability of domestic servants to such abusive working conditions – overwork, long hours, subordination, and sexual abuse by employers – was compounded by their youth and isolation. Placing these issues in a class context, Prager urged, "Hasten the day, so that the daughters of the working class will not be forced to slave at measly pay, for long hours, obeying a class that prattles of high ideals, of grand ethical laws [yet] forces their helpers to act a lie and tells them to be good."[41]

The most detailed account of the lot of the domestic servant is provided by Bertha Merrill Burns. While expressing a class perspective of the problem, Merrill Burns did not share Prager's focus on the moral well-being of domestic servants. Rather, she focused on the hard work expected of a servant:

She rises at five in the morning, and hangs out a wash of baby linen before the average working man with his eight or nine-hour day, has risen from his bed. At seven she bathes, dresses and feeds the two infants, after which she is at liberty to sweep, dust, polish grates, etc., until it is time to prepare breakfast for her mistress, her mistress' husband and his brother, who is also an inhabitant of the house. At nine o'clock she carries three well-laden trays to the bedrooms of these perfectly healthy, presumably competent members of society. I have not yet learned that she spoon-feeds them, but this will follow in due course if the working class electorate much longer permit these people to suspend all useful activities.[42]

Compared to the servant, Merrill Burns thought that the slothful mistress and the average working man were privileged. Socialism would prevent the rich woman from shirking "the useful work that should naturally fall to her to perform." It would "convert this useless, ill-bred and supercilious creature, living in luxury and idleness off the toil of her fellows, into a real woman, joyfully sharing in the productive labor of the world." For Merrill Burns, even the rich woman had something to gain from socialism. Socialism would "cultivate a spirit of fraternity and equality, for, under a system where kindness and co-operation form the only basis of exchange, the individual who would be served in one capacity must be willing to serve in another and service that no longer can be bought or commanded must be obtained by mutual fellowship and goodwill."[43] While Merrill Burns saw domestic work as naturally falling to women, she claimed for it the same dignity that working men demanded.

Even more than the working conditions of domestics, the importation of domestic servants came under fire from the left. Chinese and "Hindu" immigration was vehemently attacked by both labour and the left.[44] Given the poor working conditions and low wages of domestic servants, socialists feared that immigrant women would further drive down wages in domestic service – or worse, in other forms of employment.[45] In 1913, when the B.C. government donated $10,000 to the Salvation Army to "import" domestics, *Cotton's Weekly* claimed that this was money given to "henchmen of the labor skinners for its services in dumping jobless wage workers where the masters want to use them as a club against wage workers on the job."[46] The Salvation Army was also accused of importing strike breakers and of "speculating in goods of the feminine gender."[47] It is seldom clear whether such immigration was seen as a threat to the jobs of men or women. Clearly, working-class men feared the loss of the income of wives and daughters. One person did express concern for the consequences to women: "The wives of unemployed workmen and even employed and women whose breadwinners have been killed or injured have managed to earn enough to buy a little food by doing housework or washing for those who can afford to have it done. The McBride government and the Salvation Army are now about to relieve these women of the work by flooding B.C. with servant girls."[48]

For importing domestics, socialists accused the YWCA of preparing "candidates for houses of prostitution."[49] From Brandon, Manitoba, one person complained to *Cotton's Weekly* about Mrs Sanford, superintendent of the Winnipeg Girls Home of Welcome, who imported 101 women as domestics. The women earned $60 for six months' work, but $47 was deducted for passage: "One of these girls succeeded in securing a position in the city of Winnipeg, which would pay her almost twice as much as the position allowed her by Mrs. Sanford. The man employing her was willing to give $50.00 to Mrs. Sanford if only she would allow her to work for him, a sum which would more than pay for the girl's fare. But for some reason which no doubt Mrs. Sanford can explain, she would not relieve the girl, who is now on a farm in Manitoba working early and late with never an evening off, actually bound by the toils of legal slavery." The writer speculated that "starvation or a life of dishonour" was the fate of the girls at the end of the contract, having only $13.00 in a strange country: "Whether Mrs. Sanford knows it or not, she is without a doubt creating victims for the 'white slave traffic' … Figuring these one hundred and one girls at $5,000.00, makes it about $48.50 each. If this is what these papers and Mrs. Sanford price the life and honor of these girls at, then I am bound to say that within a year their life and honor will be sold at much below its market value."[50]

Amidst the socialist attack on bourgeois laziness and oppressive working conditions, racism fuelled further arguments against the importation of non-white workers. The labour press in British Columbia expressed concern that 90 per cent of the domestics in the province were "mongols."[51] There was some evidence of employer preference for Chinese servants because they were regarded as "sober, industrious, civil and obliging." Women especially preferred them, it was suggested, because their husbands would then be less likely to "fool around" with the maid.[52] The policy of importing Chinese workers to serve as domestics in British Columbia was attacked on the grounds that it would "force the chinks to do the dirty work for those too lazy and useless to do it for themselves, at wages which would not keep a decent daughter of the proletarian wage slave."[53] Similarly, the importation of "negresses from Guadaloupe" to serve as domestics in Montreal was criticized: "The Canadian servants won't stand for the impudence of this class of mistresses. So negresses come. The race problem is complicated."[54] Indeed. Although well aware that the lot of non-white domestics was especially harsh, the left made no serious effort to challenge the racism that exacerbated the exploitation of these women.

Efforts to solve the servant problem through domestic science education were also challenged. In the planning stages, domestic science was welcomed for providing training in home management. Once established, however, it was criticized for its manifest class bias: "The training of domestic science appears to be pushed owing to the desire on the part of the wealthy to have a large number of domestic servants. The girls are rigged out in white bonnets and aprons and are taught to cook cakes requiring such expensive materials as from four to six eggs."[55] This training was seen as impractical for a working-class family and, clearly, as being directed towards the needs of the wealthy.

While the left viewed the servant problem from a working-class perspective, not all socialists were members of the working class.

Two well-to-do socialists gave advice on how to treat one's servants. One emphasized that the ill-treatment of servants and factory hands was analogous: "We cannot pretend to be Christians and worship God sincerely, and at the same time have in our homes one or more servants whom we both so underpay and underfeed that their bodies give evidence of starvation and their garments appear as rags ... Is it any less absurd and is our hypocrisy any less heinous if, instead of going into our kitchen to view an underfed and ragged servant, we go into the slum district where live the thousands whom we employ at a wage which makes decent living impossible?"[56] Another middle-class socialist complained of the excessive demands of employers, as reflected by a request for information concerning a servant once in his employ. The prospective employer asked him, "Is she thoroughly respectable? ... Do you know whether she has any followers? ... Is she willing to be told and shown things?" To these inquiries, the socialist replied, "I wonder how the mistress would come out had her husband to reply to all those questions on her behalf! I have suggested to my wife that we reply that if the girl had all those virtues we should keep her in the family and marry her to the first son that could find sufficient money to keep such a paragon of all the perfections. It is marvellous that an inquiry was not made as to the number of teeth she had."[57]

A striking range of voices spoke to the problems facing domestic servants. They included working-class men who were concerned for the daughters of the working class; middle-class socialists who gave advice on how to treat one's servant properly; and one prominent socialist woman. Domestic servants did not speak for themselves in the socialist press, and the press ignored the efforts that were made to organize domestics in the United States, Canada, and the United Kingdom.[58] One Canadian socialist organizer considered that such efforts were futile: "It would be absurd to sacrifice a good man [organizer] for anything that could possibly be gained by Socialist propaganda in Kelowna for the population consists almost entirely of retired Manitoba capitalists, lady helps, merchants, clerks, English remittance men and Chinamen. You will do well if you have as much success here as God had in Sodom."[59] So while claiming sympathy for the condition of women domestics, socialists abandoned them to their own devices. Perhaps the best advice for the domestics, in the face of low wages and poor working conditions, was that given to a Scottish woman who was locked into a two-year contract at a mere $10 per month: "I am afraid the Scotch girl will have to serve her time unless she develops the I.W.W. spirit, smashes dishes, refuses to work, breakes mops, and creates hell generally. The mistress may threaten to jail her but if the organized slaves of B.C. take up her case there would be high times."[60] Unfortunately for women domestics, such high times were never seen.

These discussions of domestic service demonstrate the problems of generalizing about attitudes towards women and work within the framework of the family-wage ideal. The opposition to women working, evident in discussions about the family wage, is less forceful in discussions about domestic service. Socialists did not question that women had a right to work as domestics; indeed, they viewed this work as falling naturally to women both inside and outside their own homes. They acknowledged that there was exploitation in working conditions and wages, but they failed to offer any concrete support for its amelioration and they even contributed to the racism that plagued the lives of many immigrant domestics. Women's presence in this arena did not alarm socialists. It was rarely cited as an example of capitalism destroying the home. In fact, a woman domestic servant was seen to be in her "natural" place.

In contrast, socialists were very distressed about the presence of women in other sectors of the labour force. In both Britain and the United States, socialist movements served an important role in publicizing the working conditions of women in factories and shops. Specific analyses of real working conditions informed and enriched the theoretical analyses of women's work in both Britain and Germany. These accounts, which were often cited by Canadian socialists, were used to dramatize the exploitation of women workers under capitalism. Canadian socialists also exposed working conditions across Canada, but reports involving women workers were comparatively rare. The extent of coverage varied among the different socialist parties, tending to increase when the party paper had a women's column. Despite this, the left-wing press's coverage of the actual working conditions of women in Canada was sparse.

Before 1905, the socialist movement in Canada demonstrated a dramatic ignorance and naivety about the issue. In Ontario, the *Citizen and Country* provided a few enticingly brief reports of disputes involving female laundry workers in London, textile workers in Montreal, and button workers in Berlin (Kitchener).[61] It particularly condemned the poor working conditions and the subsistence wages. The *Western Socialist* provided similar coverage of local labour news in British Columbia. One issue of the paper featured a front-page story about a telephone strike in Vancouver but made no reference whatsoever to the role of the female telephone operators. We learn only of some female scabs, who were mentioned because the local telephone manager was "fiendish enough to take advantage of capitalism's crushed victims, and make poor girls luring offers to accept the places of those who demand only a little more of what should be theirs – the product of their toil." Brief mention was also made of efforts to organize laundry workers in Vancouver, and readers were asked to boycott the unfair laundries.[62]

In 1899 and 1900 the efforts of garment workers to unionize in Ontario did receive considerable attention. The most notorious firm was Eaton's. It paid its workers less than other stores and enforced rules which, according to the union, were unbearable "to ordinary human nature." In describing some of these rules, the *Citizen and Country* provided a rare published glimpse of the working conditions for women at Eaton's:

All operatives are locked out till noon if they are not at work fifteen minutes before eight o'clock in the morning – not a minute's grace is allowed although they all work by the piece. When they are in they are locked in, and are not allowed to leave the room, no matter what the cause may be, unless they procure a pass, written by one man and signed by another. If these worthies are not in the department the applicant must wait till noon or six o'clock ... If the operator comes with a lunch, not having time to partake of breakfast, the lunch is taken from them at the door and locked up till noon ... If they break more than three needles per week they are charged for them at a much dearer rate than in other stores ... If an operator stands up from her machine before the bell tolls the hour of retiring, instant dismissal follows. These are only a few of the rules which obtain in the T. Eaton Co's departmental store.[63]

The paper sympathetically announced union meetings and condemned Eaton's for paying wages on which a woman could neither live nor dress properly. "A firm that treats its work-people like The T. Eaton Co., Limited, ought not to get the patronage of decent people,"[64] it concluded. Independent of Eaton's advertising revenue, the *Citizen and Country* published correspondence about labour disputes from the garment workers' organizer, Sam Landers.[65]

Socialist papers often relied on trade unionists for reports of working conditions, but the interests of women workers and racial minorities were poorly represented. One union committee investigating the use of Chinese labour in Vancouver shops noted that orientals outnumbered whites in the garment industry. The union report stated that "a large amount of this trade is taken away from our white girls, who are thus left without a means of subsistence." The report argued that while the Chinese dominated the garment trade, this "does not affect the Tailor's union [composed of men], as these garments are made by girls in large factories, being so made they are made cheap, but the Chinamen evidently makes them cheaper. One of these factories is at Winnipeg, so the girls of Winnipeg are cut out by the Chinamen of Vancouver, with the attending consequences which any mother may easily guess."[66] Nevertheless, the impact on working girls was not a priority for this union committee; the subject was raised simply to buttress the Tailor union's case against Chinese workers.

Because 70 per cent of women who earned wages were under the age of twenty-five, the union movement often linked the problem of women with the problem of child labour. After lengthy deliberation, the Toronto Dominion Labour Council of 1902 supported demands for equal pay, equal civil and political rights for men and women, and the abolition of child labour under the age of fifteen. However, the *Canadian Socialist* criticized this platform for not being socialist enough. Its socialist solution? The abolition of child labour under eighteen years of age.[67]

The early socialist press uncritically publicized reports by factory inspectors, who tended to focus narrowly on health and morality issues that did not necessarily reflect the concerns of women. One source claimed that factory women, who were frequently overworked in comparison with seamstresses and shop girls, were a threat to "the mothers of the future workman."[68] More often, factory life was seen as a prelude to a life of immorality. The *Citizen and Country* reported the findings of Ontario's provincial inspector of prisons and public charities, Mr Noxon, who attributed the increase in drunkenness and vice among young women to their migration from the countryside to the city and the loss of the "restraining influences of home life." He argued that "the drudgery of the factory and constant nervous tension made them feel the need of amusement and excitement after the day's work was over. These influences, combined with the constant and free intercourse among the sexes, lead all too frequently to drunkenness and vice."[69] Unconcerned about women's low wages, Noxon directed his attention to the pace of work and the social life that accompanied factory work. The points he raised were characteristic of middle-class reformers: the control of "unacceptable" behaviour. That such ideas were uncritically reproduced in the left-wing press reveals a remarkable lack of editorial regard for the wage-earning woman's perspective of her own situation.

Socialist efforts to support women workers sometimes reflected the interests of male workers. While reporting the weekly proceedings of the Vancouver Trades and Labor Council, the *Western Clarion* briefly mentioned efforts to organize a factory workers' union. Attending the union's socials became an opportunity for men. "Union men," announced the *Clarion*, "this is a challenge to your chivalry and solidarity, take it up. Go in a crowd and give your sister unionists to feel that they have your help and sympathy in their endeavour to improve a condition which at the best under our social system, is far from an ideal and often a hard one. Take your sweetheart if you have one, but go anyway, and maybe you may find one."[70]

Socialists rarely conducted first-hand investigations of women's work. While travelling with her husband to establish a left-wing paper in British Columbia, Mrs G. Weston Wrigley took pains to observe the working conditions of women in Chicago, and she expressed surprise at finding married women, even middle-class women, engaged in business.[71] Her surprise is a measure of how superficially even a prominent socialist woman appreciated the average woman's working conditions. A factory in British Columbia was visited by a representative of the *Western Socialist*, who applauded the "great advance" the company had made "by casting aside the old methods of Chinese sweatshop labor" and replacing them with "the modern factory system of machine-made shirts and garments, the machines being operated exclusively by girls who belong to the garment workers' union." A detailed description of the production methods followed, but nothing whatever was said about wages, hours of labour, or working conditions. There was no evidence that the representative even spoke with the workers – either the Chinese workers who had lost their jobs or the women working the new machines. It was simply assumed that machine production represented progress over the use of sweated Chinese labour. The article concluded with an exhortation to workers to patronize this manufacturer's goods, since he used union labour.[72] Overall, one is struck both by the clever use this manufacturer made of the racism embedded in the union movement and by the socialist press's complicity in providing the manufacturer with uncritical endorsement and free publicity.

The women's column edited by Bertha Merrill Burns provided a more coherent focus on the problems of women in the labour force. Merrill Burns broached the subject by discussing a workingman who had abandoned his activities in the socialist movement and "settled down to a money making career" in order to support his family. He was worried about the need to send his daughters out to work. "My earnings are insufficient to support them as I would like," he said, "yet to place them at work for a paltry $1.50 or $2.00 a week seems to me like cruel injustice. And yet to avoid the inevitable I must do so though knowing that my temporary relief is only accentuating the difficulty ... I am fully convinced that there is a woman's labor question running parallel with that of man's." Merrill Burns urged moderation in criticizing the man's actions, explaining that his decision appealed to her "womanhood as worthy of consideration ... It is comparatively easy to make self sacrifice, but it is desperately hard to offer up those who are dependent upon you and those whom you love."[73] While she accepted that a man should earn a family wage, she acknowledged that necessity might compel children and women to work.

Merrill Burns defended women in the labour force. To the argument that they drove down men's wages, she responded, "Of course no woman goes into business life with the idea of remaining in it forever or securing sufficient salary to support a family. She expects someday to be a housewife. Her pay is small accordingly, and she becomes thus a leverage for the lowering of the salaries of her male competitors for employment." With those who argued that the solution lay in men's hands – "to marry them" – Burns disagreed. "I do not believe if all women of the working world were instantly married and settled in homes it would solve the industrial problem for the men workers and until that problem is solved marriages and homes will continue to grow appallingly less." She added that business women made better wives because they would know "what your salary costs you in physical and mental force" and would "appreciate the shelter of a home more than one who has never known what it is to miss it."[74]

Merrill Burns cited the American socialist Josephine Conger, who dismissed the idea that it was unnatural for women to work for wages: "The capacities of the women of today are so broadened that it is impossible to relegate them to the narrow limits of household duties and expect these to fill their lives ... Under Socialism the opportunity to work will be open to every man and woman."[75] Another writer, May Drummond, disagreed with Conger. In response to the question "Will a wife be allowed to work for a lazy husband under socialism?" she argued that under socialism no man, unless physically or mentally incapacitated, would have his wife work: "A man will not let a woman support him in these times ... if he is able to use the powers with which he has been endowed"; but if he could not work, it would be "a woman's privilege and joy" to supply "whatever is necessary for his as well as for her own maintenance."[76]

Merrill Burns also challenged the claim of a Toronto paper that "women teachers are unfit to mould the wilful mind of the immature man of 14 or thereabouts. He must be put under the care of male teachers at that age or dire consequences will result." She queried whether this advice applied to girls of that age as well. Women's maternal qualities, she argued, suited them to teaching: "How long [before] 'We Women' will be considered good enough to mother the race? It is time for the human incubator and electric generator, indeed, when the 'character' of mankind suffers by its early association with women."[77] She stressed that women teachers worked because of need: "I wonder what the men who oppose 'female teachers,' and those other men who cry out upon woman's entrance into the industrial world as the cause of all industrial disturbances want us to do anyway? I've already pointed out that many of us can't stay at home because we've no homes to stay in unless we make them, and we can't make them, so what are we going to do about it, O sons of Father Adam, the woman blamer?"[78]

It was Merrill Burns's belief that in the absence of equal pay, women workers drove down the wages of men, but she repeatedly contested the idea that the prohibition of female labour would solve this problem. It was the exigencies of poverty, not women, that she criticized. Women worked because they needed to support themselves and their families. Ideally, they should be able to stay at home when nursing and raising children, but this was not meant to preclude work for wages. Indeed, waged labour for women was discussed as a positive, enriching experience, of which a woman could be proud. Socialists should fight to include women workers as equals in their struggles.[79] Merrill Burns's views did not carry the day in the socialist movement prior to 1905. The early movement wrestled with the "problem" of women in the labour force while missing a crucial piece of the puzzle: the voice of working women.

After the SPC gained ascendancy within the Canadian left, the coverage of women's issues changed. With the abolition of the women's column from the party paper, first-hand descriptions of women in the Canadian labour force all but disappeared. When the party covered the telephone strike of 1906, which included female operators, it addressed its remarks not to women workers but to male trade unionists. However, the poverty of women workers continued to be a favoured illustration of the brutality and decadence of capitalism. In 1905, for instance, the party's report of a laundry strike took particular note of the financial plight of the women strikers: "Some of the female workers were so emphatically out of funds as to have nothing to carry them over Sunday, and were forced to accept the assistance at the hands of good Samaritans ... A woman with three small children had been turned into the street by the landlord, and the only breakfast her little ones got on the morning of the strike was such as came from the lunch pails of the strikers."[80]

As the SPC imposed greater consistency in discussions of women in the labour force, naivety vanished. The party eagerly exposed the class bias of reformers, yet the party platform rejected any immediate demands, including equal pay for women, minimum wage legislation, and even women's right to work. Even while sections of the labour movement in Vancouver fought for women's right to work during the depression of 1913–14, the SPC remained silent.[81] Instead of offering support, the party insisted that capitalism forced women to work – a weak footing from which to defend women in the labour force.

Individual party members often defied the SPC platform. In Vancouver, four socialist candidates running in the school board elections demanded better payment of teachers, equal pay for men and women, and the end of discrimination against married women. Frederick Urry, a candidate in Port Arthur, Ontario, was criticized by the SPC for making such demands and was told he should stand only for the abolition of the wage system. When James Simpson in Toronto endorsed, among other things, equal pay for women teachers, he was criticized by Weston Wrigley for not following the orders of the SPC.[82] The party press remained silent on the issue of equal pay for female teachers, and as late as 1910 it carried an advertisement for a teaching post – male preferred![83]

The SPC approached protective legislation in a similar manner. It debated proposals for minimum wages for women, the exclusion of women from mines and smelters, limitation of the hours of work for women, and provision of sanitary arrangements and fire escapes, but it did not believe in these reforms. Elected SPC members of Parliament found themselves in an awkward position when faced with reformist legislation. To follow the SPC platform and oppose these reforms was to side with the Conservatives and the business community. When debating the B.C. Factory Act, which limited the hours of work for women and girls, the socialist MLA Hawthornthwaite endorsed the bill but stressed the need for action that was other than palliative. Similarly, the socialist MLA O'Brien in Alberta approved of legislation forbidding women to work in mines but pointed out that women in Edmonton suffered worse conditions.[84] The SPC's emphasis on the need to educate the working class for socialism precluded its support of reforms to improve working conditions for women. However, the party's emphasis on education, the abolition of waged labour, and opposition to reform demands does not fully account for its treatment of women. One must also examine the ways in which it believed that socialism would resolve the "problem" of working women.[85]

A central problem was the concern that work, especially factory work, violated a woman's modesty, threatened her moral purity, and led to prostitution: "I have seen women scantily and improperly clad ... hauling heavy wagons by chains, past rows of men to the ovens. The heat was stifling and it was almost impossible to breath because of the gases that filled the room. Because of this women had their arms bare to the shoulders, and in order to get every bit of refreshing air to their bodies their scanty garments were thrown back at the throats, so that [t]heir persons were exposed to the gaze of the men workers, especially when they stooped to lift the chains or to empty or fill the wagons." This accusation was balanced by the claim that "a glimpse into the hall room of the social elite would show women more improperly clad than would be found in any foundry in Massachusetts."[86] Eaton's was censured for moral threats to its garment workers: "Young girls on starvation wages have been subjected to gross insults and temptations from foremen and examiners."[87] Beyond the shelter of a home, the factory hand or shop girl was seen as especially vulnerable to sexual abuse or prostitution. Socialists dramatized this threat to the moral character of working-class women in order to imply that women were unsafe in the public world of paid employment.

One male socialist criticized men's attitudes towards working women's morality: "'Virtue and a waitress' – impossible! She is usually on sale or she is a cinch." He blamed working conditions, for the waitress was "mostly repaid by sinister days of a gloomy spinsterhood, by years of dull, monotonous routine, by abject servility to patron and manager, by a slavelife in a public kitchen, by the acrimony of isolation, sexually and socially." The answer for such conditions, he argued, lay in "the teaching of working woman's class consciousness that they may sometime join the ranks of the revolutionary workers army fighting for the emancipation of all workers."[88] A woman offered a very different view of the matter:

I myself have worked in both large and small workhouses and even in offices, but have never yet come across one girl to my knowledge who had an evening dress cut low, yet the evening dress they had usually did

for Sunday and Saturday night at the show ... It's true we have bought packages of O'Phee Chee and Princess Patricia bow knots in our endeavours to tie other knots ... and we admit that we spend a small fortune on hairnets, sometimes a new one every day, on account of tearing a hole in one trying to get ahold of a lead pencil quickly for an impatient customer and a watchful floorwalker. Let us no longer be afraid of being branded "A Militant" or "Immodest" but swallow the lump once again that forces itself into our throats occasionally and learn of and work for a system wherein we hope to have time to breathe and pay a vast deal more attention on our "waist."[89]

Despite this rare and impassioned plea to those who would denigrate the morality of the working woman, the SPC continued to link immorality with single women working in shops and factories.

While discussions of single women focused on their morality, the discussions of married women centred on their abandonment of maternal and domestic duties. According to the *Western Clarion* writer Gourock, "Socialists don't believe in mothers working at all. They hold that under a sane industrial system wherein the worker would obtain the full value of his products, the man would earn sufficient to raise and maintain his family under proper conditions, and that the various exigencies which may arise, such as sickness and accident, be provided against by the community." Neither equal pay for women workers nor the provision of day care was seen as an appropriate socialist solution to the competition of women workers:

Co-operative day nurseries, where the children could be tended collectively and properly raised on sterilized milk, and I suppose predigested foods, Grapenuts and Korn Kinks and never be happy unless washed in Baby's Ownest-Own Soap, or some other conglomeration. This looks to me much like the baby farms of which we hear now and again, which are principally filled from the ranks of illegitimate and undesirable children of all classes. It would certainly be a glorious factor in cementing the home ties and in the upbuilding of a wholesome family life.[90]

Gourock's views stood in sharp contrast to those of socialist women. Josephine Conger Kaneko emphatically rebutted the idea that women were to blame for having to work. She regretted that such women had to leave "the babies to a cheaply paid guardian and let home go," but she reminded her readers that "the women of the working class have from time immemorial fed and clothed the world." It would therefore be foolish to blame women for working. "Someday society will awaken to the facts in the case. Will realize that women who have ALWAYS fed and clothed the world must of NECESSITY continue this social service. Or if not precisely this, something that is its social equivalent. It is as impossible to put the woman back into the home, if by this we mean cutting off her social usefulness, as it is to put the factory back into the home or the forge or the great bakeries and steam laundries."[91]

Working conditions that threatened woman's health were especially pernicious because they threatened maternal potential. Gourock echoed contemporary eugenists when he accused employed mothers of contributing to the "deterioration of the race." Moses Baritz reported Dr Helen MacMurchy's findings that the infant mortality rate had risen from 128.22 per thousand in 1898 to 162.54 per thousand in 1906, with an especially high rate of 196 per thousand in Toronto. He attacked the class bias of MacMurchy's study, but he did not attack the idea that married women themselves contributed to the cause of infant mortality:

Where the mother can give any attention to her child there is a greater healthiness resulting. But the mothers cannot give that attention in large industrial centres. They have to work. That, because they have to increase the family wage. It causes too a decrease in men's wages. Woman's competition with men and boys and girls competing with women cause a fall in the real wage of working-class members ... It produces poverty. Poverty means starvation. Starvation means death. And it is starvation itself, clothed many times in medical phrases, that causes infant mortality.[92]

This ostensible concern for the health of working women needs close examination. First, it was directed at the effects that a woman's health had on her family, rather than concern for the woman herself.[93] Second, although domestic work, paid or unpaid, was physically demanding, it was only with regard to work outside the home that socialists decried the consequences for a woman's physical and moral well-being. Their fears about the immoral or strenuous nature of factory work were partly rooted in anxiety about women leaving their "natural" sphere and being unable to guard the health of the working-class family.

Specific measures to alleviate the hardships women faced were not an ingredient in the SPC's socialist future. Equal pay or shared domestic chores would be peripheral if the working man earned sufficient wages to support a wife and family. "Under capitalism," it was argued, "the 'head of the house' does not receive enough in return for his labour power to support his wife and children according to the prevailing standard of living. [Women and children] sell their labour power cheaper. Thus it often happens that the mother and children, by entering industry, in order, as they think, to increase the family income, force the father into the ranks of the unemployed. He is thus compelled, by the workings of the capitalist system to live upon the industry of his wife and offspring."[94] By emphatically laying the blame at the feet of capitalism and insisting that such a class problem could be solved only by its abolition, the party dismissed consideration of issues rooted in the relations between the sexes or in men's power to exploit women, though both these perspectives were current, especially among American socialist feminists.

Alf Budden was a vocal proponent of the SPC's viewpoint. While acknowledging that capitalism did exploit women more than men, he argued that sex could not account for this: "The woman and the man of the working class have interests in common, both are slaves to the rules of capital. Woman's rights and that sort of rot are for women of the master class and those who subscribe to the *Progressive Woman*. For the she worker there is only one issue, the destruction of the wage system."[95] Socialism would not force women to work outside the home or to suffer poverty, he said. "Have these thousands and thousands of women become wage earners in revolt against the destiny laid out for them by their sex? Have they become wage earners because they loathed 'homes' and were determined to escape the hated misery of maternity?" Others agreed that women preferred to stay at home: "Is anyone so insane as to assume that women will deliberately choose to become factory slaves, or for that matter, department store slaves rather than preside over a cosy home as a beloved wife and loving mother? Doesn't every sensible person know that woman naturally and instinctively wants her place to be in the home, in the largest and broadest sense of the term? ... If [one] were to say that this woman's place is decidedly NOT in the factory we should most decidedly agree with them. Emphatically the factory is no place for a woman."[96] According to the SPC, socialism would eliminate this capitalism-created tragedy: "Men with souls and hearts should swear in the name of everything that is holy and sacred that a system that shackles motherhood to the bench of ill-paid toil and forces maidenhood to sell virtue for life, should be swept from the face of the earth."[97]

Two letters reprinted from the British *Clarion* challenged the negative view of women in the labour force. One of them questioned the idea that working women were lonely: "Leave the subject alone, and write to help women to be strong and glad they have the power to earn their own living and be useful and help one another. If they are lonely tell them to find someone who is lonelier still. Tell them to live in the 'love of comrades' – the splendid comradeship of women – none better." The second letter urged socialists to get rid of the "spirit of narrow pessimism ... more calculated to depress than to cheer" when talking of working women. The writer dismissed the idea that work was inherently bad for women or that marriage would solve anything:

Work will hurt no woman; indeed it is beneficial to them – to turn out into the world and rub shoulders with "all sorts and conditions." Is it not likely to broaden a woman's mind and open her eyes to the reforms that are so badly needed for her sex? It is not the work that cramps woman's soul but the conditions under which she works; it is these that want attacking ... It is quite clear that all cannot marry and have homes of their own; but does it necessarily follow that those who have to work must be wretched? ... Is it not possible for our women to make the leisure hours of their lives of interest, pleasure and profit to themselves and those around them?[98]

No comparable views from Canadian women were heard in the SPC press. Official editorial policy accepted the idea that men should earn enough wages to support a family; it believed that a woman's place was in the home; and it failed to provide a forum for the voice of working-class women who might have challenged these views. All this was possible since the SPC's priority was to get women out of the labour force.

In some respects, the Social Democratic Party of Canada (SDPC) approached the rights and interests of working women differently. Most important, it endorsed immediate demands, was more willing to discuss women's issues in the party press, and included them in its party platform. These distinctions were evident in *Cotton's Weekly* even before it became the official party paper of the SDPC. *Cotton's* carried on the early socialist tradition of reporting working conditions in Canada and sometimes providing sympathetic coverage of labour disputes involving women workers. A nurses' strike in Brantford in 1909 and in New Glasgow in 1910, a textile strike in Montreal in 1911, and a garment workers' strike in Montreal in 1913 were all briefly mentioned.[99] However, in comparison with the detailed coverage of labour disputes involving male workers, these brief references provided limited information about the cause, nature, or extent of women's strikes.

Like the SPC, *Cotton's* dramatized the desperate position of women. Census data highlighted the wage disparity between men and women. Women's wages were less than half that of men's; in Ontario, wages fell below subsistence level for female workers. As illustrated in C.P. Gilman's poem "The Wolf at the Door," poverty drove women to accept such low wages. Weakened by unsafe and strenuous working conditions, women's maternal capacity declined, resulting in feeble and stunted children.[100] William U. Cotton, editor of *Cotton's Weekly*, blamed the growing infant death rate on the poverty that compelled mothers to enter the labour force and abandon their children: "Bottle fed babies are the ones that die ... The babies whose mothers are in an economic position to care for them do not die ... Woman labour is responsible for the slaughter of the innocents. What woman labor? It is not the parasite wives of the parasite receivers of rent, interest and profit among whom the infant death rate is high. It is the laboring class who suffer the snatching away of their little ones."[101] Dora F. Kerr questioned the assumption that work caused women injury: "It is not the industrial work which injures women, but overwork whether in home or factory."[102]

The SDPC also held that women's morality was threatened by low wages. A poem described how a working woman resented being forced to resort to the deceits of "tight-bound hips" and "falsely blooming cheek" to keep her job. In 1913, when stenographers and clerks were laid off during high unemployment in Vancouver, prostitution reputedly increased. Similarly, it was said that wages of less than $3 per week for women workers in Saint John, New Brunswick, were the direct cause of prostitution.[103] In 1910 the average wage-earning woman in Canada over the age of sixteen made $21.75 per month. Some of them supported families on these wages. *Cotton's* asked, "Do these statistics tell you a story about the fate of your daughters? Their average pay is 83 cents per day. Many, many get far less than that. Their toil does not bring them in a living wage. To them in their poverty, if they be fair, come the sons of your robbers and lead them into shame." The employers' sons, said *Cotton's*, "promise them ease and leisure if they will but submit to infamy."[104] The paper gave further examples of their victimization:

Bestial foremen stand threateningly over the slaves and insults are offered with impunity … Is it any wonder thousands of girls each year graduate from these dens of iniquity to the street? When human nature can endure no longer the sweat shop victims take what they consider the line of least resistance. Then "society," which demands the sweatshops which produces the girl of the street, calmly proceeds to hound her from pillar to post, from police court to prison "reformatory," where jackals in human form lie in wait for their release, so they may be exploited for the benefit of that "society."[105]

Cotton's carried this argument to its logical conclusion: "Why not have the lash for the 'Christian' employer who is frequently responsible for the economic degradation of women so closely associated with the moral degradation."[106] Anxiety over prostitution became especially acute when the condition of women outside their natural sphere – the home – was under discussion. Employers were portrayed as lecherous, immoral men, heartlessly exploiting their women workers; the women, desperate to keep their jobs, were viewed as helpless against these assaults. Socialism's answer was to eliminate the economic desperation that made the women vulnerable. If the husband or father earned enough, a woman would not have to enter the dangerous workplace. She could stay home.

Although the SDPC had greater sympathy than the SPC for wage-earning women, it too sometimes blamed them: "You may not be aware that every woman working outside of the home is in part responsible for the lower rate in wages. The girls go out of the home to earn something, and gladly accept anything that is offered to them." As a result, the boss "sends away the men whom he had to pay twice the wage for which the girls will work, and employs girls instead."[107] The SDPC was unable to resolve the contradiction between the view that women worked because they had to, and that working women drove down men's wages – or worse, that they caused male unemployment. Many argued that socialism would solve the problem through the full employment of men who supported families. Under socialism, "instead of thousands of female clerks working twelve and fourteen hours a day for wages upon which they cannot live, male clerks could be employed who would work four hours a day at a salary of a hundred dollars a week."[108] Socialism would simply eliminate children and women from the labour force.

Through the women's columns in the SDPC press, women disputed this view and emphasized how important women's economic independence was to socialism. Mary Cotton Wisdom led the offensive. She was thankful that things had changed from the old days when "marriage was considered a woman's only salvation," she said. "Girls today are not dependent on fathers and brothers for their support till some other comes along to do her the honour of choosing her; giving her bed and board together with the privilege of wearing his name … The fact of sex makes no difference; woman can, and does, and will earn her own living and live her own life independent of man."[109] Dora Kerr also criticized "freeing" women from the necessity of bread winning. Noting that many women did double or triple the work of men because of the dual load of housework and paid labour, she argued:

The most efficient mother is not the woman who is "freed from the necessity of bread winning." Motherhood does not involve this dependence on others. On the contrary the experience of life which women need as much as men and in which they are so often deficient can only be gained by girls taking their part in the industrial work of this world. The years between 20 and 30 are the best years for maternity; should a girl then have no advantages or training in, and practice in some profession or handcraft in the earlier years or her adult life?[110]

Anxious to avoid the charge that if women worked, socialism would destroy the home, some writers stressed the advantages that women's economic independence could bring to marriage: "Socialism will guarantee to women as well as to men, an opportunity for employment, and at the same reward for an hour's labour. Women will thus be enabled to earn their own living, if they choose, and not be dependent on some close-fisted, autocratic lord of creation called man. Women being free can follow out their individuality, and being the equal of man, will be companions instead of mere housekeepers, playthings or sex slaves." For this writer, the demand for women's economic independence did not contradict the claim that men should support families: "Socialists believe that it is the father's business to provide for the family and since socialism will enable every man to easily do this, marriage and home life will be encouraged."[111]

Some even compared waged labour favourably with domestic labour: "The ability to earn her own living whether married or unmarried would not necessarily compel one to do so under matrimonial conditions but, whether done or not, would broaden woman's life to a degree impossible when the slave of a wage slave and isolated from the world in her kitchen or cottage."[112] One socialist argued that to exclude women from the labour force was a "common error," but nonetheless wrong:

It would be fatal to our prospects of reaching the women with the message of Socialism if we were to give the millions of wage earning women to understand that we do not intend to let them continue to earn their own living, but propose to compel them to become dependent upon men. They prize what little independence they have, and they want more of it. It would be equally fatal to our prospects of reaching the women with the message of Socialism if we were to give the married women to understand that they must remain dependent upon men. It is one of the most hopeful signs of the times that they are chafing under the galling chains of dependence.[113]

As is evident from these excerpts, the women's columns in the SDPC press provided a broader forum for feminist ideas about women's economic independence. What did this mean for the party's platform?

Party members endorsed the crucial but limited demand for equal pay, for this could reduce the fear that women would displace men and drive down overall wage rates. However, only a few articles in *Cotton's* also acknowledged that socialism had to go beyond equal pay, to challenge the waged-labour relationship itself and demand that a woman receive the "full value of the wealth she creates" or of "the labour she produces." Rejecting the liberalism inherent in equal pay demands, these articles cast the discussion within a socialist theoretical framework.[114] In answer to the question

"Would women in the co-operative Commonwealth get the same pay as men?" one writer replied, "In socialised industry each would be paid for his or her product, such value to be determined by the amount of human labour socially required for its prod·iction ... If the average woman would produce equal amount of a given product in the same time required by the average man, the result would be the same pay for the same work. If the woman would do more – produce more – than the man she would get more pay for it."[115] But there was disparity between the party's statements and actions. *Cotton's Weekly* applauded the efforts of the Vancouver teachers to organize and demand equal pay for male and female teachers as a fine example of "socialism in Canada," but in its own hiring practices it advertised for a male organizer and for an English boy to learn the printing trade.[116]

Some articles favoured minimum-wage laws for women workers. In Ontario in 1913, Newton Wesley Rowell, the Liberal leader of the opposition, spoke in favour of such laws, whereupon Premier James Whitney (who was doubtless ignorant of the proceedings of the B.C. legislature in the previous decade) declared, "Such a deliberate and intentional, considered and mature declaration of advanced socialism has never been heard in a British legislature in North America."[117] The SDPC was more discerning in its support of other immediate demands to help the woman worker. It criticized the government for being slow to introduce measures that employers opposed, such as early closing laws and minimum hours of labour for women and children. It attacked the hypocrisy of laws that forbade Chinese to employ white girls, thus reserving for "white Christian gentlemen" the exclusive right to exploit. Shelters for working girls and consumer leagues did not provide the wages women needed, it maintained. Some specific suggestions to help employed mothers, such as creches, were discussed. Prohibiting the employment of women before and after childbirth was rejected because the three-week period of "maternity leave" was too short: "That this is not sufficient is readily appreciated by whoever knows that at least two months are required for the restoration of the organ, and as a rule much more for the restitution of a fair amount of health."[118] Although the SDPC was prepared to support immediate demands, it remained sceptical about many of the reforms directed at working women.[119]

In 1911 a labour dispute inspired the SDPC to act. The garment workers' strike at Gordon Mackay's in Toronto involved forty-five members of the International Ladies' Garment Workers Union. The dispute involved piece-work rates, which resulted in a wage cut of more than 20 per cent. Union members across Toronto contributed to the strike fund, "men giving 50 cents a week and girls 25 cents." But the company carried on with the help of female strike breakers, who were duly criticized in *Cotton's*:

While it is very encouraging to see such unity among the union workers we are disgusted to find that our Canadian girls are not unwilling to slave "faithfully" and "diligently" at the very work our Jewish comrades who are in the overwhelming majority in this union would scorn to touch ... CANADIAN GIRLS ARE HANDED WORK THAT JEWISH GIRLS REFUSE TO DO. They are so selfish that they have refused the union offers. This union realizes that as they are Jewish, racial and religious prejudices are animating the girls to take their places and to decline to go out on strike with Jews. In view of this fact, Jewish unionists made a very fair offer of five dollars per week to single workers who would go on strike with them and ten dollars a week to any having someone to support ... OH TORONTO WORKING WOMEN, WHY BE SO BLIND, SO SELFISH, SO HEARTLESS? SHAME ON THE VAUNTED WARMTH OF WOMANLY HEARTS IF JEWISH WORKING MEN CAN BE REPLACED BY CHEAP FEMALE LABOUR.[120]

The union's efforts to dissuade the scabs were unusual. In allocating strike pay, the union ignored sex and distinguished between single workers and those supporting others. This did not dissuade the women strike breakers, and the strike dragged on for months. Members of the Toronto Suffrage League approached the women to show them "the injustice of their act in taking the places of these family men who cannot live on ten dollars per week, a wage that is considered exceptionally good by a single girl." Although the union acknowledged that some women might support families, the suffragists did not make this distinction. Neither did the SDPC. In support of the strike, several thousand copies of this issue of *Cotton's* were distributed, and *Cotton's* coverage was credited with assisting the union's victory. After three months, the employer was forced to accept a closed shop, and the strike breakers were laid off.[121] In the context of this labour dispute, the needs of men to support their families quickly overshadowed any sympathy for the single working woman.

Two features of the left's positions on working women stand out. First, socialists spoke *about* working women, but the women themselves rarely spoke directly about their work experiences.[122] Second, arguments about women and work were often contradictory. An article which claimed that socialism would allow men to earn sufficient wages to support a family could at the same time claim that under socialism women would have economic independence and be free to work. Compared with the spc, the sdpc was more supportive of claims for women's economic independence, but both parties unabashedly discriminated against women in their own hiring and advertising practices. None of the parties offered a coherent resolution of the contradictory claims about socialism and women's work. This reflected the low status of women's issues in the party and the relative silence of working women.

CHAPTER SIX

"Socialists Rise as One Man": The Sex Question

During the first two decades of the twentieth century in Canada and elsewhere, public debate raged over the problems of prostitution, the declining birth rate, sexual morality, white slavery, venereal disease, and the sexual customs that were thought to accompany these problems. Concern over the changing nature of sexual relations, known as the "sex question," loomed large in the minds both of the public and of state officials. For some, these problems endangered their social values and customs. They formed purity leagues, organized social and moral reform societies, undertook investigations, and lobbied politicians to raise public awareness of these problems. In their efforts to eliminate immorality, they proposed a range of reforms: laws to abolish ragtime dancing and joy rides; corporal punishment for the seducers of women; the exclusion of women from saloons; separate courts, sentences, and jails for women; and homes or reform schools for women. As well, many thought that women's suffrage and prohibition would resolve the sex question.

Although some reformers were worried about the economic causes of sexual coercion and the abuse of women, they usually concentrated their efforts on altering the moral structure of society rather than its economic or social structure. For the most part, they sought to impose their concept of "social purity" on society. Their ideal was "a white life for two": a single sexual standard for men and women, characterized by restraint. In a social milieu in which respectable women were not supposed to raise sexual matters publicly, these reformers camouflaged their efforts to educate the public, especially women, about sexuality by cloaking the entire discussion in the guise of motherhood and female reproduction. Their circumspection was not grounded in simple prudery. In the face of both the real and imagined dangers that women faced in expressing their sexuality, they sought to protect women. Campaigns such as the call for voluntary motherhood, which insisted on a married woman's right to refuse sexual relations with her husband to prevent conception, had a twofold impact. They enhanced women's autonomy over their sexuality while denying the pleasurable expression of their sexuality.[1]

Other voices emerged to challenge the conservativism of social purity. The "sex radicals" contested the view that women's sexuality was restricted to reproductive functions and insisted that pleasure was an important element. They argued that men and women should enjoy sexual pleasure and bear equal responsibility for sexual activity. From these beliefs sprang the early support for birth control, led by radicals such as Emma Goldman and Margaret Sanger. But although a few such individuals were in favour of birth control in these early years, there has to date been no evidence of any organized support for it among socialists before the 1920s.[2] Both the social purity movement and the sex radicals endorsed the idea of a single sexual standard for men and women, the former advocating restraint and the latter advocating responsible freedom. Unlike the social purity movement, the radicals did not deny or denigrate women's interest in the pleasures of sexuality.[3]

The sex question also engaged the international socialist movement. The effect of private property on marriage and sex relations, and the sexual oppression of women both inside and outside marriage were addressed by Engels and Bebel. They thought the drive to legitimate the inheritance of property imposed monogamy on women and reinforced their oppression within marriage. Bebel viewed the sex instinct as natural and insisted that men as well as women had such instincts. Capitalist society prevented their full expression, he maintained, but under socialism the satisfaction of sexual instincts would become a private matter, just like eating and dressing. Marriages would be based on love and attraction, but if "repulsion sets in ... morality commands that the unnatural, and therefore immoral, bond be dissolved." Bebel anticipated, however, that monogamy would prevail because marriages would be based on true attraction rather than on economic need.[4] The mere suggestion that people might choose to leave unhappy marriages was sufficient to offend the moral sensibilities of many socialists. Daniel DeLeon, in the preface to his English translation of Bebel's work in 1904, refused to accept Bebel's rejection of monogamy.[5]

Some feminists were initially drawn to the early socialist movement in the United States and elsewhere because a concern for equality in sex relations was embedded in the communitarian heritage of the movement; however, their ideas never came to prevail within the international socialist movement. The party hierarchies consistently refused to legitimize such issues in the United States, England, Germany, and in the early Socialist International.[6] Despite this official rejection of the sex question, critics constantly used it to discredit socialists for wanting to destroy the family. The international movement, though unwilling to consider sexual matters as an official part of its agenda, was nonetheless drawn into a defensive debate over socialism and sexual relations.

These issues reverberated throughout the Canadian left. The CSL, SPC, and SDPC all approached the sex question in strikingly similar ways. They did not make it a priority, nor did they articulate a consistent party line on many of the issues arising from it. Nonetheless, fierce debate was fuelled by politicians and church leaders, who asserted that socialists endorsed free love and wanted to destroy the family and marriage. Some of the critics indulged in gross exaggeration, notably the Catholic paper that depicted a future socialist society in which women would be rotated once a month among different husbands – those objecting being summarily killed.[7] The charge of free love was based to some extent on fact, for several well-known socialists – including Maxim Gorky, Robert Blatchford, William Morris, and Edward Carpenter – had drawn censure for their sexual behaviour; but the parties steadfastly denied that such behaviour was relevant. Canadian socialists were among those accused of practising free love, though little information is available about the nature of their sexual relations.[8] Similarly, Finnish socialists were criticized, for they refused church marriages. Associating the church with the oppressive state in Finland, many of them preferred civil marriages or marriages by custom, which were recognized by their community.[9] In 1908 the Port Arthur Finns responded emphatically to the accusations of free love:

Such a thing as free love is unknown to the Finn, but on the other hand absolute fidelity is demanded and given by both men and women. They do not recognize the necessity of having a minister to confirm or make the marriage contract binding. The practice is to procure a marriage license and then the parties to the contract, in the presence of witnesses, declare their intention to live together as man and wife. This practice is followed in Finland, but there the contract is read in court and the parties thereto are declared by the court to be man and wife. In addition a notice is inserted in the local paper announcing the contract having been entered into. Here in Canada the law does not comprehend civil marriages, but in order to secure as wide publicity as possible all marriage contracts entered into have been published in *Tyokansa* ... In no way can this practice be confounded with that of free love.[10]

A few socialists, mostly women, supported the ideas of the sex radicals and provoked a limited debate on the sex question in the socialist press. Dora Forster Kerr published a series of articles, "Sex Radicalism," in the American journal *Lucifer* – and the Canadian post office considered the articles "so suggestive and degrading" that it banned *Lucifer* from the Canadian mails.[11] In the Canadian socialist press, Kerr recommended the work of the sex radicals to her readers. She lamented that the American socialists avoided this subject and were so far behind the Europeans, and said that "nearly all the advanced thinkers on the sex question have been driven into the anarchist movement."[12] Bertha Merrill Burns also argued forcibly that socialism should address the sex question, and she recommended to her readers the works of sex radicals such as Moses Harman and Edward Carpenter, as well as the journal *Lucifer*. Merrill Burns stated that she had been influenced by Dr Amelia Yeomans of Winnipeg, a WCTU supporter and suffragist who had advocated openness in speaking about sex and who later published the pamphlet "Warning Words" on venereal disease. Merrill Burns acknowledged that some would say this was not socialism, but she insisted that it was no less important.[13] She and Kerr, however, were exceptional.

Sex radicals were not welcomed in socialist ranks. R.B. Kerr, an early proponent of birth control in Canada, complained that a young woman "found the Socialist Party so narrow, intolerant and void of an understanding of the principles of freedom that she had to get out in order to breathe." The *Western Clarion* responded with a clear rejection of the sex question: "For the present we must leave to Moses the things that belong to Moses, I mean, of course, Moses Harman and his journal *Lucifer*. I believe he is doing useful and necessary work ... Inasmuch as the first and vital condition of life is a material base, so it follows that to make the material or economic basis of life ample and secure is the factor that conditions all further progress ... Let us seek first the kingdom of an assured physical life, and all other really good things will be added as fast as they can be assimilated."[14] The SPC characterized the concerns of sex radicals as irrelevant to socialism:

Socialism is not a social reform or a sex reform movement. It makes no attack upon marriage as an institution. It no more criticizes matrimony than it criticizes eating peas with a knife. Socialist writers may have individual opinions with respect to the action of economic change upon institutions of which marriage is one. Such opinions however are not authoritative, and they often bring it about that the sex vagaries of individuals are laid at the door of the movement to its hurt. The person who occupies the platform of the Socialist Movement in order to express his individual ideas on the sex question is out of place and should find some other vehicle for the publication of his doctrines.[15]

Other socialists were uncomfortable with the sex radicals. One person who sold subscriptions for *Cotton's Weekly* said that readers objected to discussion of free love in the paper.[16] *Cotton's* was anxious that socialism should not be identified with the advocacy of free love: "There are of course, occasional individuals in the socialist ranks who are unfortunate in their domestic arrangements; but that proves absolutely nothing and is no argument against socialism ... It is declared policy and programme which counts. And the policy and programme of the socialist party does not and never has stood for promiscuity and the abolition of family and home relations. On the contrary, we are declared in the last analysis for just the opposite."[17]

One issue that engaged socialists was a growing concern over the birth rate. In Europe, eugenics was gaining currency as a result of the threat of overpopulation. Its advocates expressed anxiety about the quality of children being born, and they argued that poverty and the quality of life would be significantly improved if there were limitations on family size and restrictions on the fertility of unfit parents. In North America, the fear of "race suicide" – the declining birth rate of the white middle-classes as a result of birth control – was voiced by many social leaders, most notably Theodore Roosevelt in the United States. Parts of Canada had noticeably lower rates of marital fertility, with Anglo-Ontario leading the world in this decline by 1900. Lacking the modern techniques for birth control, couples used traditional methods with some success; but these methods were not always reliable and, in any case, church leaders and others reviled birth control as a sin. Consequently, women still resorted to the desperate, illegal acts of infanticide and abortion.[18]

The declining birth rate among the white upper and middle classes led to a concern that the racial and class balance would leave the "best people" outnumbered by those of the "inferior" classes. In *What a Young Wife Ought to Know*, Emma Drake argued that this alarming "evil" imperilled "the best instincts of the moral nature of our time" and was "threatening to the future of our land, when we consider the very few children born into our better homes, while in the byways, among the lower classes, the little ones swarm in hot-beds of sin."[19] This idea developed some currency among social reformers in the United States and Canada, feeding on the fears the white community had towards industrialization, urbanization, and the massive waves of immigration that had hit the shores of North America. The concern over race suicide wedded both racist and class-based prejudices with an insistence that women of the "right" class and race must not neglect their duty to bear children.[20] Typically, these concerns conflicted with the feminist goal of allowing women to control their own reproduction, a pattern that persisted in the birth control movement well into the century.[21]

Although the socialists opposed the efforts of the eugenists and moral reformers to impose their solutions on the working class, their dominant response was defensive, for the socialists were aware that outright advocacy of birth control would lead to the charge that they wanted to destroy the family. Overall, they maintained that race suicide and unfit children were caused by capitalism. Working-class people, they insisted, were paid such low wages that they could not afford to marry; or, if married, they avoided having children. Women forced into the factory lost their ability to have children or contributed to higher rates of infant mortality. Moral exhortations to alter this trend were futile, they held. Only socialism could halt the declining birth rate and the high rates of infant mortality by making marriage possible among the working class and by restoring women to the home. Since capitalism caused race suicide, any efforts to alleviate the problem through reform were scorned. The eugenicists' proposals to limit the birth rate of the poor and the unfit were deemed impractical. Pseudo-scientific proposals to breed the working class selectively were tantamount to treating people like cattle. A suggestion that women undergo artificial insemination in order to replenish the population after a war was similarly ridiculed. In short, efforts to control the birth rate socially were viewed as an assault by capitalists on members of the working class. As one writer quipped, this was not race suicide but "race homicide."[22]

In these discussions, the socialists' primary concern was neither capitalism's impact on women nor their right to control family size; it was the negative impact on the working-class family. This is an important distinction, because concern for the working-class family was often based on the assumption that women wanted to be in the home and wanted to have children. While this may have been true for many women of this period, it does not address the feminist concern for woman's sexual autonomy. Only a few articles in the socialist press were sympathetic to the right of women to refuse to bear children in circumstances of extreme hardship and poverty, or simply to replenish the labour market with factory fodder: "If the capitalists want slaves, they will have to ask their own class of women to breed them, for the working class are about through with the game ... The enlightened working woman knows her business and she knows that that business is not rearing children to replace the worn out slaves in the sweat pens of the capitalists. And the Socialists rise as one man and say that she is right."[23]

Unlike the Finnish press and some magazines, which openly advocated birth control through advertisements for pessaries and other devices, the English socialist press did not publish explicit information on the subject.[24] While socialists acknowledged that women and men practised birth control, none admitted doing so personally, though one writer contended that virtually everyone, even prostitutes, employed some form of contraception: only ignorant girls did not. Another discussed how working-class men were "deliberately and with morality aforethought preventing the conception of their wives." Native Canadians were thought to know how to prevent pregnancy.[25] While all these uses of birth control were acknowledged in the socialist press, they were never criticized. *Cotton's Weekly* discussed the widespread use of contraception and the futility of laws to punish the practice and to censor information about it. Under socialism, "race suicide" would be a matter of free choice.[26]

Nevertheless, birth control had little actual support from the socialist movement. In the years before the war, although birth control advocates in Canada found a medium for debate in the socialist press, the socialist parties themselves were ambivalent and were limited by their assumptions about a woman's place within the home and her maternal functions. Only a small handful of socialists publicly supported birth control. They were few, isolated, and certainly represented a minority within the Canadian left.[27]

By contrast, the left was eager to embrace the issue of prostitution, which it used as a symbol to demonstrate that capitalism, not socialism, was the cause of immorality. Some communities in Canada regarded prostitution as a necessary evil to be contained and regulated, and they established segregated districts for brothels. Social purity reformers were outraged by such tolerance and by its implicit double standard. From Halifax, Toronto, Hamilton,

Winnipeg, Vancouver, and other cities across Canada, these reformers ardently vied in their claims that their own city had more vice
than any other in North America. Wanting a total ban on prostitution, they launched punitive attacks on the "fallen women,"
urging the authorities to arrest or sentence them, or drive them out
of town. Some attempted to reform the prostitutes and direct them
to appropriate work, such as domestic service. In the early years,
the socialist press endorsed greater penalties for seduction,[28] but it
increasingly became critical of reform efforts. Nonetheless, it was
eager to use the social purity reports to establish that prostitution
was a significant problem across Canada.[29]

As early as 1903, the *Western Clarion* reported a campaign to
get Vancouver officials to move the red-light district, noting with
disdain that the underlying purpose of the campaign was probably
to accommodate the real estate speculators, who wanted to profit
from proximity to the railway route. The moral reformers helped
business interests, it was said, by driving down the price of the
land. Meanwhile, the logging and mining camps of British Columbia brought in prostitutes with the sanction of lawmakers and
police: "Boats leave Vancouver on Sundays and visit the camps,
and on their arrival, put up the red flag." There were similar
accounts about other western cities. "Calgary Worse than Chicago"
headlined one article, while another claimed that Edmonton also
was "infested." Vice was deemed to be rampant in Winnipeg, where
police drew revenue from the profits of the trade. Efforts to drive
the prostitutes out of town were criticized for wanting to "club the
girls into the Red River" rather than considering them as victims.
In fact, the attacks on segregated districts simply spread the brothels
throughout the city.[30]

Socialists claimed that Ontario also had its share of this social
evil. In 1899 the *Citizen and Country* criticized the campaign to
expel prostitutes from Port Arthur, declaring that the women were
"more sinned against than they are sinning." Raids in Chatham
were similarly attacked. The provincial inspector of prisons and
public charities reported that the 50 per cent increase in inmates at
the House of Refuge were mainly "young girls who had been led
astray." Toronto was indeed a centre for prostitution. There were
numerous brothels, and its theatres, ice-cream parlours, and restaurants were considered venues for men seeking prostitutes. According
to some estimates, as many as two hundred victims a year were
lured into Toronto's white slave trade. Moreover, prostitution
reached into the highest echelons of power. It was alleged that when
Parliament was in session, its members kept the trade active.[31]

In Quebec, Montreal was cited as the centre for prostitution and also for supplying the brothels of Chicago with "girls." *Cotton's Weekly* covered the arrest of prostitutes in Montreal and explicitly attacked both the judge and the man responsible for bringing the women to court. The courts and the police were viewed as corrupt, taking bribes and protection money from the prostitutes. As in Toronto, the theatres were cited as corrupting the youth of the city. East of Montreal, there was only one brief reference to prostitution – in Saint John, New Brunswick.[32]

The left dramatized the problem with stories about the international scale of prostitution, accompanied by lurid headlines such as "One Woman's Shame Another's Fortune," "Auction Block in America," "The Slaves of Sensuality," "Brutal Treatment Meted Out to Women at Spokane," and "Betraying and Selling Girls for Profit One Aspect of the Capitalist System." These melodramatic headlines were matched with sensationalized estimates of the numbers of victims plying the trade: 100,000 prostitutes in London England; 15,000 imported to the United States per year; 300,000 white slaves in the United States, 37,000 of whom were from Chicago alone. One article inflated the claim to fantastic proportions, stating that 10 per cent of women in the United States were prostitutes.[33]

Only a few articles offered explicit evidence of the racism that pervaded the trade and arose from distinctive Canadian conditions. For example, one article reported that Indian girls had their skin bleached to look white and were "bought and sold as slaves" and sold to the logging camps.[34] Women from racial and ethnic minorities sometimes worked as prostitutes under the most deplorable conditions, but panic about the "white slave trade" obscured their plight. This term was first used by factory workers during early industrialization in England and the United States "to describe their 'slavery' to wages and industrial discipline."[35] By the turn of the century, social purity reformers had transformed the meaning by applying it to the forcible capture of women, not necessarily white women, and their subsequent sale and initiation into prostitution. Ernest Bell, secretary of the Illinois Vigilance Association and author of *Fighting the Traffic in Young Girls, or The War on the White Slave Trade*, stressed that only a small portion of the girls were prostitutes of their own volition and stated that a "small proportion are of the degenerate class who are born with a screw loose somewhere." He explained to his readers that the "term 'white slave' includes only those women and girls who are actually slaves – those women who are owned and held as property and chattels – whose lives are lives of involuntary servitude." Underscoring the racism embedded in the white slavery panic, he stated that this was a "business of securing white women and of selling them or exploiting them for immoral purposes. It includes those women and girls who, if given a fair chance, would in all probability, have been good wives and mothers and useful citizens."[36]

The left publicized accounts of white slavery as proof of the immorality and corruption of capitalism. The trade was depicted as part of an international network, with girls being kidnapped from Canada, the United States, England, and China. It was viewed as a highly monopolized, concentrated, commercial enterprise, like all business interests under capitalism.[37] Procurers, madames, pimps, property owners, merchants, liquor interests, and others profited from prostitution. Moreover, the state and public officials were seen to play their part in this system. In cities that tolerated red-light districts, municipal politicians and police benefited by pocketing bribes. Judges played their part by imposing fines rather than sentences. City officials were accused of living off the avails of prostitution, since the fines paid their salaries.

Prostitutes in Montreal established a fund for their legal defence, which allowed them to be released from custody rather than sentenced to jail: "If thirty or forty women are sent to prison for six months, just that much revenue is lost to the people who fatten on the degradation of the women. Landlords, grocers, butchers, cigarette vendors, boozemakers, stand to lose easy money when women of ill repute are sent to prison. The law says they must go to prison, so a common fund has been formed to fight the law with money. People who live in brownstone houses in the select section must not have their revenues of rent taken from the houses of shame in the slums which they own."[38]

The left-wing press did not query the validity of such reports, nor did it challenge the assumptions embedded in the racist concept of "white" slavery – that it was far worse than black slavery, that it especially imperilled white women, and that the procurers were foreign or non-white (French, Jewish, Chinese, etc.).[39] White women were cast as the sexual ideal for the clients of prostitutes; pimps and procurers were often cast as "foreigners." It was said, for example, that white women were held captive to work as prostitutes for the Chinese in Vancouver and Nanaimo. The *Western Clarion* reminded its readers that capitalism was to blame, not the Chinese, but it remained oblivious to the real plight of Chinese women prostitutes in British Columbia.[40] Thus, while socialist concern escalated for the white girls who were drawn into prostitution, it ignored the even worse situation of the black, Chinese, or Aboriginal women and did little to attack the racism that pervaded the trade and the social purity movement.[41]

Socialists were roused to defend a more "appropriate" victim – Mrs Napolitano, an Italian woman from Sault Ste Marie, who became a celebrated cause for the left and for women's groups in 1911. Mrs Napolitano was twenty-eight years old, a mother and pregnant, when her husband Pietro beat her and demanded that she earn money through prostitution. She tried unsuccessfully to commit suicide, and then after further beatings she hacked her husband to death with an axe while he was sleeping. She was tried, convicted, and sentenced to death within three weeks. Both *Cotton's Weekly* and the *Western Clarion* exploited Mrs Napolitano's plight to illustrate how capitalism forced women into prostitution and how the courts colluded in this crime. *Cotton's Weekly* urged the socialist women of Canada to circulate petitions for the release of Mrs Napolitano, and indeed her death sentence was commuted after a concerted campaign was launched by women's groups from around the world. As Karen Dubinsky and Franca Iacovetta argue, she brought together potent signifiers of sexual danger: "Even the obedient wife at home, mother of several children, was not immune from the threat of 'white slavery.' And Pietro Napolitano provided a fitting villain: the 'foreigner' who preyed on women's bodies."[42]

While eagerly publicizing the lurid accounts of the moral reformers, the left challenged many of their assumptions about the nature of prostitution. The SPC rejected social purity reforms as it did any other reforms that might be construed as immediate demands. Consistent with its platform, the party press emphasized that the cause was capitalism and that unless the reformers were prepared to oppose it, they would never eliminate prostitution. The social purity advocates were accused of punishing the working class while ignoring the sins of the wealthy. In fact, this was not a fair characterization. Some of the reformers were genuinely concerned about the low wages paid to working women and the unhealthy and penurious living conditions that were thought to lead to prostitution. Some were motivated by feminist concerns for the autonomy of women. However, the SPC ignored any such distinctions and attacked them all for failing to care about the conditions of the working class and for blaming its women: "The reformer again takes no care about the young woman, until she is forced, by economic necessity, upon the street. She is then hunted from place to place. The evil, however, cannot be got rid of in that way. She has to live, and for a time at least, she is offered a good standard of living by the sale of her virtue."[43] The SPC insisted that change would come not from crying shame but from the efforts of proletarians to overthrow the economic system that produced poverty.

The SDPC, too, rejected moral exhortations. *Cotton's Weekly* declared that morality flowed directly from economic conditions and that unless these changed, moral reform was useless. Roscoe Fillmore, an SPC organizer who published in *Cotton's*, attacked the Council of Women meeting in Toronto for moralizing about prostitution while "thousands of young girls were being ground into mire." When the Edmonton Women's Council declared its intention to build a home for working girls, *Cotton's* pointed out that the members of the council derived their living from the exploitation of the working class. Also, providing refuge for a small number of women still left many more without adequate shelter. The YWCA's plan to build a home for girls in Montreal was criticized because working women needed decent wages, not a home for a few. Similarly, efforts in Toronto were deemed inadequate: "Toronto the good will not put into force laws that will give a chance to women not to live obscene lives. That would interfere with the revenues of the aristocratic moralizers whose revenues are derived from slave labour."[44]

The left's mistrust of the class bias of the reformers was shared by some sections of the labour movement. Although the Trades and Labor Congress cooperated with the Moral and Social Reform councils, other labour organizations were more suspicious.[45] The Edmonton branch of the United Brotherhood of Carpenters and Joiners refused to lend its support to the National Committee for the Suppression of the White Slave Trade. The Carpenters maintained that prostitution had not existed in Canada a generation earlier and said that conditions had changed with the development of factories. "The natural aversion of the girls to the damnable drudgery of the factory," their dislike of unhealthy working conditions, and their reluctance to perform "dangerous and brutalizing tasks" made women workers "easy victims to the wiles of the procurer." The Carpenters declared, "Prostitution and the white slave traffic will disappear when the system of production for profits is succeeded by one of production for use, and we invite all earnest among you to lay your theology on the shelf and join with us to overthrow class ownership, thereby making the world a more desirable abode for human beings."[46] The Carpenters voted overwhelmingly (83 out of 86) to circulate their letter, and it was published by the SPC and the SDPC press. This incident underscores the extent to which the left concurred in the view that reformers were profoundly misguided and self-serving. The left's disdain for the reformers was well illustrated in *Cotton's Weekly*'s terse response to the establishment of a federal commission into the white slave trade in Canada: "Bah!"[47]

Although the social purity reformers were in fact a disparate group, they were viewed as monolithic by the left. Their reforms were considered profoundly inadequate because they did not attack the wage system and the low wages paid to working women. In one respect, the left-wing criticisms were well founded. The efforts at reform did fail, for they were rejected by the prostitutes. Police attempts to disband the red-light districts did not end prostitution; they simply moved it to other locations. Furthermore, it is likely that the end of the era of brothels marked a dramatic decline in the prostitutes' quality of life. Without the security and social network of the houses, the women were forced into the streets, where they were more vulnerable to exploitation and victimization by pimps and customers. Those of the social purity reformers who sincerely desired to improve the life of the prostitutes failed miserably in their efforts. Their failure was marked by an inability or unwillingness to recognize that although real alternatives were not the only solution, they were essential to solving the problem. Prostitutes needed viable and attractive alternatives.

The socialists kept prostitution in the forefront of their discussion of the sex question and offered a competing analysis of its cause. Rather than blaming the moral weakness of prostitutes or their working-class clients, they blamed capitalism. The urban working woman was depicted as the most likely candidate because she did not earn adequate wages.[48] When Montreal launched an attack on its red-light district in 1909, *Cotton's Weekly* criticized the prosecutor, Recorder Wier. Instead of bringing women to court, the paper urged him to go

to the departmental store proprietors, the mill owners and other employers of girl labour, and force them to pay a living wage to girls who work under them. If he will do this he will remove the first cause to a great extent of the social evil of Montreal. The respectable church going philanthropic business men of Montreal through low wage, force many girls into a life of ill fame. Then French, the Minister of God of love jumps on the girls with both feet and gets patted on the back by employers through whose greed the evil exists.[49]

While employers justified the payment of low wages by arguing that many working women lived at home and did not need to support themselves, socialists seldom acknowledged this when discussing prostitution. Rather, they emphasized the need to pay women wages that would enable them to be self-sufficient. Sometimes they made the case for equal pay or minimum wages for women; more often, they demanded that women be paid the full value of their labour.[50] This emphasis on women's need for a living wage, which arose repeatedly in discussions of prostitution, was never reconciled with the socialist assumptions about the family wage, which arose in other contexts. The two conflicting ideals – the family wage and women's economic independence – were expedients that were used to advantage in some contexts and discarded in others. This underscores the importance of taking into account the larger set of issues that shaped ideology about women. A focus on women in paid labour might erroneously lead one to believe that assumptions about the family wage prevailed within the left. But by examining its ideas about prostitution, one can see that the left abandoned this ideal at times in favour of women's economic independence.

The emphasis on low wages as the cause of prostitution was not always posed in the extreme terms of a woman choosing between starvation and prostitution. A few articles alluded to it as the only way for women to get clothes and adornment; for example, the "shop girl" who "likes pretty things and cannot afford buying them and finally barters her purity and good name for money."[51] These articles were sympathetic to such desires (unlike some of the social purity reformers, who often viewed love of finery as evidence of a woman's wickedness),[52] and they acknowledged that some working women made a reasonable choice because the alternatives were so limited. While prostitutes were seen as victims of a system that created limited alternatives (prostitution or starvation), to some extent they were also seen as people who actively made choices from among limited alternatives.

The distinctions between white slavery and prostitution are important. The usual arguments about prostitution – those focusing on women's low wages – depicted women as having a subjective being. The women chose between starvation, suicide, and a life of prostitution. With white slavery, this small element of choice disappeared, for starvation and suicide were not among the alternatives. The white slave became the ultimate commodity of capitalism – an object devoid of any human subjectivity. This helps to explain why socialists so readily embraced the white slavery panic, for it provided a dramatic, compelling, and at times romanticized illustration of the dehumanization of the working class under capitalism.

Several articles explicitly noted the parallels between waged slavery and white slavery, and linked the dehumanization of women as prostitutes to the exploitation of men and women as workers:

The white slave trade is just as moral and clean as any other part of the world's trade and commerce. It is all based upon the enslavement and robbery of the working class, and where wage slavery exists, every power, faculty and attribute of the slave is a legitimate article of barter and sale in the market. The money gained by the white slave dealers is as free from taint as any of that which flows from the exploitation of slaves under the rule of capital. The curse of the thing does not lie in the turning of woman's virtue into profitable account. It lies in the enslavement of labour which alone makes such beastly traffic possible.[53]

For socialists, prostitution was basically an economic problem. They emphatically rejected the moral view held by some social and moral reformers that the prostitute was a "fallen woman" who should be either punished or reformed. Rather than blaming the woman for her behaviour, the left-wing press empathized with her plight. The prostitute became a socialist symbol of the extremes of exploitation and dehumanization which capitalism thrust upon the working class.

Through economic independence, socialism would give women sexual autonomy, and this would eliminate the supply of prostitutes. But what about the demand for prostitutes? This came from two types of customers: working-class men and capitalist or wealthy men. The ways in which capitalism was seen to create a demand for prostitutes varied dramatically between these two types of men. The capitalists were characterized as sexually immoral. For evidence, the socialist press drew on widely publicized scandals about the disreputable exploits of the wealthy: divorce, homosexuality, marital infidelity, "licentious carousals," and sexual assaults.[54] One article concluded that "our precious and exalted rulers themselves are far more promiscuous and infinitely less decent in their sex relations than a drove of hogs."[55] Rich men were depicted as procurers or as clients of prostitutes, and their sexual exploits were described in vivid terms. Working-class women were pictured as "playthings of wealthy sports" and victims of "the lusts of leisure class men" and "tyrannical foremen."[56] One article lamented how the domestic servant was the most vulnerable of all:

Every male member of the household has a right to insult her. No matter who or what he is – raw and drivelling youth, burly master, or drooling and senile grandpa. Driven to bay by these the gentlemen, she may call for help. But there is no help. Only mistress can hear her cry. She knows that "her boy" wouldn't do such a thing. "You are the brazen baggage." "Leave my house – hussy!" No reference. No "character." When attacked by foreman or employer, the factory girl may save her soul at the price of her place and bread, but many a time the "domestic" must give up all on the altar of slavery.[57]

Thus, as well as causing prostitution by paying low wages, capitalists were directly responsible for the sexual exploitation of working-class women. The employer who paid low wages and the rich who lived off the profits were deemed to be no different from pimps.[58]

Although male socialists were keen to expose the immorality of capitalists' use of prostitutes, they showed remarkable blindness to the sexual exploitation of women by working-class men. Roscoe Fillmore urged working-class men to defend their women: "You are responsible for the poverty which has ground these women into the mire and until you wake up it will continue to go from bad to worse. While you continue to lick the hand of the capitalists, thus signifying your satisfaction with conditions, your daughter and sisters will be sacrificed to the hell-hound lust. Think of it! Let it sink into your soul if you have any."[59] Although Fillmore was concerned for the women drawn into prostitution, he had an extraordinarily limited perception of the role that working-class men might have in the matter; and while he urged the men to defend women as fathers and brothers, he did not suggest that they might protect women by refusing to be their customers. Neither did he mention how women themselves might organize to fight such sexual exploitation. When another man acknowledged that working-class men were the clients of prostitutes, it was not the men but the reformers whom he addressed: "You organize 'purity leagues' and hound the unfortunate women down. You fairly froth at the mouth when you are discussing the 'low, beastly man' who may occasionally visit a house of ill fame."[60] By blaming the economic system, socialist men could transfer blame away from working-class women and, significantly, from the male working-class clients of prostitutes.

The low wages paid to men were sometimes cited alongside women's low wages as a cause of prostitution. Since the men's low wages prevented them from marrying, they became the clients of prostitutes.[61] The best illustration of this argument is from the article "Who Destroys the Home?" and its accompanying illustrations. The article was clearly addressed to working men:

YOU DON'T GET MARRIED BECAUSE YOU CAN'T AFFORD TO GET MAR-
RIED. WHY CAN'T YOU AFFORD IT? BECAUSE SOMEBODY IS ROBBING
YOU OF WHAT YOU EARN. SOMEBODY IS TAKING FROM YOU WHAT
YOU CREATE. WHO IS THIS SOMEBODY? CAPITALISM ... Your working-
class sister is just as unfortunate as you are. You can't afford to marry
her, so she is forced to seek employment ... The miserable wages paid her
by the exploiting employers barely keep her alive. After bravely breasting
the industrial world to keep her independence and womanhood unsullied,
WANT sooner or later drives her to accept the "easiest way" ... Thus
capitalism systematically manufactures prostitutes and forces our young
men and women to become Sons and Daughters of Shame.[62]

The article asked whether the man would abandon his dream of a
home and continue to "act as traitor" to his "working-class sister"
or whether he would exercise his right to vote an end to capitalism.

Important assumptions were embedded in this article and those
like it. First, the force that capitalism exerted on men and women
was different. Women starved if they tried to live on women's wages
without a husband or family to support them; men could survive
on men's wages without starving, but they could not support a
family. Both were perceived as being victims of capitalism. Second,
the solution presented was the family-wage ideal: men ought to be
paid enough to support a wife and home. Socialism would give the
male worker the full value of his labour. This solution placed less
emphasis on the autonomy of women than the alternative – that
women be paid a living wage representing the full value of their
labour. Third, there was a presumption that once the working-class
male married, he would not need the services of a prostitute. While
it was never openly stated, the wife was seen as a sex object,
existing to serve man's sexual needs. None of these arguments
questioned whether the working-class man who treated a prostitute
(or his wife) as a sex object was exploiting his working-class sister.
Like the prostitute, the single working-class man was depicted as
a victim of capitalism: deprived of sex without marriage, he was
"forced" to resort to prostitutes.

In other ways, socialist men claimed their right to have sexual
access to women. The *Western Clarion* opposed attempts to censor
a certain degree of female nudity in the media. One article criticized
as "prudes and hens" those who objected to a cigar advertisement
depicting a semi-nude woman. Another objected to efforts to censor
motion pictures and shows: "True, now and then the slaves are
treated to a leg show and a little dancing in short frocks and gauzy
coverings but there is always someone to cry shame and remind

The Dream of Home   But Capitalism Gives This Instead

Who Destroys the Home?

the assembled plugs that work and not such evil pleasures are their natural bent." Socialism would mean the release of women (no mention of men) from "present conceptions of morality."[63] In such a context, the release of women from bourgeois morality did not entail liberation for them; it simply increased access to women as working-class men's recreation. Although socialist men defended their sexual privileges when threatened by social purity advocates, their rhetoric in defence of their working-class sisters stopped far short of calling their own sexual privileges into question.

Socialist women did not stand for this. One woman accused the "dominant man," including working-class men, of profiting from the exploitation of women. Men acted as "self-styled capitalists" in refusing to concede rights to women, and even socialist men were "in the old rut of quiet tolerance and condensation" towards women. To illustrate her point, this writer asked whether a house of "questionable character" with six inmates could survive on six visitors.[64] Alf Budden responded at length to her letter, but he refused to acknowledge that working-class men contributed to the sexual exploitation of women: "Suppose a man does visit a house of questionable character ... does this touch the question of slavery?"[65] Typically, his response failed to distinguish between prudish criticism towards all expressions of sexuality and criticism of the sexual exploitation of women. Socialist men were quick to reproach rich men when they engaged in such behaviour, but they failed to reproach their own.

This failure was further illustrated by those male socialists who insisted that the working-class man's sex drive was a strong, natural hunger that needed to be satisfied.[66] Men who used prostitutes were not seen as immoral or beastly: "The so-called bestial behavior of men is but the perverted strivings for expression of the divine ... fatherhood."[67] Deprived of the chance to marry, men would inevitably seek out the services of a prostitute: "The average man, for instance finds it hard enough to scratch for himself. Naturally enough therefore he 'shies off' the proposition of marriage, which entails the keeping of someone else. But, of course, he has, as a normal healthy animal, certain desires. Since society – or the ruling class in society – prevent the satisfaction of those desires in one way, the normal man satisfies them in another."[68] This implied that men would be abnormal if they could not satisfy their sexual desires.

Wilfred Gribble, who had served in the navy and claimed to have treated hundreds of cases of venereal disease, discussed the issue in more depth. He noted that there was too much focus on the female victims of prostitution: "Where there is one victim of the female sex there are at least ten of the male sex." Men were victims, he claimed, because they acquired venereal disease from the prostitutes. To the moralizer who would argue that this was their own fault, Gribble replied, "It is not their fault, for in becoming customers of the girl victims they are obeying a demand that is insistent, irresistible, older than the wage system, older than society, old as the human race and older ... the demand for species perpetuation, it is an appetite calling for satisfaction, normal and as decent as the appetite for that good meal you are going to sit down to today." Recognizing that this argument could be used to justify all men (even the capitalists) using prostitutes, Gribble clarified his point: "Understand I am writing this not in defense of the overfed plutocrats, who being overfed, go in for excessive sexual indulgence as *a natural consequence*, but in defense of the normal unmarried male of the working class." Thus, Gribble perceived that there were natural and unnatural expressions of the male sex drive; the working-class male's sexual drive, even when using a prostitute, he deemed to be natural.

Gribble viewed the female prostitute in a different light: "While the customers of the 'Red Light' district are driven there by sexual desire, which is physically normal, the sellers of the sexual commodity are physically abnormal in submitting themselves to all and sundry for pay. If both male and female were animated by passion, both being uninfected by disease, no physically harmful effects could follow, but when a female submits to the sexual demands of many men in a day, and day after day, she is bound to become diseased in the end, and once diseased, can and does infect many men."[69] Thus, while Gribble understood that either the man or the woman could contract venereal disease, he clearly viewed the man as normal, the woman as abnormal.[70]

Similar arguments about the naturalness of man's sexual urges were presented in *Cotton's Weekly*. Gerald Desmond insisted that prostitution was essential in order to protect women from sexually frustrated men: "As soon as you do away with the 'scarlet woman' your wives and daughters will find it unsafe to travel alone after dark or even in daylight in lonely places. In short, doing away with prostitution, provided it were possible under capitalism, you endanger the virtue and even the lives of those who are near and dear to you."[71] One may wonder whether such views were typical among working-class men. Martin Baker, a worker in British Columbia, expressed a similar opinion when recalling efforts to drive the prostitutes out of the red-light district in Fernie. With considerable hesitation, he argued that prostitutes were necessary to protect virtuous women:

I think they had their good features about them. These lumberjacks and trappers and what not that came out from the woods and that after five, six months or something like that, they had a place to go for relief. Now they hadn't got those places so they'd get a lot of girls in trouble over it, I mean young girls. On the other hand married women too get taken. No, I think that those places, properly examined and run like they used to be, I think they should be a necessity here. I think they have a place in every community wouldn't you agree?

To Baker, the advantage of having brothels was that they were inspected regularly for venereal disease: "They had an inspection certificate hanging right over the bed and before you got too far you could read it."[72] (Like those who discussed this issue in the socialist press, he claimed that his knowledge of these things was not first hand!)

Thus, the left almost universally viewed the sexuality of the working-class man as natural and as uncontrollable if not satisfied. It was a drive analogous to hunger. Seen in this light, the prostitute as victim disappeared, as did any feminist concern for the women themselves. Given the economic arguments about prostitution presented in the socialist press, as well as its keen sense of the victimization of the prostitute by capitalism, the arguments absolving working-class men of responsibility for participating in the sexual exploitation of women are especially striking. Unlike hunger, sexuality is a human urge that compels us to interact with others and enjoins us to mutual responsibility and obligation. With their analogy to hunger, male socialists absolved themselves of any acknowledgment of the other partner in sexuality. In short, their arguments about the "naturalness" of men's sex drive justified the sexual exploitation of women by working-class men.

Socialist women challenged these views and expressed a very different perception of male sexuality. The drive to clean up prostitution in Montreal evoked the most passionate responses. The front page of *Cotton's Weekly* bitterly attacked efforts to reform or punish the Montreal prostitutes, contending that one must attack the cause of prostitution – the low wages paid to women workers.[73] Mary Cotton Wisdom wrote:

It raises my indignation to the boiling point when I think of a man of God hauling those poor sinful creatures, those down trodden women, those women made outcasts by man's sin, up before the courts to be judged by a man, imprisoned by a man, for what? For committing a sin for which man is responsible. I am not condoning their sin. I loathe it intensely. But my indignation knows no bounds when I read in the reports of these proceedings that the men found in these houses are given a slight fine and allowed to go free. Why should these men go free? Each one of these men (no, I will not call them by the name of man. Beast or reptile is far more applicable) should be punished to the full extent of the law and if the law provided no punishment for the man the law should be changed ... women must stand shoulder to shoulder. Together we must insist upon the right to control the conditions under which we live.[74]

Unlike her brother, Wisdom focused less on the economic exploitation of women than on male sexual domination. She did not think these "beasts or reptiles" followed natural urges.

Other women concurred with her depiction of prostitution as a male crime stemming from man's depraved nature. Rosa Gabriel took particular exception to the courts releasing the men found in brothels and even protecting their identities. She insisted that immoral traffic was not possible without these men and that they should bear the responsibility for their actions: "I know of many causes which eventually drives a woman to those depths; I know of none which drives a man there except his depraved nature. It is certainly not a moment of forgetfulness but deliberate sin."[75] Kate Richards O'Hare referred to those who "exalt motherhood and praise virtue; but, nevertheless they demand woman to become the machine to gratify their beastly passions and provide the machine of prostitution."[76]

It was not just the single man these women feared.[77] They were concerned that married men using prostitutes would catch venereal disease and contaminate their wives and children. This was not a fanciful fear, for the consequences of venereal disease in an era lacking early diagnosis and adequate cure could mean severe illness, disability, infertility, and eventual death.[78] Mrs Jane Brown asked how a woman could remain pure and undefiled when she lived with a "bestial man."[79] The sanctity of their homes and their bodies were imperilled by husbands who used prostitutes, and some even made veiled references to the unwanted sexual demands of husbands. For example, one article spoke of how "we have perverted nature in submitting the mothers to the lusts of brute beasts who monopolize the power and means of life under our brutish system."[80] R.B. Kerr described a mother who "suffered from the tyranny and brutality of her husband during pregnancy, and was rebuked and told to submit by a doctor to whom she complained."[81] While Kerr was circumspect in his description of the husband's behaviour, he was sympathetic to a woman's right to refuse sex when pregnant.

Although experts urged restraint within marriage, a husband's right of sexual access to his wife was reinforced by the weight of the medical community, by religious beliefs and the law, and implicitly by much of the left-wing press.[82] Socialist women deployed the maternal image to contest the widely held view that a wife should be sexually passive and should submit to her husband's sexual desires:

The Christian marriage of today is a crime against the nature, and thousands of women find themselves bound by their prejudices and so-called religion to an indescribable torture. The nature of a man and woman is different, it was said by the celebrated professor Mechnioff: "that nature was unjust against the woman, making her unable to be adequate to the man from the sexual point of view." This means that the marriage of today is not a healthy, normal, joyful life for the wife, but just an abnormal existence, worse than the life of a female animal, which follows sincerely and simply upon the call of her nature, but does not tolerate the insane obedience to its "hubby" as are doing millions of women. Why are they so foolish? Why do they go against their nature and spoil their health and that of their children?[83]

Women who depicted male sexuality as bestial or abnormal demanded woman's sexual autonomy, including the right to refuse sex, inside or outside marriage. Unfortunately, this maternalist framework at the same time denied them acknowledgment of woman's sensual pleasures and desires.

Few socialists admitted that women might find sex pleasurable. Some social purity reformers were convinced that women turned to prostitution because of their sinful nature – hence, the emphasis on the moral salvation of the fallen women. Sinful nature was a euphemism for sensual pleasures, ranging from the love of finery to sexual desire. Socialists rejected this view entirely. Their belief that women would never take up prostitution because they found it attractive or willingly chose it, or because they were innately wicked was reinforced by the poems and stories about women who had to choose among starvation, suicide, and prostitution. As one writer put it, it was unthinkable that a prostitute had any "love of the game."[84]

An interesting exchange of letters in 1902 illustrates this attitude. A woman wrote to Dorothy Drew (the pen name of Bertha Merrill Burns as editor of the women's column), asking what socialism might do for her daughter:

I have an adopted daughter, taken from an institutional home when she was seven months old. I know nothing of her parentage, but at a very early age she developed tendencies of a very depraved nature, and at seventeen she is, to all intents and purposes, a prostitute. I live in agony of terror lest at any time she may openly take to the streets. She has had every advantage, the adoring love of her adopted father and brothers, and, I think I may say, she has not lacked the faithful counsel and tender admonitions of a mother. Now what will socialism or any other "ism" do for such cases as hers? You claim that it will do more for women than for any other class of humanity, but how will it redeem girls who are evil simply from no stress of circumstances, but simply from vicious tendencies, and how can mothers be happy when their daughters are going astray.[85]

It should be noted that it is by no means clear from the above that the girl was a prostitute. Since she was still living at home and had not yet taken to the streets, we can only speculate about the kind of behaviour that might have led to the mother's judgment. The paper published several letters from readers who responded to the mother's query. One writer advised several changes in her living habits, such as more exercise, loose clothing, and avoidance of certain foods, since these might have the effect of "feeding the fires."[86] Another wrote that socialism could not do much for the depraved daughter: "The laws of heredity are too strong for us, and who shall say what were the pre-natal influences at work on the poor girl. I believe that sin is just as much a disease as consumption."[87]

Bertha Merrill Burns provided an extensive response to the question. She suggested that it was not a girl of low ideals who turned to prostitution but one with high ideals and the longing for a better life:

I am far from believing that the girl of low ideals is the one who oftenest becomes a victim to sex criminology. It is rather the girl with an unsatisfied heart hunger; an hunger that is perhaps due to the absence of love at her conception, or perhaps to the absence of any expression of love in her home life. Why, I know of many children who do not know the taste of a father's kiss, and who have forgotten the caresses of a mother because none have been bestowed since they parted from the breast from which they drew their first sustenance. To such girls temptation in the guise of love is almost irresistible, and the seducer has always love's phraseology on his lips and a lust light in his eyes that cannot easily be distinguished from love's fond glow by an untaught and ignorant girl.[88]

In rejecting the social purity and eugenic models in favour of a theory of childhood deprivation, Merrill Burns was in advance of the mainstream educational and medical authorities of 1902.

Other articles echoed the view that some women were "deceived" by the men they loved;[89] outcast by respectable society, they were thought to turn to prostitution for survival. Sympathetic reference was also made to women who resorted to it to escape the drudgery and oppression of factory life:

There are so many tendencies, so many emotions, so many desires, and so many temptations. Only those who have worked among that class which we call "The Fallen Sisterhood" know this, and who are we to judge them? … Then we have … the woman who is fond of fine clothes and the pleasures of life. The drudgery of the factory and the workshop pall on her; her wages are insufficient to procure fine food and clothing even of the plainest. She is not strong enough to overcome her desires and needs, and toil on. So much we could say in justice and defense of these unfortunate sisters. We do not uphold the sin. It is loathsome, and those of us who are strong know that, although we love the sunshine, luxury and comforts of life, we would rather spend our days at the wash tub or die in a garret, chaste – but we are not all strong.[90]

Although the socialist press rarely mentioned sensuality in women, it did acknowledge that some women engaged in sex because they were in "love" (as distinguished from "lust"). Nevertheless, within marriage, there was little if any acknowledgment that the woman might be an equal partner sharing in the pleasures of sex. Husbands were thought to impose their sexual demands on their wives. Women were thought to turn to prostitution for several reasons, all connected to economic and emotional deprivation. For the most part, the left rejected the view that these were immoral "fallen women" who were enjoying the life of a prostitute.

Socialist women articulated important links among the experiences they shared with nonsocialist women. The respectability that was so important for women was understood as a tenuous virtue, dependent on things beyond one's control. Illness, injury, or the death of a breadwinner might bring a respectable woman into the world of disrepute. More important was the link between prostitution and married life. The women writers often described marriage as a form of prostitution, where "woman sells her sex life in return for her keep."[91] Whether a woman married for love or for support, by drawing attention to the social convention which insisted that women submit to their husbands's sexual demands, these socialist women demanded sexual autonomy – inside and outside marriage. Unlike the sex radicals in the United States, this was not a demand for a woman's right to enjoy sex. Rather, it was a demand for a woman's right to participate in sex at her own choosing: "The Socialist believes love should be free in the sense that woman shall not be forced to surrender in matrimony or outside of it for the sake of a living."[92] The emphasis on woman's maternal role was crucial in securing sexual autonomy. Once a woman was economically free, she could "naturally select the father of her children, and determine when she was prepared to become a mother"; and she would no longer be compelled "to tolerate a drunkard, a bully, or a sensualist."[93]

This was a distinct view of woman's sexuality. Given economic independence, women would be free to love as they chose – but not in the sensual, libertarian sense that opponents of socialism interpreted. Indeed, socialist women rarely expressed any concept of women being capable of or desiring sexual pleasure.[94] Rather, their insistence on women's freedom to love as they chose was both a positive freedom to choose a good husband and a negative freedom – freedom from the unwanted overtures of men, inside and outside marriage. Socialism would allow men and women to be free to marry whom they loved and to sustain a monogamous married life. Few articles even questioned the naturalness of monogamy.[95] From the male perspective, this often represented an unreflective view of a man's right to seek sexual gratification in marriage and outside it. A few people within the left – mainly though not exclusively women – challenged socialist men to question these views and to address sexual as well as economic exploitation.

Some socialist women argued that the solution to the sexual exploitation of women extended beyond economic matters to a recognition that women must act collectively to assert their freedom from this form of oppression by men. One insisted that only women could solve the problem of prostitution: "Let women make the laws to govern punishment of their sisters and let a woman judge and minister the woman-made laws against women. Perhaps then the un-Christian, inhuman laws against women which Wier enforces will be considerably changed."[96] Another insisted, "Women must stand by women. Women must go forward to free their sisters from the awful conditions imposed upon them by man's brutality and selfishness."[97] To protect their sisters and themselves, women needed the vote.

CHAPTER SEVEN

"Descent from the Pedestal": Women's Suffrage and the Left

As demands for women's suffrage grew,[1] the early socialist movement threw its support behind the cause. In the Maritimes, a Fabian society was formed in 1900, supported by a contingent of suffragists in Saint John, New Brunswick.[2] In Ontario, the Canadian Socialist League (CSL) featured the issue prominently in the provincial election of 1902, declaring that socialists were "the only advocates of woman suffrage." The nomination of Margaret Haile as the CSL candidate in North Toronto demonstrated their "belief in the right of women to take part in the making of the laws under which they have to live." They also hoped that her candidacy would attract votes from suffrage advocates, for prominent suffragists were invited to support the CSL campaign. At one election meeting, the paper reported that Dr Emily Gullen [sic][3] addressed the crowd in support of socialism and women's suffrage. However, Margaret Haile declared herself "a Socialist candidate rather than a woman suffrage candidate," explaining that although she believed women should have the franchise, "that is only a short step towards the ultimate object of socializing the means of producing and distributing wealth." It was reported that this meeting "closed with cheers for the candidate."[4]

The Socialist Party of British Columbia also supported women's suffrage (though its support was as short-lived as the party itself).[5] In the fall of 1902, with members of the Revolutionary Socialist Party attending, it held its second annual meeting to debate a new platform and constitution. No women were present. Some men lobbied for the inclusion of immediate demands in the party platform, but the majority preferred to drop them, including the immediate demand for women's suffrage. The new platform was accepted by a large majority of the membership of both parties.[6] The absence of women at the convention did not go unnoticed. Under her pen name Dorothy Drew, Bertha Merrill Burns reported: "Not a woman delegate was present, not a woman's name appeared in the proceedings report and, apparently, not a woman's hand or tongue or brain in any way influenced the convention, unless indeed some good sister brushed her husband's Sunday coat and curtain [sic] lectured him into a proper frame of mind concerning 'immediate demands' before he went forth to conclave with his brethren."[7]

As support for suffrage disappeared from the platform, the party began to ridicule it along with other immediate demands. When the Independent Labour Party of Manitoba included suffrage in its platform, the SPC declared this move to be "one of the choicest from the fragrant bouquet of nostrums offered the unsuspecting electorate," which needed "not woman suffrage, but freedom from Exploitation for man and woman alike."[8] Socialists were urged to ignore immediate demands: "We are not interested in 'grafters,' 'Votes for Women,' 'Right to Work' and the rest of the nonsense that is heralded as immediate demands. We have only one 'immediate demand,' and that is the abolition of capitalism. We proletarians have no time to waste on 'Votes for Women.'"[9]

Despite these protests, women's suffrage was unlike other immediate demands because it "fitted" the SPC's agenda. The party had a concerted focus on educating the working class for socialism, and also an idealist conception of the transition to socialism. If the working class was educated to its class interests, a simple majority vote by its members could bring in the era of socialism. Control of the state would lead to control of wealth production. In those early years, socialists had absolute faith in the democratic political process. The task of the party was thus to educate the working class to its class interests.[10]

With emphasis on democratic political action through the franchise, it would have been entirely consistent for the party to acknowledge the importance of enfranchising the entire working class, including women. This line of reasoning would also have given the party some strategic grounds for expanding its educational efforts among the working class – which ostensibly was its prime objective. This was not, however, a course of action that the SPC chose to pursue. One woman derided this lack of consistency: "When the Socialist speakers advocate political action as the means of changing the present conditions how do they expect to approach the industrial woman worker with Socialism?"[11] The party never adequately answered her question. Yet nothing in its single-minded focus on education and the transition to socialism necessarily precluded support of women's suffrage. In fact, the enfranchisement of women fitted in well with this agenda. To explain the party's official failure to endorse women's suffrage, we must look elsewhere – to the hostility towards women reflected in the masculine ethos of the SPC. The party leaders did not consider women to be central to the socialist project. As noted above, no women were present when the party platform was revised. Masculine privilege was thoroughly embedded in the way the leading socialists articulated resistance to capitalism and in their view of the transition to socialism.[12]

It will be remembered that shortly before the formation of the SPC, in 1904, the *Western Clarion* stopped printing its women's column. As men assumed control of the paper, their antagonism to suffrage surfaced in the articles. One editorial cited Kant's edict that sexual equality was nonsense. Men and women were not equals but were complements which together made up a whole unit in society: "Being complementary, there is no question of equality between them and no basis of comparison, any more than between the violin and the bow which go to make up the musical instrument ... There is absolutely no foundation in fact to the sex equality upon which the feminists insist and no reality to the sex war as some of them proclaim. The normal functions and characteristics of the two sexes do not compete or clash. They dovetail into and complete one another." Accordingly, the editor ascribed to women the characteristics of passivity, conservativism, and reproduction of the species; to men he ascribed characteristics of variation and unrest. Women who agitated for change were deviating from nature. For this, capitalism was to blame. It perverted women from their natural functions by forcing them out of the home and into the labour force to compete with men as "packages of labour power." With a flourish of Marx's terminology, this writer argued that women received "the exchange value of an inferior grade of labour power. And it is this commodity inferiority, mistaken for sex inferiority, that is at the bottom of the so-called sex-revolt." Since women misconstrued the origins of their discontent, he concluded, socialists could, and indeed should, ignore their protests: "This is no affair of ours as Socialists. Ours is a revolt of the exploited class. Incidentally, of members of this class, many are women. Incidentally also, many of that class are vegetarians. The one fact is of as much bearing on the class struggle as the other."[13]

Some of the SPC's editorial comments were similar to those of conservative antisuffragists.[14] D.G. McKenzie, who was editor of the *Western Clarion* from 1908 to 1911, argued that the "average woman may desire a hat or a husband or some other trifle, but it cannot truthfully be said that she is pining away for lack of a vote."[15] However, unlike the more conservative critics of women's suffrage, he insisted that unless women were prepared to take radical action to demand the vote, they would not deserve it. He was, he said, "one of those malevolent individuals who is unwilling to endow woman with a vote at any time, on the ground that there is no vote coming to her ... [unless] she is prepared to make life unliveable on this footstool if she doesn't get it."[16] Like many socialists, he feared that women were inherently conservative and would pose a threat to socialists at the polls. Although he considered the British suffragists radical enough to warrant the vote, he thought that Canadian women lagged far behind their British sisters.[17]

However, not all socialists agreed that the conservative nature of women was grounds for denying them the right to vote. For many, the conservatism was proof that socialists needed to step up their efforts to appeal to women in particular and educate them to the cause of socialism. Several leading women socialists, including Edith Wrigley, Ruth Lestor, and Lena Mortimer, argued in this fashion. They also reminded the editor that men – who currently had the franchise – were failing to use their vote in a class-conscious manner.[18] Regardless of such arguments, editorial antagonism prevailed. While the *Western Clarion* frequently reprinted articles from the international socialist press, especially from British and American sources, it avoided reprinting material in favour of suffrage. When the American socialist party voted to set up a separate branch within the party to address women's issues, and especially women's suffrage, the *Western Clarion* ignored the arguments in favour of doing so and reprinted only the minority resolution opposing the move. Similarly, it reprinted antisuffrage articles from the *New York Call* and the *Socialist Standard*.[19]

Some women supported the spc's position on women's suffrage. Ruth Lestor was one, though she was not always consistent. She regarded the demand for suffrage as the direct result of the development of capitalism, which had reduced women to "simply breeding slaves for the capitalist market." In one instance she disputed the idea that women were particularly reactionary, reminding her audience that it was men who sent the reactionaries to Parliament; but at other times she took the opposite position, arguing that women, especially those not in the labour force, were "reactionary and disruptive." At times she stated that the demand for suffrage sprang mainly from "a desire to perpetuate permanently woman's follies and slavery to capital." At other times, she said that once women had the vote, they would have the means of becoming class conscious. Even without a political voice, she maintained, "the mother's instinct for the protection of her young ought to send them forth on a holy crusade against the evils [of capitalism]." In the meantime, women could "nevertheless hurl countless votes through their influence with their friends and relatives of the opposite sex. The man who will not listen to the plea of woman for the child is not entitled to receive woman's co-operation in producing children."[20]

The SPC's opposition to women's suffrage extended beyond its editorial pages. Sometimes it went out of its way to antagonize the suffrage organizations. In Vancouver, the WCTU wrote to all the candidates in the 1908 election asking for their support of several causes, including women's suffrage. Impossibilism framed the SPC's terse response. The ladies of the WCTU were informed that SPC candidates were not entitled to "the support or influence of any organization not having the same end [cooperative ownership of the means of wealth production] in view." The WCTU in turn supported all those nonsocialist candidates who did endorse their causes. Consequently, the SPC came to view the WCTU even more critically for using its influence to defeat socialists in elections.[21]

SPC member M.H.T. Alexander complained about the Political Equality League in typical impossibilist fashion. She had refused to join the league because she viewed the issues it supported (for example, changing the dower rights for women and instituting a mother's allowance) as simply defending the interests of private property. Furthermore, she claimed that the league did not address the causes of women's problems in society and that their having the vote would do nothing to alter the conditions that produced such problems.[22] In Vancouver, the representatives of the Political Equality League approached the SPC to seek its "sympathy and financial assistance" in securing the franchise for women. The party's response was decidedly unsympathetic: "Not that we are violently opposed to your having the vote, even though we know you would use it against us. We know of no good reason why you should not have a vote and it would matter nothing if we did. We simply don't care a cuss ... We know only two kinds of people. Not men and women but masters and slaves. Our 'financial assistance' if any is devoted to making slaves aware of the fact."[23]

While the party paper was hostile, some SPC members wanted women to have the vote, though they doubted the claim that suffrage would cure society's ills. SPC member Mrs Scott of Victoria debated with Dorothy Davis of the Political Equality League on the question "Will Woman Suffrage Solve the Economic Problem?" Mrs Scott, taking up the negative side of the debate, argued that women would be no more intelligent in their use of the vote than men were. The suffragists were mistaken, she said. The sex struggle "upon analysis resolves itself into a class struggle. I think when women get the vote they will vote with their class, just as the men do and that sex has no part in politics." She further objected to those suffragists who exhibited their class bias by demanding property rights for women. But although she took the negative side in the debate, she did not argue against the right of women to vote; she objected only to the suffragists' claims that the enfranchisement of women would change the economic problems of the day. Dorothy Davis concluded with disappointment that she did not have the opportunity to debate a real antisuffragist, for her opponent wanted the vote as much as she did.[24]

Other members of the SPC who supported the suffrage movement included Dora Forster Kerr and R.B. Kerr, the well known sex radicals and advocates of birth control. Both were active suffragists. Mrs Kerr was nominated to the provincial executive committee of the SPC, and both wrote articles on women's issues for the socialist press. Mrs Kerr was also organizer and secretary for the Political Equality League in Kelowna, British Columbia. She organized a suffrage meeting in 1912 (chaired by her husband, with Dorothy Davis as speaker) which resulted in thirty-four new members for the league. As the Kerrs were strongly committed to women's issues, one would expect to find them strong supporters of the SDPC, but Mr Kerr complained privately that the split of the Social Democrats from the SPC "spoiled an interesting experiment by the formation of a new party, as ... impossibilism had never so good a chance of showing what it could do as in B.C."[25]

Socialist MLA James Hawthornthwaite introduced suffrage bills into the British Columbian legislature in 1906 and 1909. He claimed that the first bill was "one of the most important measures ever introduced into the house."[26] While he admitted that women's suffrage would not mean economic freedom, he presented several arguments in its favour, one of which mirrored the racism evident in British Columbia's labour and socialist movements. He reported that some considered it an outrage "that one-half of their population should be deprived of the franchise, while Indians and Hindoos (whom they were now importing) might have it." He "knew no greater civilizing force than the enfranchisement of their mothers, wives and sisters."[27] Racism pervaded suffrage debates in all classes.

When Hawthornthwaite's bill was voted down on second reading, he concluded that it required more support from Canadian women and said they should learn some lessons in tactics from their British sisters. He was disappointed that so few of them were present in the visitors' gallery during the debate. However, his efforts did not escape notice, for the Vancouver branch of the National Council of Women commended him for his efforts. Nevertheless, the second suffrage bill he introduced suffered a similar fate in 1909.[28]

SPC members supported suffrage in a variety of ways. Some locals held propaganda meetings on the issue, featuring well-know socialist speakers such as Hawthornthwaite, Irene Smith, and Sam Atkinson. Charter members continued to support suffrage, despite the party's platform. After a heated debate, in 1908 the Ontario SPC convention voted to endorse women's suffrage and to encourage locals to bring in women lecturers, and it urged the dominion executive to follow suit and provide literature on working women.[29] Despite such pressure from party locals, the dominion executive, centred in British Columbia, refused to change party policy – though, as with other reform issues, it was not always able to enforce compliance from its members.

The SPC never changed its official position. Prominent suffragists were disparaged for their upper-class background and political allegiance. Nellie McClung, for example, was criticized for lending her support to the Liberals. After 1912, the party press did not cover or endorse suffrage politics, nor did it acknowledge the attainment of suffrage at the federal and provincial levels. However, it noted that working women's influence in the 1917 federal election had hurt the party. The SPC concluded that it had been right all along: "Women need to be educated to use the vote."[30]

The discontent within the SPC that led to the formation of the SDPC sprang from disagreements over many issues – most notably, immediate demands, affiliation with the international socialist movement, autonomy of ethnic locals, and internal democracy within the party.[31] But women's suffrage also had its place in the vituperative disputes that led to the formation of the new party. Ethnic locals differed in their support of this cause. Finns and Ukrainians cited it as one of their reasons for dissenting from the SPC. Many individual members expressed discontent with the party line well before an official break with the SPC. Ernest Burns, for example, gave the SPC's stance on women's suffrage as one of his reasons for not supporting the party.[32]

The 1908 SPC convention in Ontario debated a resolution urging the party to support several immediate demands, one of which was universal suffrage. Some members of the Toronto English local opposed the motion because they feared that the party would thus be endorsing "palliatives," but G.W. Wrigley defended it, arguing that universal suffrage was not an immediate demand but was a concession "to be wrung from capitalist legislators in order that the workers will be better equipped in the struggle to secure control of the law making power." The convention unanimously adopted the resolution and instructed "all speakers and Local organizers to make a more direct appeal to the workers for universal suffrage."[33] The *Western Clarion*'s response to this move was characteristic:

Now, every Socialist, as a matter of course, stands for the enfranchisement of women and equal rights for the sexes in every department of life. But that this should be made an issue of by the Socialist party can only be accounted for upon sentimental grounds. Just how the enfranchisement of women is going to enhance the triumphs of the working class or contribute to its economic enlightenment is difficult to make out ... The economic issue is clouded by a political issue and the struggle between the classes overshadowed by the struggle between the sexes.[34]

The English local in Toronto voted to endorse women's suffrage on the grounds that if men needed to use the ballot to attain socialism, women should also have it. Local 1 of Toronto voted to extend full political rights to women at the municipal level, demanding that the existing franchise for "spinsters and widows" be expanded to include married women. In addition, it endorsed the right of women to hold political office at the municipal level. These resolutions were not recognized by the dominion executive of the SPC in Vancouver. The Ontario locals were summarily read out of the party, leaving a small handful of socialists in Toronto who supported the SPC platform.[35]

When the expelled members from across Canada combined to form the SDPC, their new party's platform rejected the impossibilism of the SPC and supported measures to improve conditions under capitalism. The SDPC platform specified four demands: the reduction of hours of labour; the elimination of child labour; universal adult suffrage; and initiative, referendum, and right of recall.[36] Not surprisingly, the SPC's response to this new party was hostile. Roscoe A. Fillmore, a leading propagandist for the SPC, ridiculed the SDPC's platform by targeting each of the political demands. His criticism of the suffrage issue was particularly vehement: "Keep your eyes on the blackboard boys! Our next number is a hell-cracker. Woman suffrage! What an inspiring theme! [T]he dream of poets and philosophers since time began! How we have all dreamed of the day when woman would descend from her pedestal and take part in the more prosaic things of life! When she would scrap with hubby over the relative merits of the two or more labor thieves who were running for office."[37] Understandably, some people confused the two parties, and the SDPC made efforts to distinguish itself from the SPC by announcing, "Social Democrats do not sneer at woman suffrage."[38]

Because the SDPC supported suffrage, there was more extensive coverage of the issue in its party paper. Some of the arguments were grounded in the egalitarian principle that women had an equal right to the vote. One article endorsed the "absolute equality of the sexes [in] every department of life," and there were many short pieces claiming that only socialists stood for the equality of women.[39] But few articles argued exclusively in terms of the justice of extending equal political rights to women and men. Equal rights were certainly not the primary argument justifying suffrage. Indeed, considerable caution was expressed on the issue. One article explained that the "old 'equal rights' argument" was "fast becoming obsolete" and that its place was being taken by economic necessity: women needed the ballot to protect themselves and their families from the various ravages of capitalism.[40] While this particular article was a reprint from an American paper (and certainly reflected the influence that American socialists may have had on the Canadian movement), it captured the socialists' ambivalence over the adequacy of equality arguments. This was not, as some might anticipate, simply because the arguments reflected individualist and bourgeois values, though at times this was the case.[41] It was because the SDPC press had other – and in its view, better – reasons for endorsing suffrage.

Like the suffragists, the SDPC saw the ballot as a means to an end, and to some extent it shared the goals of the suffrage movement, for it believed that suffrage could address three key problems. First, suffrage could redress the legal status of all women under capitalism. The suffrage movement had produced a groundswell of criticism about the subordinate legal position of women under Canadian law. Accorded the status of lunatics and criminals, women were denied homestead and dower rights, custody rights, and property rights within marriage. The suffragists believed that with the vote, women would be able to act to right these injustices.[42] The chief proponent in the SDPC of altering the status of women was Mary Cotton Wisdom (a propertied woman). She was appalled that a woman had to die before she received her rightful share of matrimonial property.

Second, women voters would change the laws and conditions of prostitution and white slavery. They presumed that only women would make these changes because men, who had the franchise, had failed to do so. Third, women's suffrage was linked to prohibition.[43] Both Mary Cotton Wisdom and William Cotton, editor of *Cotton's Weekly*, were strong proponents of prohibition and were affiliated with the wctu. On at least one occasion, William Cotton addressed the wctu on temperance, and his paper often attacked the brewery interests. Mary Cotton Wisdom was an avid prohibitionist all her life.[44] All three issues were raised by the suffrage movement, and in this respect the SDPC echoed their concerns, differing only in their view that capitalism caused these evils.

Suffragists across Canada had an uneven and ambivalent record in relation to working women. Dominated by middle- and upper-class women, some suffrage organizations were hostile to the labour movement and treated working-class women as "passive recipients of the philanthropic endeavours of others." However, some of them overcame this patronizing view and supported working-class women.[45] The SDPC emphatically believed that wage-earning women were capable of deciding for themselves how to improve their lot. Several articles from *Cotton's Weekly* provide us with ample illustration of this argument. One typical article outlined the contrast between women in primitive society and women under capitalism. In primitive society women did not desire the vote. Only in capitalist society did women want the vote, because all their traditional work, such as spinning and weaving, was no longer done in the home: "As the women are affected by conditions which obtain in the industrial world it is quite natural that they desire to have a voice in determining these conditions ... The only way in which women can influence legislation directly is by the use of the ballot; hence the demand for suffrage and political equality."[46] This argument neatly side-stepped the issue of whether they should be earning wages. Since they were present in the paid-labour force, they needed the same rights as men:

Women of leisure must demand the ballot for abstract reasons, justice and equality: but the working women need the ballot. They need it as a means of self defense in the terrible competitive struggle that marks our present industrial system. They need it to protect their very health, the life and the future of their children ... Give working women votes and you will give them an opportunity to help themselves as no charity or welfare work or middle-class attempts at reform can ever help them. Give working women the votes and they will legislate child labor out of existence. Give working women the votes and they will shorten their long workday and establish a decent living wage ... To give women political freedom as a means of winning economic freedom, it is for this that the Socialist Democratic party demands votes for women.[47]

The emphasis on low wages, long hours, child labour, and unsafe and unhealthy working conditions was similar to the suffrage arguments presented in the labour press of the time.[48] In this light, suffrage was not required in order to help or control unfortunate others. The ballot was an economic necessity for women to defend themselves from capitalism and to achieve socialists goals.[49]

In addition, the SDPC echoed the suffrage movement in its belief that women would bring unique feminine qualities to politics. Sharing the prevailing belief in women's superior moral, maternal, and domestic virtues, it held that enfranchised women would "house-clean" politics. Mary Cotton Wisdom often relied on the language of domestic labour to exhort her readers to become politically active. In doing so, she presumed that men and women differed in their interests and that they would contribute different skills and qualities to politics:

When we return home after a week's absence, during which time our men folk have done all the house-keeping, we will want a good cleaning up of affairs. We don't pretend to understand political economies and we don't want to understand them. But we have a great deal of common sense and we are practical and are used to housecleaning ... We will not go about our governing by having a cigar or a glass of wine ... If we adopted that system of preparing our meals, or mending the family clothes, or doing the week's washing, our homes would soon be in a state of chaos ... Man's government has brought a state of chaos upon the country ... We women must come to the rescue of the generations yet unborn, and the only way for us to do this is through the ballot.[50]

Such examples of maternal feminism were common in Wisdom's "Woman's Page." She regarded politics as unscrupulous and unclean: "The dust and cobwebs of ages seem to have accumulated in our council halls to such an extent that even the dim dirtiness of the political corridors are deemed sacred."[51] Political corruption was well countered by her image of house cleaning.

The domestic metaphor also beckoned women into the political arena, where they were sorely needed, for men had not eliminated alcohol and prostitution: "If a housekeeper should conduct her household along the lines of throwing mud on her floor in order to clean it, of breaking her china in order to mend it ... she would be considered of unsound mind. Yet, this is exactly the mode of housekeeping on which our legislators conduct the larger home of the nation. Through legalizing the selling of rum they make criminals, then build penitentiaries and jails to shut them in."[52] Suffrage would aid women "in solving the problems in which they are so closely interested."[53] Other SDPC women also embraced the rhetoric of maternal feminism. As late as 1918, long after Wisdom had stopped editing the "Woman's Page," the SDPC paper *Canadian Forward* still talked about "housecleaning politics."[54]

Maternal feminism often appeared alongside egalitarian arguments. In an article entitled "Woman the Equal of Man," Wisdom argued that a woman deserved to have equal rights of citizenship as a man had, and she also said she believed that a woman would exercise this right to "say how and when and where *she and her children* shall be governed" (emphasis added).[55] Socialists combined egalitarian feminism with maternal feminism, as did the suffrage movement. Women had an equal right to suffrage, and they would use suffrage to protect and improve the domestic sphere. The two forms of feminism were not considered mutually exclusive. The socialists' maternal feminism in no way diminished their radical critique of the status quo, nor did they seek to confine women to narrow prescriptions of a woman's place. Their presumptions about the maternal role were not linked to conservative ends. While maternalism justified women entering politics and politicized the home, this did not in itself govern or limit in a conservative way the kinds of change which they thought women could achieve with suffrage, particularly in defense of the wage-earning women.

The SDPC also attacked common antisuffrage arguments: that suffrage would unsex women; that husbands should publicly speak for women; that women should be denied the vote because they did not bear arms; that some women were not intelligent enough to vote; that suffragists by their agitation had proved themselves unworthy of the vote; that a woman's place was in the home; and that the franchise would lead to a disrespect for the law. To each of these arguments the party paper provided stiff and witty rejoinders, rejecting each in turn.[56]

In British Columbia, the SDPC member of the legislature Jack Place introduced suffrage bills in 1913, 1914, and 1916. Each of his bills was voted down, but it is not clear that this was entirely because of lack of legislative support. In 1914, Place was approached by a delegation of women, who asked him to withdraw his suffrage bill so that a Conservative member of the house could introduce one. Place refused to do so. Since the Conservative majority in the house was reluctant to support a bill proposed by an opposition member, Place's bill was defeated.[57] The suffragists did not necessarily blame the Social Democrats for this defeat. Dorothy Davis, a prominent British Columbian suffragist, predicted that the government's position might lead people to support the socialists.[58] Although Place's efforts failed, they provide us with evidence of socialist support for women's suffrage, tinged as it was by the partisan considerations that shadowed the suffrage movement across Canada.

Despite these tensions, the SDPC was much more cordial than the SPC in its treatment of requests from suffrage organizations. At the SDPC's annual convention in British Columbia in 1913, delegates from the Political Equality League were given the floor to speak in favour of a suffrage resolution. The resolution was adopted unanimously. In contrast to the SPC, the SDPC was not only willing to endorse women's suffrage, but it organized meetings in support of the cause. An SDPC social in Alberta, for example, featured a lady comrade who reportedly gave an "excellent talk on woman suffrage," after which the local auctioned off box lunches that had been prepared by its women. In Vancouver, the Social Democrats organized a public meeting that included speeches on "Votes for Women" and "Suffragettes and Socialists." One address linked suffrage to the attainment of socialism. Prominent Social Democrats such as Jack Place also endorsed women's suffrage in public speeches.[59] Although the SDPC members were not numerous enough to have a very strong influence on the suffrage movement in Canada, they nonetheless championed the cause publicly.

Even though the Social Democrats were favourably disposed towards suffragists, tension erupted on several occasions. In 1913 two party members who addressed a suffrage meeting in Saint John, New Brunswick, were criticized by two women in the audience, who attacked their socialism, insisting that workingmen earned good wages.[60] Another woman felt that the party could do more. Margaret Allen, an employee of *Cotton's Weekly*, submitted five resolutions to its business meeting. Details of all the resolutions were not published, but at least one addressed women's suffrage, and the paper's response to it was to inform Allen that suffrage was "covered by the constitution of the SDPC"[61] and thus required no further action.

There may have been others who were not happy with the extent of the SDPC's support. Even the Social Democrats who appeared to be most supportive were not always consistent. William Cotton, for instance, did not include suffrage in his list of political demands when he ran in the municipal election in Montreal in 1911, even though Montreal suffragists made zealous efforts to mobilize voters. And in British Columbia, Jack Place, despite his legislative initiatives, was reluctant to endorse the women's participation on a government labour commission.[62] Not surprisingly, the SDPC paper did not air criticisms of these matters in its columns. But in spite of this evidence of some reluctance to give women's suffrage its full support, the the SDPC was not vituperative or hostile when addressing the issue, though it often distinguished between middle-class and socialist grounds for supporting women's suffrage. The SDPC thus avoided the acrimony which the SPC engendered on the suffrage issue.

We have seen, then, that although the early socialists initially endorsed suffrage, the SPC never formally did so. It insisted that the issue was irrelevant and detracted from the socialist struggle. The SPC carried little favourable suffrage coverage after its women's column was discontinued, and on many occasions it antagonized suffragists. Many party members who supported the cause deserted the SPC for the SDPC. This is not to suggest that suffrage was the crucial issue in the split between the two parties, but it was certainly an issue that contributed to the split, and it doubtless was important to some socialists, especially women. The SDPC provided more favourable and extensive coverage of suffrage issues. It supported women's suffrage on equal rights grounds and as a means of ending prostitution, white slavery, and the liquor traffic, and enabling women to defend themselves in the labour force. Embedded in this support were the assumptions of maternal feminism – that women would bring their unique maternal qualities to politics. Maternal feminism certainly overshadowed egalitarian arguments, but it did not diminish the SDPC's radical critique of capitalism or its defence of wage-earning women.

CHAPTER EIGHT

The War Years
and the Decline
of Feminism

With the outbreak of World War I, events in Europe overwhelmed and transformed the agenda of the left.[1] Interest in women's issues paled as war events and the repression of radicals dominated the headlines. When women's issues did arise, they were recast in the light of the war and the Russian Revolution. After the events of August 1914, the SPC immediately took a strong antiwar stance and issued a manifesto stressing the need for workers to battle against class enemies, not one another. The SPC was against war because it served only imperialist and class-based interests.[2] Suspicious of all political radicals, the Canadian state rallied quickly to accuse Germans, Ukrainians, and Russians of sedition. Press censorship was increased, and socialists across Canada were arrested. By 1918, orders-in-council had effectively banned left-wing organizations, as well as papers published in "enemy alien" languages and meetings at which those languages were spoken.[3]

The SPC was usually spared the worst effects of this repression. Key ethnic groups – notably, the Finns, Ukrainians, and Russians – had already abandoned the party. While some pockets of ethnic groups remained, an English-speaking, Anglo-Saxon leadership controlled the party, and state officials regarded these British-born radicals as nonthreatening.[4] This view of the SPC became a crucial factor in its survival. As was pointed out by William Pritchard (who was editor of the *Western Clarion* from 1914 to 1917), although the SPC was badgered, it managed to keep going throughout the war years, unlike the SDPC.[5] Nonetheless, its support declined, and in April 1915 the party paper was reduced to a monthly publication. Members of the SPC who supported the war either abandoned the party or were duly expelled, and this caused a decisive shift to the left. The party platform no longer condoned reforms that would later lead to socialism: it now called for socialism and nothing else.[6] In this more extreme position, the SPC's antipathy to feminism was confirmed.

Ignoring the small but significant contingent of suffragists who were pacifists, the SPC was outraged by women who supported the war. When Mrs Pankhurst, the famous British suffragist, suspended her suffrage campaign in favour of the war effort, the SPC attacked her and claimed that she was as duped by the government and the commercial classes as German women were. The Canadian women's movement did not suspend its suffrage campaign, but many prominent suffragists followed Pankhurst's lead. Nellie McClung, who was already disliked by the SPC for her backing of the Liberal party and her disdain for socialists, was outspoken on behalf of the war effort, advising women that they could "knit while discussing suffrage" at their War Auxiliary meetings.[7] Meanwhile, she fostered serious division when, claiming to speak for the entire movement, she advised Prime Minister Borden to grant the franchise to all women of British and Canadian birth while denying it to foreign-born women. Branches of the National Council of Women voted in support of this limited franchise, but other leading suffragists protested McClung's actions.[8] A male socialist ridiculed her for exposing the true base of the suffrage movement – women who "wanted political expression for their property ownership." Working-class women who wanted the vote were sentimental dupes of bourgeois feminists, he said. For a socialist to support women's suffrage was "probably a very gallant thing to do, and very expedient too, especially in the pairing season. But the scientific socialist ... waves all obligation to this movement ... The suffragette ... must not expect the same caresses in the political arena that she receives on lovers lane." He concluded that the scientific socialist must explain that women's suffrage has nothing to do with socialism and that she "needs to understand capitalist society more than she needs votes; that she needs to think more and, for the time being, talk less."[9]

Women enfranchised by the Wartimes Elections Act first voted in the federal election of 1917. When the outcome of the election was announced, William Pritchard, the editor of the *Western Clarion*, declared the results a foregone conclusion, given the Elections Act: "The woman's vote was a working woman's vote for the most part and all the comfort we can draw from it is that our attitude again has been proven correct. That is: education only will ensure success."[10] In later years, Pritchard recalled that 1917 "was the time when the ruling class decided that women were people so long as they were related to somebody who was overseas, so they granted the vote to women who had relatives overseas. My wife had four brothers so she could vote ... The ruling class needed those women's votes because they could count on the loyalty of those women whose men were overseas."[11] The suffrage movement's support of the war and the partial franchise confirmed the SPC's view that suffrage was a bourgeois cause hostile to the interests of working-class women. Its paper did not report McClung's retraction of her support for the partial franchise, nor did it publicize the views of leading suffragists who were adamantly opposed to the partial franchise – for example, the president of the Canadian Suffrage Association. For the SPC, suffrage, like all feminist concerns, deflected working-class women from the class struggle.

The large number of women who entered the labour market during the war alarmed the SPC. Male trade unionists feared that women would use the vote to keep their jobs when the war ended, thus creating unemployment for returning soldiers. The *B.C. Federationist* stopped publishing its suffrage column in 1915.[12] The fourth edition of the SPC's manifesto declared, "The influx of women into the fields of waged labour hitherto occupied by men is remarkable. By virtue of their cheapness they will stay. At the end of the war some 20 million men will be thrown upon a glutted labour market."[13] Ignoring the fact that women needed to be able to support themselves, the SPC was eager to criticize those who joined the wartime labour force. When female munitions workers in England and France were praised for their abilities, one article called this "the screech of the militant [suffragist] breaking out anew in another quarter." This author dismissed the claim for women's right to work as a superficial demand for "equity and justice" or "idiocy and tarradiddle."[14]

J. Harrington, the only SPC candidate in Vancouver in 1916, noted that the "mouthpieces of capitalism" praised women for their entry into "industries formerly monopolized by men" because women were more efficient, cheaper, and drove down all wage rates. This development distorted age-old relations: "At no period since man has recorded his needs and deeds is it apparent that his entire waking life need be monopolized in procuring his subsistence (excepting, of course abnormal disturbances). Women, therefore, were never called upon to take part in the actual production or procuring of food. (Again allow for a few specific exceptions)." In Harrington's opinion, war was just such an abnormal disturbance, drawing women into male activities. He predicted that when the war ended, hostility would reappear, because women would refuse to relinquish their jobs. They were allies of the capitalists, who had granted them the vote to keep returned soldiers from voting them out of office. Harrington concluded that the only hope for the "sane woman at present earning an independent living, however meagre, but still better than she has ever hoped for, owing to the war ... lies in her lining up with her class to overthrow the capitalist era."[15] His class struggle would, if it could, drive women out of industry. These views against women workers are especially noteworthy in view of the shift in support of industrial unionism that is reputed to have occurred in the SPC during the war years.[16]

As the war decimated the young male population and the ratio of women to men increased, various proposals for repopulation were offered. The concern about prostitution and white slavery took second place to anxiety about the declining birth rate and the plight of unwed mothers. Soldiers leaving for the front were urged to marry and start families. In the name of patriotism, women were urged to "do their duty" and bear more children.[17] Pritchard criticized the move to legalize "bastardy" and the "very lenient attitude towards Tommy's moral mis-demeanours" in Britain. Canada also was affected, he reported, because "eighteen hundred unmarried girls and women in Toronto ... expect to give birth to children whose fathers are now in Flanders." As the "sanctity of the marriage contract" and the "beauty of the hearth and home" were swept away, these women would be seen as pawns in a hollow farce serving the nation's need for "cannon fodder." The masses would lose their reverence for these institutions, and morality itself would become further grist to the "mill of the revolutionary proletaire."[18] One farmer, W.J. Battershall, responded in SPC spirit when filling out his daughter's birth registration. In answer to the question "Occupation of mother?" he replied, "Raising slaves to be skinned." He refused to retract his answers and spent fifteen days in the Portage la Prairie jail.[19]

Pritchard linked the legalization of "bastardy" with the "desperate need of the masters for re-population after the war" and the "utter impossibility of attaining such an object without ruthlessly destroying the existing moral fabric of society." He argued that legitimizing illegitimate children and encouraging the marriage of soldiers were examples of the immorality of capitalism. Motherhood was called upon to serve the immoral needs of capitalism, he maintained: "In some quarters it is urged that EVERY WOMAN ABLE TO FULFIL HER NATURAL FUNCTION SHOULD, AS A DUTY, BECOME A MOTHER; and so, for this FIRST time in Christendom, we get a hint that PARTIAL POLYGAMY IS TO BE PARDONED IN

THE INTERESTS OF THE STATE, and more boldly the demand that the UNMARRIED MOTHER should no longer be regarded as a sinner." He concluded that such blatant manipulation of women's maternal functions in the interests of the capitalists would serve to radicalize working-class women.[20] The war years did radicalize some women, but not necessarily in the way Pritchard anticipated.

Sonya Levien shared Pritchard's perspective that capitalism and war were the cause of immorality, but she stressed the need to respond humanely and compassionately to the plight of women and children. She disparaged the inconsistencies of English puritanism as "church morality tries to justify economic expediency," and she ridiculed reformers (including Mrs Pankhurst) who, she said, were calling for the state endowment of motherhood because they had just discovered that "the child has an equal claim on society whether the mother is married or single." Levien asserted that "none but the bigoted and cruel would deprive illegitimate infants of the healthy birthright that is due all children, but to justify and encourage their coming into being because a nation desires more men is barbaric in its cruelty to both the children and the mothers that bear them." She objected to calling the soldier-fathers of illegitimate children heroes. When men "permit themselves to become irresponsible fathers and burden their women and the next generation without any real guarantee from society that there will be a new attitude toward their carelessly begotten children, they are not heroes, nor are the women heroines." Pritchard had not addressed the social need to provide for such women and children, nor did he insist that the men take responsibility for their behaviour. Levien, on the other hand, declared that society had a responsibility to care for its children, whether they were war babies or slum children, and that men and women should be responsible for the consequences of their sexual activities.[21]

While deploring the patriotic efforts to promote an increase in the birth rate, the SPC did not support the demand for birth control or abortion; it viewed both as further evidence of capitalism's corruption. During these years, rather than bear the unwanted children of soldiers, many women relied on abortion and infanticide. The works commissioner in Toronto reported that two hundred prematurely born babies had been found in the screens at the sewage disposal plant, and this was regarded as an underestimate of the numbers of "slaughtered innocents," for many had gone through the sewage system without being detected.[22] Birth control was attacked by Moses Baritz, a member of the tiny Socialist Party of North America. He maintained that "small breasted women and fat headed men" foolishly advocated birth control "as a means of allaying the sufferings of the working class." He explained: "The main idea advocated is that the smaller the family, the greater the happiness, and the more secure the economic condition ... Poverty will not be abolished by 'Birth Control' whatever the method used." Baritz acknowledged that working-class women were using birth control "because it is hard to keep a family in decency when wages only hover above the cost of subsistence." He concluded that the people advocating contraception were merely justifying robbery of the working class. His argument, which placed sole emphasis on economic pressures, ignored the feminist grounds for the use of birth control – the issues of choice and control over one's body.[23]

Further criticism of capitalism's effects on family life was expressed in the discussions of venereal disease. Pritchard insisted that it was "bound up with capitalism." He reviewed army reports on the extent of the problem and warned the wives of soldiers that they risked contracting syphilis. With the aid of the YWCA, the army provided local women and prostitutes for the soldiers. Pritchard asked, "And the women? What of them? Can women, that is women of the working class, receive any great or lasting benefits by taking a mere 'anti-male stand,' the futile policy of denouncing the tyranny of man-made laws? Have working-class women anything to gain by lining up in a sex fight?" Pritchard contended that woman's position was identical to man's. Both sold the one commodity they had, their labour power, to capitalist interests. The only remedy was to break the bonds of wage slavery.[24]

The war confirmed the SPC's antipathy to feminism. Birth control, women's right to work, and women's suffrage were now viewed more starkly as bourgeois demands designed to distract the working-class woman. Lacking a feminist vision, the SPC's socialist future would reverse the effects of capitalism on family life, return women to the home and re-establish the male wage earner's position as head of the household. The party's spurious attempts to lay claim to a scientific understanding of the woman question paralleled contemporary attempts to use scientific evidence to prove whites superior to other races. This "scientific" socialism provided a specious rationale in support of pre-existing prejudices and male privilege. It limited the definition of socialism to the experiences of male waged labourers, and it deflected feminist criticisms that challenged male privilege within the home, at work, and in society at large.

The SDPC's response to the war was more complex. The prewar years saw a significant increase in support; after *Cotton's Weekly* was turned over to the SDPC in 1911, its circulation rose dramatically, reaching 30,000 by mid-1913.[25] But with the continuation of the war, membership steadily declined. Some members of the party were swayed by the wartime propaganda and could not support the party's antiwar stance. Those of German background were subjected to public hostility and government repression, which forced them to limit their political activities or refrain from them altogether. By October 1916, the SDPC reported a mere two thousand members across Canada, fragmented into different ethnic locals, the largest contingent being Finnish. Ontario claimed only three hundred party members. Small numbers of Jewish, Finnish, and Ukrainian members reported themselves still active in 1917, and the party press complained that there were not enough English comrades to carry on the struggle. By the end of 1914, the party paper was bankrupt. No other English-language Social Democratic paper was published until the *Canadian Forward* appeared in October 1916 as a bimonthly publication. Once again, the party press had to struggle for its survival, since the Canadian post office denied the paper the standard reduced postal rates it afforded others.[26]

The SDPC initially appeared united in its opposition to the war,[27] but divisions soon appeared in its ranks. Some party members, notably those with links to the trade union movement, abandoned the party and lent their support to the war effort. Those who stayed were against the war for a variety of reasons. Some believed that socialists should fight their common class enemies, not each other, but others opposed the war on pacifist grounds, maintaining that all war was immoral. These views coexisted within the SDPC, but as Russia moved towards revolution, pacifism was increasingly challenged. The party also split along ethnic lines, the Anglo-Canadian leadership leaning towards pacifism while the Eastern European members tended to support revolutionary internationalism. Because the prominent German and other ethnic locals in the SDPC were regarded as "enemy aliens" by both the public and the government, the state ruthlessly targeted the SDPC for suppression. This led directly to its demise and to the scattering of its supporters among the labour movement and the Communist Party, or out of the left altogether.[28]

Since the SDPC had given voice to feminist concerns, how did these developments influence the future of feminism on the left? While the party declined and fragmented along ethnic lines, women struggled to establish an organizational framework to encourage female participation. British Columbia voted in 1913 to permit women to have separate women's organizations within the party. In an effort to encourage the wives of socialist men to join the party, in 1916 the SDPC held a referendum on a proposal for twin stamps that would allow married couples to join at reduced rates. Members voted 665 to 195 in favour of the proposal, and the party paper urged locals to order supplies.

A Women's Social-Democratic League was formed in 1914 in Ontario, with an initial membership of thirty women. Its purpose was to promote socialism through an autonomous women's organization that would be open to all progressive women, but in fact most of its members were from the SDPC. Despite the party's refusal to provide funding, the league organized lectures, study sessions, and socials, such as the reception held for socialist and labour candidates in 1916, and it raised significant sums of money for the party during the war years. In Toronto in 1915 and 1916, a Christmas bazaar raised $300 to be shared equally among the women's league, the SDPC, the Jewish organization, and the municipal election campaign.[29] The league was viewed by some as simply an auxiliary organization for the party. At its organizing meeting, the Rev. W. James emphasized that there was a need for women socialists because men needed wives who would approve and support them in their socialist work. He concluded by referring to the "Queen Mother of Socialism, Mrs Karl Marx," without whose "inspiration and sympathy Marx could never have laid the foundations of Socialism."[30] But the women served other important functions for the party. By organizing social activities that included the various locals, the Women's Social-Democratic League provided a unifying influence for the organizationally and ethnically diverse party.

As mandatory conscription loomed on the political horizon in 1917, the SDPC vehemently opposed it and organized rallies across Canada. Women were visible in this campaign. The women's league in Ontario debated "Is Patriotism a Virtue?" and Winnipeg's women's locals declared themselves against conscription. Mrs Prentor spoke to a large anticonscription rally, Rebecca Buhay reported to the party paper on anticonscription rallies in Montreal, and the SDPC commended Laura Hughes, who was affiliated with the Independent Labour Party, for her public stance against conscription. Socialist women were also active in peace organizations, most notably the Women's Peace Crusade and the Council for the Study of International Relations to Prevent War.[31]

Some women feared the consequences of political radicalism during these years. More than one wartime socialist blamed his wife for the loss of his treasured socialist library, and John Bruce lamented his wife's burning of his 1886 edition of *Das Capital*.[32] Spouses now had a well-founded reason for objecting to their partners' political activities, since these posed the threat of imprisonment and physical danger. The government drove many socialists underground or out of the country, or forced them to abandon their left-wing activities. Opposition to the war did not have popular support, and soldiers attacked socialist meetings across Canada, doubtless deterring many from attending. In Edmonton, a party meeting was broken up by soldiers, and the members – including one woman – were beaten.

As state repression against "enemy aliens" escalated, the attacks on the SDPC increased. The editor of the party paper, Isaac Bainbridge, was charged, convicted, and served a prison term for sedition in 1917. In the same year, socialist meetings were broken up by police, who particularly targeted the ethnic locals; in Winnipeg, the police raided socialist and labour organizations, closing down the Russian and Ukrainian socialist papers. The earlier orders-in-council were considered inadequate for curtailing the activities of socialists of non-German background, so in September 1918 the government issued an order-in-council that effectively outlawed the Social Democratic left in Canada. From this point on, the party papers were closed, meetings were banned, and members' homes and offices were raided. During this sweep, twenty-five-year-old Mrs Sarah Knight of Edmonton was arrested and charged with sedition for having given a speech criticizing American involvement in the war. Mrs Armstrong, a prominent activist in the labour movement in Winnipeg, arranged for her bail and pledged the support of the Winnipeg labour movement in defending her at trial.[33]

Harassment also threatened the livelihood of individual socialists. Miss Anna Held's loyalty to "British ideals" was questioned by the Board of Education in Toronto because of her distant German heritage, her pacifist activities outside the classroom (which were considered socialist), and her refusal to sing the second verse of "God Save the King." She objected to the lines "Scatter our enemies," "Confound their politics," and "Frustrate their knavish tricks." In fact, church leaders and one provincial government also objected to this verse. The investigators, however, assumed that Held's pacifism was evidence of "dirty German socialism." The party press complained that Held could not prove her loyalty by joining the armed forces and dying overseas, like a male teacher who had been similarly accused. The charges against her were vague, difficult to prove, and no action was taken against her, but she resigned her post, declaring, "Any effective work I might have done with the children and parents has been denied me." The investigation had cost her "her position and means of livelihood and detached her from a profession for which she had spent many years of training and to which she was strongly attached." The party paper ranked her with Jack Reid, Wilfred Gribble, and Isaac Bainbridge as martyrs to the cause of free speech and democracy.[34]

The SDPC continued its women's column, but women's issues were transformed as a result of the war and the Russian Revolution. The party was not as openly critical of suffragists or feminists during the war as the SPC was. Although Mrs Pankhurst was criticized for representing bourgeois interests, her daughter, Sylvia Pankhurst, was admired for her socialist leanings. The *Western Clarion*, sniped that SDPC candidate G.E. Winkler even packed "a sparring partner around with him in the shape of a suffragette ... [who] justified the Allies participation in the war."[35] The SDPC often distinguished between bourgeois imperialist suffragists and working-class socialist suffragists. The SPC damned both, using the pro-war suffragists to vilify all feminists.[36]

The SDPC opposed the partial franchise for women and protested the disenfranchisement of "enemy" citizens that accompanied the legislation. The first reading of the Wartime Elections Act was announced with no commentary. Socialist women of Eastern European background, who constituted the majority of Social Democratic women, could not share in celebrating this victory, for not only were they explicitly denied the vote, but their husbands, fathers, and brothers were disenfranchised by the same act that gave the vote to their Anglo-Canadian sisters. The SDPC expressed restrained enthusiasm for the act and stressed the need to educate women for the future use of the ballot.[37]

As public attention focused on women in war industries, the defence of wage-earning women became difficult. While the Women's Employment League publicized the plight of the hundreds of unemployed women on its rolls, James Simpson addressed a gathering of the Political Equality League and declared that women were "unfair competitors in the industrial field against the men."[38] Under fire from men who were fearful of losing their jobs, one article used the war to defend women's employment:

Parents have no right to keep back their girls from the factory than their boys from the ranks. The moral advantage of service far outweighs the moral danger of changed conditions. But, above all, you will escape the moments which come to any self-respecting girl or woman when she asks herself whether it is right or fair or decent that she should be having a good time while our men are facing and suffering what we hear of – and much too that we do not hear ... For any able-bodied Canadian, whether man or woman, a life of leisure, at such a time as this, is a life of disgrace.[39]

Wartime events also coloured views of sexuality. Armies were criticized for procuring women to serve as prostitutes and for creating such conditions of desperation and need. Capitalist militarists were held responsible for this, as well as for venereal disease, the regulation of the birth rate, and the prohibition of birth control: "More and better births are not wanted in order that there may be more and finer joy in human life, but, implicitly in order that the 'kannonenfutter' may be sufficiently plentiful and effective."[40] Discussion of prostitution in Canada dwindled to one article that reproduced the report of the secretary of the Canadian Vigilance Association, who had toured Canada and the United States. It included an account of a woman who had earned a weekly salary of $200 while travelling the vaudeville circuit but had had her income drop to $60 per week at the outbreak of the war. "She said it was utterly impossible, upon the lesser salary, to pay travelling expenses and keep up the necessary elaborate wardrobe, unless she obtained revenue by violating the moral code. She, therefore, decided to run a sporting-house. She now has three in British Columbia, to wit, at Fernie, Elke, and Caithness, all wide open." In Fernie, British Columbia, it was reported that "a wide open vice district was found. Here girls called to men 200 feet distant." One prostitute from Moose Jaw, Saskatchewan, said that she had tried to work in a factory but the "starvation wages had forced her to become publicly immoral." To this, the party paper replied that only abolition of the wage system would solve the problem. In the meantime, the "Norwegian system" was advocated, in which doctors were required by law to report any cases of venereal disease to the public health authorities.[41]

The SPC had ridiculed any suggestion that women had special life-bearing, maternal qualities which led them to oppose war. It ignored the antiwar activities of socialist and nonsocialist women around the world, preferring instead to deride the British and German women who supported the war. In contrast, drawing on the intellectual heritage of the turn-of-the-century women's movement, maternal pacifism flourished in the SDPC press.

Gertrude Richardson was its most published proponent. Her correspondence appeared regularly in the *Canadian Forward* from

July 1917 until the paper ceased publication in August 1918. While she appealed directly to women in maternalist language, her analysis of the cause of war was socialist.[42] Richardson had been born in Leicester, England, of parents who "suffered poverty in order to assist the social outcasts of their native city." Although deeply religious, she "found herself in conflict with conventionality and the shallow veneer of church-going people, and ultimately concluded that many atheists were better Christians than professors of that faith." During the Boer War, she came into contact with socialists for the first time; she became the first woman to join the "Stop the War Committee" and published her antiwar views. Her father was mobbed for taking part in a peace meeting and died a few days later. In 1911 she and her mother came to Canada to assist her brother on his farm. In 1912 she married a farmer and settled in Manitoba, but marriage did not stop her political activism, for she continued her weekly contributions to the socialist *Leicester Pioneer* in England. Having been a suffragist in England, she continued her activities in Manitoba. She spoke to the Grain Growers of Dozeng and the Women's Labour League in Winnipeg, helped organize the Women's Suffrage Society of Manitoba, and was elected president of the Swan River Suffrage Association.[43]

Richardson did not view the war in class terms; to her, the enemy was war itself: "The enemy is neither Germany nor Austria, the enemy is the spirit of cruelty and conquest developing in the condition of war and militarism, the oppression of the mother and of all weak and unprotected persons – the institutions of slavery in every form ... We are enfranchised women and have power to-day to make our demands for righteousness." She appealed to women with "mother hearts" to join her in fighting militarism at home and abroad, explaining that motherhood deployed against the war was not limited to mothers; it included anyone who possessed the spirit of motherhood, a "deep spiritual possession, a love for humanity, a glorious, self-giving longing to protect, conserve and guard and save."[44] To all such women, said Richardson, the sons overseas cried out as they died: "Women of Canada, women with mother hearts, they are crying to you, to us all ... They are asking us to save them, to put an end to the horror that is claiming them, destroying their beautiful young bodies, closing their keen and piercing eyes in death."[45]

She described women as "purer" than men and thus more able to bring peace to the world. This purity was not a faint-hearted quality:

So here's to the new era of Militancy –
Hold, ye faint hearted! Ye are not alone!
Into your worn-out ranks of weary men
Come mighty reinforcements, even now!
Look where the dawn is kindling in the East
Brave with the glory of the better day,
A countless host, an endless host all fresh
With unstained banners and unsullied shields
With shining swords that point to victory
And great young hearts that know not how to fear
The women come to save the weary world.[46]

Other socialists women agreed that through pregnancy and child-birth, mothers displayed great acts of heroism and endurance: "Every corpse on the battlefield represents nine months of physical discomfort and suffering often culminating in hours of the most excruciating agony which mortals may know ... She, the natural conserver of life has brought forth babies only to have men destroy what she, out of the boundless depths of mother love has sought, throughout the long, long years to preserve and prepare for life's duties."[47] Childbirth provided a powerful image of female strength in a country where maternal and infant mortality rates surpassed those of comparable industrialized nations.[48] The ability to overcome fear and pain in childbirth drove mothers to oppose a war that would destroy the lives they had created. In letters from Richardson's supporters around the world, women confirmed their pacifism. This correspondence highlighted the efforts of German socialist women and the women's peace organizations in England, America, and Australia to end the war.[49] It reinforced the impression that women had a common, worldwide bond that made them natural enemies of war.

In 1915, after attending the Women's Peace Conference at The Hague in Holland, Laura Hughes joined with other feminists and with the Toronto Suffrage Association and the Women's Social-Democratic League to form the Canadian Women's Peace Party, an affiliate of the Women's International League for Peace and Freedom. These wartime pacifists were sustained by their feminism and their radical commitment to social and economic justice.[50] Richardson urged Canadian socialist women to join the International Women's Crusade to oppose militarism. The platform of the crusade was published in the *Canadian Forward*:

We, the members of the Women's Crusade, believing that the men and women of all nations are the Brotherhood and Sisterhood of the great family of humanity, assert our opposition to all war, conscription and slavery. We pledge ourselves to support, by our influence and voting power, only those who will work for freedom and peace, and the suppression of militarism under all forms. We desire social and political equality – the world for the workers, to whom life of international Socialism it has it belongs [sic], the true religion, which is the fulfilment of the Golden Rule, the creation of a safe and happy world for the unborn.[51]

A second printing of the Women's Crusade pledge appeared in June 1918. It no longer stated its opposition to conscription but called for "social and political purity, the world for the workers (to whom it belongs), the true religion, that is the fulfilment of the Golden Rule, and the creation of a safe and happy world for the unborn."[52] Richardson claimed that socialist women outnumbered all others in the Women's Crusade in Canada. They organized letter-writing campaigns to secure the release of imprisoned conscientious objectors, including Richardson's brother and Isaac Bainbridge. They also opposed the growth of militarism, for example, the introduction of military training in Canadian schools.[53]

Richardson and many other socialists linked their pacifism to Christianity. They often found themselves at odds with fellow church members, for the war was supported by religious leaders across Canada, including those belonging to the more radical Methodist Church.[54] Pacifists and opponents of the war were denounced from the pulpits. The SDPC believed that these churches had abandoned the true values of Christ. It urged women to boycott the "jingoist newspapers" and to rise "quietly and leave every religious service where war is preached in the name of Christ."[55]

The use of maternalist rhetoric did not prevent socialists from having a class-conscious understanding of the war. Rebecca Buhay wrote a sentimental article about a mother who died of "a broken heart" when she received news of her son's death. At the same time, Buhay displayed a sophisticated grasp of class analysis and a clear enthusiasm for the "stupendous" victories in Petrograd. After the war, she was involved briefly in the One Big Union and then became an active member of the Communist Party of Canada.[56] Isolated from the pro-war feminist community, socialist women within the Women's Peace Crusade found a camaraderie in their socialist, feminist, Christian, and maternalist beliefs. They readily wedded the imagery of mothers against war with resistance to the tyranny of class oppression in their call for "the world for the workers to whom it belongs" and an end of "slavery in every form."[57]

Maternalism did not, however, provide a concrete foundation for pacifism.[58] To argue that all mothers were naturally opposed to war became a hollow cry when one was confronted with issues of self-defence. The Russian Revolution was just such a case. The claim that women as mothers were opposed to war in any form left the "mothers' sons" slaughtered in Czarist Russia. Socialist women from Eastern Europe, who had closer ties to the class warfare there, doubtless found it difficult to relate to the maternal pacifism espoused by Anglo-Canadian socialist women. Many pacifist Social Democrats were deeply torn between their socialist convictions (which applauded the struggle of workers against their oppressors) and their pacifist convictions (which disdained war in any form). This conflict took on particular significance in the face of the Russian Revolution. The revolution, more than the war, tested the ideological convictions of those socialist women whose political heritage rested in church organizations and the women's movement. Already under threefold pressure from the pro-war propaganda, the virulent animosity directed against pacifists, radicals, and Eastern Europeans, and the church-based support for the war effort, some of these women were further alienated from socialism by the Russian Revolution. Not surprisingly, some of them chose to abandon socialism altogether. One such person was Mary Cotton Wisdom.

Before the war, Wisdom had urged women to overcome their fear of "foreign" socialists. Little is known of her activities during the war, but her correspondence after it leads us to conclude that she became a supporter of the conflict. Her brother William maintained his commitment to socialism and moved to Nova Scotia to establish the *Maritime Labour Herald*, the miners' official newspaper. He was fired in 1922 for stating that the union leaders were members of the Communist Party and that he "refused to follow the party line as laid down by Moscow."[59] He was arrested, and his sister's letters to him provide an interesting insight into how her political views changed during the war years. She told William, "I don't object to your radical ideas or your defending the weak." But she said that she did object to the strong language he used in his papers, reminding him that he was a gentleman and "a gentleman doesn't call names" to people one disagrees with.[60]

Mary Cotton Wisdom believed in spiritualism and claimed to have psychic powers that enabled her, by means of "automatic writing," to relay messages from their dead father. As the mouthpiece of their father, she informed William: "The idea has been impressed upon me to tell you that you had better impress upon your readers that you are *not* any immigrant, – for by the taunting you have been doing they may think you are – say you are a staunch Britisher and

Mary Cotton Wisdom, 1902

you had better wave the dear old flag (figuratively) pretty lively – you honour the King and love your Country but dislike the way the laws are administered." She reminded William of their distinguished ancestors to prove that he was no "foreigner" but was descended from "*British* loyal, educated gentlemen." As "Father," she further instructed William: "When your head is in the lion's mouth be careful, be polite until you crack his jaw."[61] She insisted that if he remained a loyal Britisher he could not be called a "seditionist," "disloyal," a "Red or some other dreadful character."[62]

By the end of the war, Wisdom had abandoned her tolerance of foreigners. Her sense of racial superiority, which was doubtless heightened by the anti-immigrant fervour of the war years, may have been an important part of her rejection of socialism. Although she remained sympathetic to her brother's efforts, her later politics were decidedly Liberal. She remained active in various women's organizations, including the local Women's Institute, the Women's Guild, and the Woman's Christian Temperance Union.[63]

There were undoubtedly a number of women who, like Wisdom, abandoned socialist politics as a result of the war years, but others weathered the storm and remained committed socialists. In spite of the vacuum created by the erosion of maternal feminism, some of them tried to articulate a perspective of the Russian Revolution that challenged maternalism while retaining a gender-distinct identity for socialist women. An article by Ida Crouch Hazlett marked the breach between maternal pacifism and socialism, and charted a distinctively new course for the women of the left.[64]

Hazlett criticized those who deplored the entrance of women into the Russian army, praising the Russians for having "shattered the sentimental traditions about women with their bayonets" by showing that when "their homes and their loved ones can only be preserved through war they have never wavered in courage and intrepidity of spirit." She saw this as the entrance of women into humanity, throwing "their all, themselves, into the struggle for ultimate liberty." She described women as superior to the "less developed personality of men." Women showed courage as they faced death in childbirth, whereas "men's only contribution to that event is pleasure." Women, she said, face "worse than death whenever they are forced to submit their body and the sacred functions of love, by law, necessity, physical compulsion or any other power, to a man whom they despise. Going into battle must have been a glorious exaltation compared to that." When Russian male soldiers attempted to assault and rape women soldiers, she praised the women for forcing them back with their bayonets. With this act, the Russian women "severed forever the cords of bondage that had bound their sex to the harem psychology, namely that women cannot back up their independence with physical force." This action "vindicated womankind forever from the disabling implication of impotency and subordination." As the "preservers of life," women could now fight to hasten the "advent of a free world."[65] Hazlett and others used rhetoric that represented the mother as a fierce defender of her young. In declaring their support for the Bolshevik revolution, they rejected Richardson's pacifist maternal images. Maternalism was indeed a malleable image that served different ends.[66]

The war years put enormous pressure on the SDPC. Differences among ethnic locals exerted a centrifugal force. The party's diversified structure, which had been useful in the prewar years, proved too weak to provide the organizational or ideological coherence to surmount the growing pressures on the party. Some of the Anglo-Canadian members succumbed to wartime propaganda and nativism. Government repression increased, and public attacks on the left grew under the blind eye of the Canadian state. Women members were as affected by these forces as the men. Those who were active in the Ukrainian, Finnish, Russian, Jewish, and other locals continued to be guided by the exigencies of the survival of their families and communities. Despite the rhetoric of women's common interests and despite organizational structures such as the women's league, women's support of the party also fragmented. With a few exceptions, the unity of women is noticeably absent during these years as women rejected socialism altogether or shifted their allegiance in concert with their ethnic organizations, or as they struggled to stay united within the crumbling ranks of the party. These disintegrating forces were compounded by growing ideological rifts among socialist women. The SDPC had provided a brief home for women who strove to forge links between feminism and socialism, but these links were shattered during the war years.

By the spring of 1918 the SDPC faced open dissolution. Some members were in favour of supporting a revolutionary socialist party, while others favoured a party similar to the British Labour Party. In September 1918 the Canadian government effectively outlawed most of the Canadian left. Although the English branches of the party were exempt from the ban of November 1918, they could not survive for long. In 1920 the SDPC, the party that had provided a voice for the concerns of feminists, finally collapsed. This did not bode well for the survival of feminism in the Canadian left.

CHAPTER NINE

Conclusion

Radicals, labourites, socialists, and women who had been active in, or influenced by, the women's movement were all drawn to the early Canadian left. The Canadian Socialist League (CSL) was broad and flexible enough to embrace people from such disparate political circles. This flexibility worked to the advantage of women as they strove to make sense of capitalism's impact on their lives. In developing their political voice, women drew on their domestic experience and religious convictions, on the socialist classics, and on the feminist ideas of the communitarian socialist movement. Strengthened by these and by the vitality of the women's movement, they were able to place their concerns on the early socialist agenda.

With the triumph of the Socialist Party of Canada (SPC), greater organizational and ideological rigidity was imposed on the socialist movement. In the minds of its advocates, this development strengthened the socialist base of the movement and purged it of reformism. But it also weakened its appeal to women by excluding many of their concerns. The majority of socialist men used their dominant positions within the SPC to articulate and defend a masculine view of socialism. In the name of socialism, they rejected immediate demands and refused to support women's fight for suffrage. Some even denied women the right to participate as equals within the party. They demanded the full value for men's labour but failed to call for women's right to the same. They called for an end to prostitution, but they refused to examine their own sense of sexual entitlement and privileges which contributed to women's oppression. They promised that socialism would transform society, but they stopped short of any serious consideration of a transformation of the domestic realm that would alter male dominance within the home. They did not even seriously entertain proposals to lighten the burden of work for women within the home. While laying claim to the authority of scientific socialism, they held views that were far from scientific. The socialist men who articulated these arguments were protecting their privileged positions over women in politics, in the labour force, in the home, and in sexual relations.

Their views did not go unchallenged. A few exceptional men, such as R.B. Kerr and Weston Wrigley, called on their male comrades to reconsider. More important, socialist women challenged the male left and offered pointed criticisms of these masculine views. Drawing on women's experience in the home, they offered a feminist version of the socialist agenda that might best be described as a radical variant of maternal feminism. This was a feminism that spoke to women's lives, lives that were dominated by the promise of marriage and domestic labour, but that also seemed threatened by the encroachments of capitalism.

Socialist women demanded the socialist and materialist transformation of the domestic sphere. Not wanting to work in the paid labour force while raising a family, they supported the working-class man's demand to be paid a family wage. But this did not weaken their support for working women. They also challenged the economic dependence of women under capitalism and called for decent wages for working women and even for "state support of motherhood." They demanded the right to work, insisting that it should be a woman's own decision whether or not she engaged in paid labour. As well, socialist women demanded sexual autonomy: freedom from the unwanted overtures of men, both inside and outside marriage, and the political and economic tools with which to claim this right. Finally, socialist women demanded women's suffrage, both on egalitarian grounds and because they believed they had particular interests, related to their maternal and domestic lives, which gave them the right and the obligation to participate in politics. Taken together, their demands challenged the masculine vision of socialism in which women remained dependent on men and isolated within the home. Although their ideas were rooted in the domestic sphere, this did not render them conservative or ineffective. Rather, these concerns became the common ground upon which they built their vision of a socialist future – a future far more radically transformed along socialist lines than many of their male comrades could envision.

Yet socialist women failed in their attempt to transform the agenda of the SPC. How do we account for this failure? In part, they faced the same constraints of domestic and maternal duties that inhibited the political activity of other women. As well, they met with opposition within the left itself, usually from their male comrades, who used their majority and their control of party hierarchies to establish a socialist agenda with an implicit, and often explicit, masculine bias. Loath to acknowledge their bias, the men were unwilling to share control of party structures with women. Thus, a women's column, women's branches, and legitimacy for women's concerns were denied within the SPC.

Finding the SPC too hostile, some socialist women joined the Social Democratic Party of Canada (SDPC) because it was more willing to include issues such as suffrage as a part of the socialist agenda. As well, it was willing to permit women to organize separately in their own groups and to publish women's columns in the party press. Feminists flourished briefly in the ranks of the SDPC, until the party was shattered during the war years.

The combination of social forces that nourished prewar socialist feminism were faltering. The great expectations of the suffragists were not realized. Women voters did not transform the world, nor did women rush to claim a seat in Parliament. The maternalism of the prewar years was increasingly undermined in the 1920s as young women turned away from this seemingly "old-fashioned" cause. With suffrage won, feminism "survived strongly as an individual creed, but faltered as an organized movement."[1] Individual socialist women retained their commitment to the cause, but they were especially hurt by this weakening of the organized feminist movement from which they had drawn strength. In its absence, the left was no longer compelled to speak to women's issues as it had been in the past.

The altered political landscape of the postwar decade offered little promise that the left would champion women's concerns. The SPC in British Columbia shifted decisively to the left and confirmed its rejection of feminism. The newly formed Communist Party of Canada raised women's issues, but it subordinated them to the primacy of the class struggle.[2] Some left-wing activists turned to the Canadian Labour Party and the One Big Union, hoping that an alliance of Canadian labour would advance the cause of socialism in Canada, but these efforts failed.[3] Where did the interests of socialist women fit in this development? Although the numbers of women entering the labour force was certainly on the increase, waged labour was not yet central to women's lives as it was for men. Wage-earning women continued to toil in segregated, low-paying jobs, often without the support of unions. Most women's lives, even those of wage earners, continued to be shaped by marriage, child rearing, and domestic labour. Dominated by men, the labour movement did not fashion an agenda that addressed the concerns of women.[4]

In the prewar years, a particular form of socialist feminism had flourished, one that sprang from the domestic realities of women's lives, calling for the socialist transformation of the domestic sphere and a redress of the power imbalance between the sexes. Socialist women turned maternal feminism to socialist ends. In so doing, they articulated a vision of socialism that was far more radical and egalitarian than the "scientific" socialism of the SPC. After the war, their vision went into eclipse. But their feminist challenge echoes to this day as a legacy that socialists must address.

Notes

CHAPTER ONE

1 Other works have examined the organizational history of the left in detail, paying little or no attention to the role of women. See Fox, "Early Socialism in Canada"; Robin, *Radical Politics and Canadian Labour*; Troop, "Socialism in Canada"; Penner, *The Canadian Left*; Bercuson, *Fools and Wise Men*; Angus, *Canadian Bolsheviks*; Avakumovic, *The Communist Party*; Tadeusz, "Canadian Socialism"; Homel, "James Simpson"; Kawecki, "Origins of the Canadian Communist Party"; O'Brien, "Roots of Canadian Radicalism" and "Maurice Spector"; Penton, "Ideas of William Cotton"; Peter Campbell, "Making Socialists"; McCormack, *Reformers, Rebels and Revolutionaries*; Saywell, "Labour and Socialism in British Columbia"; M. Smith, "Development of Socialist Opposition"; Grantham, "Some Aspects of the Socialist Movement in B.C."; Seager, "Socialists and Workers"; Ross Johnson, "No Compromise, No Political Trading"; Makahonuk, "Class Conflict in a Prairie City"; Mills, "Single Tax, Socialism and the ILP"; Frank and Reilly, "Socialist Movement in the Maritimes"; Steeves, *Compassionate Rebel*.
2 The CSL was likely modelled after the British Socialist League. See S. Pierson, *British Socialists*.
3 The voting laws in British Columbia required a 12-month residency period in the province and a 60-day residency period in an electoral district. This law was used by employers to disenfranchise men who were socialists. Before an election, workers would be laid off, thus making it very difficult for them to settle and build homes. Mining companies also had restrictions on workers building homes on company land. These actions added

to the difficulties workers faced in establishing a settled family life in the logging and mining camps of British Columbia and reinforced the masculine character of the early socialist movement. See *Western Clarion*, 9 Nov. 1907, 3; 5 Oct. 1907, 2; and 13 Jan. 1904, 4.

4 *Western Clarion*, 28 Jan. 1905, 3.

5 Barman, *The West beyond the West*, 357.

6 Initially called the Canadian Socialist Federation, the party soon changed its name to the SDPC. Its platform supported trade unions, the eight-hour work day, and further democratization of the political system to include initiative, referendum, proportional representation, and the right of recall. See *Cotton's Weekly*, 4 May 1911, 8.

7 Lindstrom-Best has published several works on the role of Finnish women in the socialist movement. L. Kealey also examines women's role, in "Women in the Canadian Socialist Movement."

8 These roots predate the activities discussed by Vickers in "Intellectual Origins of Women's Movements in Canada."

9 Cleverdon, *The Woman Suffrage Movement in Canada*.

10 Bacchi, *Liberation Deferred?* 148.

11 Forbes, "The Ideas of Carol Bacchi" and "Battles in Another War." The relationship between middle-class women's organizations and the working class is complex, and I do not find that Forbes provides a convincing and thorough assessment of it. Fingard offers a more nuanced discussion of the relationship in *Dark Side of Victorian Halifax*.

12 Hale, "British Columbia Woman Suffrage Movement."

13 Backhouse, *Petticoats and Prejudice*, ch. 5.

14 A. Prentice et al., *Canadian Women*, 174–5.

15 It is difficult in the Canadian context to separate the suffrage movement from the other groups that supported suffrage. Many women's organizations, such as the WCTU and the National Council of Women, became active in the suffrage campaign, and at the local level they took the lead in suffrage activities. Other organizations also could take the lead, as the United Farmers did in Alberta (Holt, "Woman's Suffrage in Alberta").

16 L. Kealey, *A Not Unreasonable Claim*, 7.

17 W. Roberts, "Rocking the Cradle," 27.

18 Valverde, *Age of Light, Soap and Water*.

19 By A. Prentice et al.

20 Strong-Boag, "Ever a Crusader," 181; *New Day Recalled*, 192; and "Pulling in Double Harness."

CHAPTER TWO

1 "Four Plain Women," *Cotton's Weekly*, 4 Feb. 1909, 7.
2 The Victoria local reported that half of its members were women; Sointula, B.C., reported that its female membership increased by 80 per cent in 1914 (*Cotton's Weekly*, 26 March 1914, 4); Hamilton reported the first two women to join its local in 1914; and Berlin, Ontario, reported its first woman member in 1913 (*Cotton's Weekly*, 11 Dec. 1913). See also *Western Clarion*, 10 Oct. 1908, 4, and "Reach the Women," *Cotton's Weekly*, 1 April 1909, 7.
3 For the role of women in the Finnish socialist community, see Lindstrom-Best, *Defiant Sisters* and "The Socialist Party of Canada and the Finnish Connection, 1905–1911"; Sangster, "Finnish Women in Ontario, 1890–1930"; and *Western Clarion*, 22 June 1907, 1.
4 *Western Clarion*, 22 June 1907, 1. By one account, the Toronto Italian local consisted of 300 to 400 members. See *Western Clarion*, 8 Aug. 1908, 1, and 20 April 1907, 4.
5 Of the 376 women mentioned in the English left-wing press whose marital status can be identified, 76 were married. See Newton, "Enough of Exclusive Masculine Thinking," app. 4.
6 *Cotton's Weekly*, 16 Oct. 1913, 3, and 20 July 1911, 1; *Canadian Forward*, 13 Jan. 1917, 5, and 24 March 1917, 4. See also *Der Yiddisher Zhurnal*, 25 Aug. 1919, 1, and 31 Aug. 1919, 3 (citation courtesy of R. Frager); and Frager, "Uncloaking Vested Interests."
7 According to the 1911 census, women were roughly 13 per cent of the paid labour force (Meltz, *Manpower in Canada*). Undoubtedly the census underestimated the numbers of women, married and single, who earned an income through household activities. These may have been as financially significant as waged labour for supporting the household. For a fuller discussion of these issues, see chapter 5.
8 N. Fillmore, *Maritime Radical*; P. Campbell, "Making Socialists"; Akers, "Rebel or Revolutionary?"
9 S. Mann Trofimenkoff, "Feminist Biography," and Sangster, "The Making of a Socialist-Feminist."
10 He was active in the temperance movement and was editor of the *Citizen and Country*. See his biography in the *Western Clarion*, 9 Feb. 1907, 4.
11 *Citizen and Country*, 13 April 1900, 1.
12 Ibid., 13 May 1899, 1; 13 April 1900, 3; and 27 April 1900, 4.

13 See *Ontario Socialist Platform* (adopted by the Ontario Socialist League by referendum vote, Jan. 1902), National Archives of Canada; *Citizen and Country*, 9 May 1902, 1; 16 May 1902, 1–3; 23 May 1902; and 30 May 1902, 1–3; *Canadian Socialist*, 6 June 1902, 1–3; and 20 June 1902, 3.

14 *Citizen and Country*, 16 May 1902, 2.

15 Buhle, *Women and American Socialism*, 94, 105, 117.

16 *Citizen and Country*, 9 May 1902, 1.

17 For a discussion of early women's groups in Canada, see Bacchi, *Liberation Deferred?*; L. Kealey, *A Not Unreasonable Claim*; Strong-Boag, "Setting the Stage" and *The Parliament of Women*; Bliss, "Neglected Radicals"; Baines, *Women's Reform Organizations in Canada*; Brandt, "Organizations in Canada"; Mitchinson, "Early Women's Organizations"; D. Pedersen, "Building Today for the Womanhood of Tomorrow"; and Kinnear, ed., *First Days, Fighting Days*.

18 Phillips Thompson and George Wrigley are two such people discussed by Cook in *The Regenerators*. See also S. Pierson, *British Socialists*; Brouwer, "Transcending the 'Unacknowledged Quarantine'"; Marks, "The Knights of Labour and the Salvation Army" and "The Hallelujah Lasses"; and Fishbein, "Radicals and Religion."

19 Bacchi, *Liberation Deferred?* 59; Cook, *The Regenerators*, 70; John Thomas, "Servants of the Church"; Brouwer, "Transcending the 'Unacknowledged Quarantine'"; and Baines, *Women's Reform Organizations in Canada*.

20 Valverde, *Age of Light, Soap and Water*, 58–61; Tyrell, *Woman's World, Woman's Empire*.

21 Brandt, "Organizations in Canada," 86.

22 Valverde discusses this in *Age of Light, Soap and Water*, 35.

23 Mitchinson, "Early Women's Organizations," 87; D. Pedersen, "The Scientific Training of Mothers."

24 D. Pedersen, "Building Today for the Womanhood of Tomorrow," 229.

25 Quoted in Valverde, *Age of Light, Soap and Water*, 64.

26 Mitchenson, "Early Women's Organizations," 85.

27 Fingard provides a nuanced discussion of the ways impoverished people made use of the services offered by reformers and charities (*Dark Side of Victorian Halifax*), and Horodski discusses the way the YWCA assisted women left homeless during the Winnipeg General Strike ("Women and the Winnipeg General Strike," 31).

28 See Valverde, *Age of Light, Soap and Water*, and Tyrell, *Woman's World, Woman's Empire*.

29 Alice Chown's biography, *The Stairway*, provides us with one example of a woman making the transition from conventional women's organizations to activism within trade unions. See also Cook, *The Regenerators*, 232.

30 Buhle, *Women and American Socialism*.

31 I. Howard, *Struggle for Social Justice*; Lacombe, "Theosophy and the Canadian Idealist Tradition"; Homel, "Fading Beams of the Nineteenth Century"; Wilson, "Matti Kurikka and A.B. Makela"; Cook, *The Regenerators*, 82–4, 167.

32 Penner, *The Canadian Left*, 45.

33 For examples of SPC attitudes on prohibition, see *Western Clarion*, 2 May 1908, 4; 7 Dec. 1907, 1; and 26 Feb. 1910, 1.

34 *Cotton's Weekly*, 4 May 1911, 1; *Western Clarion*, 13 Feb. 1909, 4; 13 March 1909, 3; 16 Oct. 1909, 3; 24 May 1913, 3; and Oct. 1915, 13.

35 The widely circulated book *Safe Counsel: Light on Dark Corners* advised in its rules on etiquette, "Don't bring the smell of spirits or tobacco into the presence of ladies. Never use either in the presence of ladies" (Jefferis, 59). When Lady Aberdeen, head of the National Council of Women, served drinks at official functions, she came under criticism (Valverde, *Age of Light, Soap and Water*, 62). The WCTU had some early success banning women from serving liquor in taverns and restaurants, and in preventing married women from holding liquor licences (Backhouse, *Petticoats and Prejudice*, 290–1).

36 "The Woman's Place," *Western Clarion*, 10 Dec. 1910, 1.

37 Lindstrom-Best, "Defiant Sisters," 362.

38 S. Pierson, *British Socialists*, 71–9.

39 For example, see *Western Clarion*, 6 June 1908, 1, 2; 15 May 1909, 1; and 19 Dec. 1914, 3.

40 This was argued by Moses Baritz, a Jewish member of the small, sectarian Socialist Party of North America (*Cotton's Weekly*, 6 Oct. 1910, 3). Another socialist, Fred Faulkner, recalled that "many socialists in those days, spent too much time (killing God) as it was called" (Fred Faulkner, letters, 5 March, Angus MacInnis Collection, UBC).

41 For example, see *Western Clarion*, 6 June 1908, 1, 2; 15 May 1909, 1; and 19 Dec. 1914, 3. For a discussion of the appeal of the Salvation Army within the working class, see Fingard, *Dark Side of Victorian Halifax*, and Marks, "The Hallelujah Lasses" and "Knights of Labour and the Salvation Army."

42 The articles by William Shier, before he left the Socialist Party, are a good example of this. See *Western Clarion*, 31 Aug. 1907, 4; 29 May 1909, 2; and 1 Aug. 1908, 4.

43 Mrs W.D., *Western Clarion*, 28 Jan. 1911, 3.

44 *Western Clarion*, 22 Dec. 1906, 3.

45 This discussion of Ruth Lestor is based on the following sources: *Western Clarion*, 13 March 1909, 3; 19 June 1909, 3; "The Woman's Place," 10 July 1909, 1; "How Capitalism Breeds Lunacy," 11 Dec. 1909, 1, 3; 23 July 1910, 4; "With the Reds of the Prairies," 4 March 1911, 1; 1 April 1911, 2; "Woman and the Socialist Party of Canada," July 1911, 21–5; and Sept. 1917, 12; *Cotton's Weekly*, 6 May 1909, 3; 13 May 1909, 5; 6 Jan. 1911, 3; and 19 Jan. 1911, 3.

46 We know more about Lestor's husband, Charles, than we know of her. He was born in England in 1876 and had turned his hand to many occupations: blacksmith, solicitor, labourer, showman, actor, and waterworks manager. He touted himself as a socialist, a writer, and a student of history and social problems. He joined the Canadian Socialist Party in 1908.

47 "The Woman's Place," *Western Clarion*, 10 July 1909, 1.

48 *Western Clarion*, July 1911, 24–5.

49 "How Capitalism Breeds Lunacy," *Western Clarion*, 11 Dec. 1909, 1.

50 "Woman and the Socialist Party of Canada," *Western Clarion*, July 1911, 21–5.

51 Smith-Rosenberg, "Female World of Love and Ritual," and Tyrell, *Woman's World: Woman's Empire*, 114–45.

52 For a more extensive discussion of Sophie Mushkat, see L. Kealey, "Sophie," *New Maritimes*, Nov. 1987, 12–13, and Newton, "Enough of Exclusive Masculine Thinking," 426–35.

53 *Western Clarion*, 9 Oct. 1909, 1; *Cotton's Weekly*, 30 Sept. 1909, 4.

54 N. Fillmore outlines the Maritime socialist movement in his biography of Roscoe, including brief mention of Mushkat's activities (Fillmore, *Maritime Radical*, 42–92).

55 *Western Clarion*, 7 Aug. 1909, 3; 4 Sept. 1909, 3; 12 March 1910, 2; and 27 Sept. 1913, 7; *Eastern Labour News*, 4 Dec. 1909, 2; Roscoe Fillmore, "Strike Situation in Eastern Canada," *International Socialist Review*, 10 May 1910, 1007; and *Cotton's Weekly*, 30 Sept. 1909, 3; 11 Sept. 1913, 4; 25 Sept. 1913, 3; and 9 Oct. 1913, 3.

56 *Cotton's Weekly*, 24 March 1910, 3.

57 *Western Clarion*, 9 Oct. 1909, 1, and 24 March 1910, 3; *Cotton's Weekly*, 30 Sept. 1909, 4.

58 *Western Clarion*, 5 Nov. 1910, 3; 20 April 1912, 3; 29 June 1912, 3; 19 July 1913, 3; 14 March 1914, 2; and "The Argument

of a Russian Serf," 18 July 1914, 2. See also *Cotton's Weekly*, 15 May 1913, 3.

59 The matter was apparently resolved by the local involved. See *Western Clarion*, 16 Aug. 1913, 3; 14 July 1914, 3; and 16 Jan. 1915, 3.

60 If the SPC was consistent, Mushkat was probably expelled for supporting prohibition or local option. Several party members in British Columbia had been expelled for the same reason. See *Western Clarion*, Aug. 1915, 14.

61 This discussion of Merrill Burns is drawn from the following sources: articles by Bertha Merrill Burns and Ernest Burns published in *Western Clarion; Cotton's Weekly; Citizen and Country; Canadian Socialist; Western Socialist; Vancouver World; B.C. Federationist; Independent;* Angus MacInnis Collection, UBC; and Ramsay MacDonald Collection, National Archives of Canada (hereafter cited as NA).

62 Merrill Burns's column will be discussed in greater detail in subsequent chapters.

63 Born in Birmingham England, Ernest studied a range of Marxian, utopian, and ethical socialists, including Edward Bellamy, Henry George, William Morris, Edward Carpenter, and H.M. Hyndman. In 1885 he became a socialist and a charter member of the Birmingham Social Democratic Federation. In 1889 he left England for Washington and became active in the Knights of Labor and the Populist Party, endorsing socialism from their platforms. He returned to British Columbia in 1899 and worked in logging and fishing. As president of the Fisherman's Union, he was prominent in its strike of 1900 and 1901. From 1900 on, he was active in socialist politics in British Columbia. See *Western Socialist*, 14 Feb. 1903, 2.

64 *Canadian Socialist*, 19 July 1902, 4.

65 Ernest did not retain this distinction, for the SPC expelled other members. See *Western Clarion*, 2 March 1907, 3, and 9 March 1907, 2; *B.C. Federationist*, 20 May 1912, 3; and Bertha Merrill Burns to Mrs Ramsay MacDonald, 29 April 1907, Ramsay MacDonald Collection, NA.

66 Merrill Burns to Mrs MacDonald, 29 April 1907, Ramsay MacDonald Collection, NA.

67 Ibid.

68 Merrill Burns to Mrs MacDonald, 26 July 1906, Ramsay MacDonald Collection, NA.

69 Merrill Burns to Mrs MacDonald, 29 April 1907, ibid.

70 Phillips Thompson mistook her for a man in *Western Clarion*, 18 May 1907, 1.

71 Merrill Burns became a public speaker for the Social Democratic Party and she was elected as provincial secretary to the party's women's committee in British Columbia. However, her activities were cut short in 1914 because of illness.

72 William Shier criticized the party for its crudeness and its attacks on Christian socialists, then shifted his allegiance to the Social Democrats. See *Western Clarion*, 31 Aug. 1907, 4; 29 May 1909, 2; and 1 Aug. 1908, 4; and *Cotton's Weekly*, 28 Nov. 1912, 3.

73 *Cotton's Weekly*, 12 Jan. 1911, 3.

74 For example, *Cotton's Weekly*, 7 May 1914, 4, and "Poverty the Cause of Intemperance," ibid., 2 July 1914, 3.

75 This account of the life of Mary Cotton Wisdom is based on information drawn from *Cotton's Weekly* and from the following manuscripts in the author's private collection: Mary Cotton Wisdom's letters to her brother William Cotton, c. 1922; letter to author from granddaughter Harriet Beech, 30 Aug. 1983; interview with niece Mary Ford, 1983; "Family History," compiled by Mary Ford, 1983; and manuscript by William Cotton, 1943.

76 "Socialism and Ignorance," *Cotton's Weekly*, 20 May 1909.

77 S. Ross, in "Struggles for the Screen," discusses the emergence of antisocialist films in the United States during this time which reinforced this view of socialists.

78 "My View of Socialism," *Cotton's Weekly*, 30 Sept. 1909, 7.

79 *Cotton's Weekly*, 28 Oct. 1909, 7.

80 Wisdom continued to be active in women's organizations, such as the local Women's Institute, the Women's Guild, and the Woman's Christian Temperance Union, and she continued her religious commitment as a devout Anglican and as a philanthropist and supporter of the Salvation Army. Surviving her husband and two children, she died at the age of 84.

81 Material for this discussion of Mary Norton is drawn exclusively from an interview, Women's Labour History Project, Public Archives of British Columbia, 1973.

82 C. Wright, "Feminine Trifles."

83 D. Pederson, "Building Today," 230.

84 For a fuller discussion of Gutteridge, see Howard, *Struggle for Social Justice*, and Wade, "Helena Gutteridge."

85 Interview with Mary Norton, Women's Labour History Project.

86 Roscoe Fillmore's biography provides an example of how a male socialist could exercise his political activism despite his wife's opposition. See N. Fillmore, *Maritime Radical*.

CHAPTER THREE

1   Gerald O. Desmond, "Women and International Socialism," *Cotton's Weekly*, 15 April 1909, 7.
2   "Women and the Socialist Party," *Cotton's Weekly*, 18 Feb. 1909, 7; "Women," ibid., 18 Feb. 1909, 7.
3   *Canadian Socialist*, 30 Aug. 1902, 4, and 16 Aug. 1902, 4; *Western Socialist*, 27 Sept. 1902, 4; 4 Oct. 1902, 4; and 3 Jan. 1903, 1.
4   *Western Clarion*, 31 July 1903, 1; 11 Sept. 1903, 1; 29 Oct. 1903, 3; and 5 Nov. 1903, 1, 2.
5   Ibid., 13 Aug. 1904, 1, and 5 Nov. 1903, 1.
6   Ibid., 5 Nov. 1903, 1.
7   Manley captures this masculine atmosphere in his description of the Communist Party headquarters in Glace Bay with its floor "littered with pipe dottle, cigarette ends and match sticks" ("Preaching the Red Stuff," 85).
8   Miss M.M. Heir, *Citizen and Country*, 13 May 1899, 1; Miss C.A. Steadman, ibid., 18 May 1900, 4; *Western Clarion*, 14 Sept. 1907, 1, and 16 Nov. 1907, 3.
9   *Western Clarion*, 16 Nov. 1907, 3. Women were deterred from attending meetings of the Vancouver Trades and Labor Council by the men who stood on the steps outside smoking. Socialist meetings were sometimes held in this hall. See Vancouver Trades and Labor Council Minutes, 5 Oct. 1905, 379.
10 *Western Clarion*, 8 Aug. 1908, 2. For other examples of vulgarity, see the following in *Western Clarion*: O. Lee Charlton, "Letter From Victoria," 23 May 1903, 1; "Home Truths," 14 Nov. 1908, 4; letter from Mrs Clark, 7 May 1910, 3; and Dec. 1915, 9. See also *Cotton's Weekly*, 22 June 1911, 3.
11 See *Western Clarion* as follows: 9 April 1910, 3; "That Convention," 15 July 1905, 2; 7 July 1906, 3; 16 Dec. 1905, 3; 8 Aug. 1908, 1; J.N. Hintsa, "Anti-Nationalist," 18 Sept. 1909, 3; 4 Dec. 1909, 2; and 19 April 1913, 4. Similar language occurs in *Cotton's Weekly*, 6 Jan. 1910, 4.
12 W. Gribble, "A Blister," *Western Clarion*, 23 April 1910, 2.
13 See the following articles in *Cotton's Weekly*: Mrs Krupp, "A Word of Advice," 27 May 1909, 7; Gustav Prager, "A Letter to Canadian Workingmen," 20 May 1909, 6; Roscoe A. Fillmore, "Change the System," 26 Aug. 1909, 4; 21 April 1910, 1; "It Is for You," 9 June 1910, 4; "Are You a Socialist?" 24 Aug. 1911, 4; John A. Randolph, "All Roads Lead to Socialism," 21 Sept. 1911, 4; and "Socialist Women Needed," 15 Oct. 1914, 2.

182 Notes to pages 43-7

14 George Toseland, "Are You a Man?" *Cotton's Weekly*, 13 Jan. 1910, 3; Roscoe A. Fillmore, "Show Your Colours," ibid., 17 June 1909, 8.

15 "Home Truths," *Western Clarion*, 14 Nov. 1908, 4; E.E., "Are Women Wanted in the Party," *Cotton's Weekly*, 8 April 1909, 7, and Franklin Wentworth, "Man's Duty," ibid., 25 March 1909, 7.

16 G.W. Wrigley, *Western Clarion*, 26 Sept. 1908, 4; see also "Socialism Women's Hope," *Cotton's Weekly*, 4 June 1914, 2.

17 "Home Truths," *Western Clarion*, 14 Nov. 1908, 4.

18 Stella, "Time We Got Busy," *Western Clarion*, 21 Nov. 1908, 3.

19 "Clear as a Bell," *Western Clarion*, 4 July 1908, 2; J.N. Hinsta, ibid., 18 Sept. 1909, 3. In 1908, when the American Socialist Party voted in favour of establishing the Woman's National Committee, the *Western Clarion* expressed its opposition to the decision by ignoring the arguments in favour of separate organizations and reporting in full detail the minority report "[as ringing] a note that was too seldom heard at the convention." For a fuller discussion of the American situation, see Moller, "The National Convention and the Woman's Movement"; Buhle, *Women and American Socialism*, 145-75; and Freedman, "Separatism as Strategy."

20 *Western Clarion*, 17 Oct. 1908, 4, and B.O. Robinson, "Women's Study Club," ibid., 15 May 1909, 3; see also E.M. Eplett, "Women and Socialism," *Cotton's Weekly*, 4 Feb. 1909, 7. This study club was similar to the independent self-supporting reading circles that were encouraged by American socialist feminist Josephine Day Nye ("Women and Socialism," *Cotton's Weekly*, 3 June 1909, 7).

21 "Report of Resolution Committee," *Western Clarion*, 26 Sept. 1908, 1.

22 Ibid.

23 *Western Clarion*, 10 Oct. 1908, 3; Buhle, *Women and American Socialism*, 150; G.W. Wrigley, *Western Clarion*, 26 Sept. 1908, 4; "May Wood Simons at Berlin," *Cotton's Weekly*, 16 Feb. 1911, 3; and "May Wood Simons Touring in Canada," ibid., 26 Jan. 1911, 3. A series of lectures on the woman question were also held in Montreal, with the guest speaker, Elsteen of Philadelphia, giving his address in Yiddish (*Cotton's Weekly*, 16 Sept. 1909, 5).

24 "Ontario Convention," *Cotton's Weekly*, 4 May 1911, 1, 4.

25 "Report of B.C. Executive Meeting of SDP," *Cotton's Weekly*, 28 Aug. 1913, 3; "B.C. Executive," ibid., 6 Nov. 1913, 3; *B.C. Federationist*, 7 Nov. 1913, 5, and 24 Oct. 1913, 5.

26 *Cotton's Weekly,* 27 Nov. 1913, 4; 2 April 1914, 1; 1 Jan. 1914, 4; and "In Hamilton, Ont.," 12 March 1914, 4. See also *Canadian Forward,* 27 Jan. 1917, 5.

27 *Cotton's Weekly,* 27 Nov. 1913, 4; *Western Clarion,* Oct. 1915, 9.

28 *Western Clarion,* 3 Jan. 1902, 4.

29 "Attention," *Cotton's Weekly,* 22 June 1911, 3.

30 C.M. O'Brien, *Western Clarion,* 15 Jan. 1910, 3.

31 "An Appreciation," *Western Clarion,* 24 Oct. 1913, 2.

32 *Cotton's Weekly,* 11 Dec. 1913, 4; 14 Aug. 1913, 3; and 4 May 1911, 3.

33 Doubtless this is due, in part, to editorial laxity in identifying authorship or the source of material borrowed from other journals or newspapers. It is difficult to discern whether an article written by a woman had been written by a Canadian woman or reproduced from elsewhere. Where possible, names of women who wrote articles were cross-checked with known American and European writers.

34 *Cotton's Weekly,* 24 Aug. 1911, 2, and 13 July 1911, 2; *Canadian Forward,* 29 Oct. 1914, 4.

35 *Western Clarion,* 31 July 1909, 3; Krawchuk, *The Ukrainian Socialist Movement in Canada*; Kazymyra, "The Defiant Pavlo Krat"; Martynowych, "The Ukrainian Socialist Movement in Canada," parts I and II.

36 Merrill Burns's article, "The Woman in the Case," first appeared in the *Western Clarion,* 13 and 20 Aug. 1904.

37 *Cotton's Weekly,* 23 Nov. 1914, 2.

38 Interview with John Bruce. It is known that King did frequent socialist meetings in Toronto. See Cook, *The Regenerators,* 197–213.

39 Fanny Levy and Sophie Mushkat are two such women. See also *Cotton's Weekly,* 14 Aug 1913, 3; and the comments of Irene Smith on her first experience at "soap-boxing" from a hack, in *Western Clarion,* 24 Sept. 1903, 4.

40 See, for example, Mrs Cockett, *Cotton's Weekly,* 12 Dec. 1912, 1; also *Cotton's Weekly,* 19 Dec. 1912, 3, and 16 Jan. 1913, 3.

CHAPTER FOUR

1 Strong-Boag, "Keeping House in God's Country," "Discovering the Home," "Pulling in Double Harness," and *The New Day Recalled,* chs. 4 and 5; Luxton, *More than a Labour of Love*; Corrective Collective, *Never Done*; Riley, "Six Saucepans to One"; Barber, "Help for Farm Homes"; D. Pedersen, "The Scientific

Training of Mothers"; Light and Pierson, *Not an Easy Road*, ch.
5; Hobbs and Pierson, "A Kitchen that Wastes No Steps"; Arnup
and Pierson, *Delivering Motherhood*; Reilly, "Material History";
and Gorham, "History of Housework." Strasser's *Never Done* provides an excellent overview of the changes occurring in housework
in America and is especially useful in identifying the dates at
which certain innovations came into popular use.

2   Folbre, "The Unproductive Housewife."

3   Arnup, "Educating Mothers," 203, and Benoit, "Mothering in a
Newfoundland Community," 186–7. The hospitalization of
women for childbirth initially led to an increase in maternal mortality. Hospitalization did not address the health risks associated
with poverty or the illegal abortions that contributed to maternal
deaths. See Strong-Boag and McPherson, "The Confinement of
Women"; J. Oppenheimer, "Childbirth in Ontario"; and McLaren
and McLaren, "Discoveries and Dissimulations."

4   Strong-Boag, "Discovering the Home," 40, and Luxton, "More
than a Labour of Love."

5   For a discussion of the family wage debate, see Humphries, "Class
Struggle and the Persistence of the Working Class Family," "The
Working Class Family, Women's Liberation and Class Struggle,"
and "The Working Class Family: A Marxist Perspective." See also
Barrett and McIntosh, "The Family Wage"; Barrett, *Women's
Oppression Today*; Land, "The Family Wage"; and Connelly,
"Women Workers and the Family Wage in Canada."

6   L. Kealey, "Canadian Socialism and the Woman Question," 78.

7   Gosse makes a similar argument in the American context, claiming
that the focus on home and family created potential space for feminist action within the American left. See Gosse, "To Organize in
Every Neighbourhood."

8   B. Taylor's *Eve and the New Jerusalem* outlines the inverse relationship between the decline of the feminist component in the
early socialist movement and the ascendancy of more orthodox
Marxian socialism in Britain. See Bellamy's *Looking Backward*,
ch. 25, for a description of his utopian vision of the transformation of women's work. Many of the socialists involved in these
early experiments at the turn of the century became active in the
formation of Canada's socialist parties. See Newton, "Enough of
Exclusive Masculine Thinking," ch. 2.

9   Hayden, *The Grand Domestic Revolution*.

10 Folbre, "The Unproductive Housewife."

11 This argument is based on Hayden's discussion of the rift between
the Marxian socialists and the "material feminists" who sought

to transform domestic labour (*The Grand Domestic Revolution*, 1–29). See also Landes, "Marxism and the 'Woman Question.'" A good illustration of controversy between the Marxian socialists and the material feminists can be found in Kotsch, "The Mother's Future," and M. Thompson, "The Value of Woman's Work."

12   "A Word to WCTU Ladies," *Citizen and Country*, 13 April 1900, 1.

13   The column "Woman Is Man's Social Equal" appeared in the *Citizen and Country*, 9 May 1902, 1; 16 May 1902, 1; and 6 June 1902, 4. The column "We Women" appeared in the *Canadian Socialist*, 5 July to 13 Sept. 1902, and in the *Western Socialist*, 20 Sept. 1902 to 7 Feb. 1903.

14   Miss B.E. Merrill, "Why Women Should Be Socialists," *Canadian Socialist*, 20 June 1902, 2; see also *Western Socialist*, 22 Nov. 1902, 3.

15   *Citizen and Country*, 12 Oct. 1900, 2, and 9 May 1900, 1.

16   Dorothy Drew (pen name for Bertha Merrill) *Western Socialist*, 3 Jan. 1903, 3.

17   Similar arguments for cooperative laundries and bakeries were discussed by women's farm organizations in the 1920s but were deemed impractical. See Barber, "Help for Farm Homes."

18   Much of the literature on motherhood in this era focuses on the role that doctors and the medical profession played in undermining women's traditional skills. The impact of commercial advertising on mothering has not been studied as intensely, but it also likely undermined women's traditional mothering skills.

19   Many of the socialist ideas for the scientific transformation of the household echoed similar ideas expressed in the campaign for domestic science. See D. Pedersen, "The Scientific Training of Mothers."

20   "The Woman in the Case," *Western Clarion*, 20 Aug. 1904, 3. See also "Woman and Social Problem," ibid., 13 Aug. 1904, 4; *Citizen and Country*, 9 May 1902, 1; *Western Socialist*, 15 Nov. 1902, 3; and the following in *Canadian Socialist*: "A Woman's Sphere," 30 Aug. 1902, 3; 6 June 1902, 4; 5 July 1902, 2; and Josephine Conger, "Socialism and Working Women," 22 Oct. 1903, 3.

21   *Western Socialist*, 24 April 1903, 1.

22   *Western Clarion*, 31 July 1903, 1.

23   Ibid., 22 Aug. 1908, 3.

24   "A Woman's Column," *Western Clarion*, 12 Sept. 1908, 2.

25   *Western Clarion*, 17 Oct. 1908, 4.

26   J.G.M., "Plenty," *Western Clarion*, 7 Nov. 1908, 3; see also 31 Oct. 1908, 4.

27 Rural George, "Begs to Differ," *Western Clarion*, 19 Sept. 1908, 3.

28 "Another One," *Western Clarion*, 26 Sept. 1908, 3.

29 B.O. Robinson, *Western Clarion*, 12 Sept. 1908, 2.

30 Edith Wrigley, ibid.

31 G.W. Wrigley, "Too Few Revolutionary Women," *Western Clarion*, 10 Oct. 1908, 4; see also 26 Sept. 1908, 4.

32 George Paton, "Woman in Society," *Western Clarion*, 3 Aug. 1912, 2. See also N.M.T., "Socialism Would Destroy the Home," ibid., 7 Aug. 1909, 1.

33 *Western Clarion*, 23 Sept. 1905, 1. See also M.D. Armstrong, ibid., Oct. 1915, 9. The paper also ridiculed the timid husband of a suffrage speaker, "a mild-looking man in spectacles," who did domestic labour (*Western Clarion*, 14 Oct. 1905, 1).

34 *Western Clarion*, 18 Sept. 1909, 1. Numerous articles presented this argument. See, for example, "Some Striking Phenomena: Census Bulletin Shows How Home and Family Are Safeguarded," 20 May, 1905, 1; Gourock, 12 Dec. 1908, 1; "Would Destroy the Home," 7 Nov. 1908, 2; "Objections to Capitalism," 25 Nov. 1905, 1; and "Homeseekers, B.C.," 3 May 1913, 1.

35 S. Ross, "Struggles for the Screen."

36 Joy Parr discusses the contrast between two such towns in *The Gender of Breadwinners*.

37 *Western Clarion*, 22 Dec. 1906, 4; see also 24 Aug. 1907, 2, and 21 Aug. 1909, 3.

38 Desmond, "For Sale," *Western Clarion*, 26 March 1910, 1.

39 See the following articles in *Western Clarion*: "Woman Ware," 26 March 1910, 2; "Socialism Will Destroy the Home," 25 Aug. 1906, 1; and 9 March 1907, 1.

40 Gourock, "Effect of Socialism: Absurdity of Anti-Socialist Prognostications of Disaster," *Western Clarion*, 2 July 1911, 1.

41 "Can Socialism Destroy the Home," *Western Clarion*, 23 March 1912, 1.

42 Karl Kautsky, "Abolition of the Family," *Western Clarion*, 29 April 1905, 3; see also 4 July 1908, 4.

43 Buckley, "Search for the Decline of Maternal Mortality."

44 "Socialism and Motherhood," *Western Clarion*, 22 June 1912, 1.

45 *Western Clarion*, 25 Sept. 1909, 2.

46 "Socialism and Sex," *Western Clarion*, 14 Dec. 1907, 4.

47 For a discussion of state support of motherhood in Britain and the United States, see S. Pedersen, "The Failure of Feminism," and Sarvasy, "Beyond the Difference versus Equality Policy Debate."

48 Alf Budden, "The Woman's Place: From a Proletarian Rather than Sex Standpoint," *Western Clarion*, 10 Dec. 1910, 1.

49 "Charlotte Perkins Gilman," *Western Clarion*, 24 June 1905, 1; see also 1 July 1905, 3, 4. The Victoria local ignored the poor review and invited her to speak.

50 Alf Budden, "The Woman's Place."

51 "To the Wives of Workingmen," *Cotton's Weekly*, 31 Dec. 1908, 6.

52 *Cotton's Weekly*, 22 April 1909, 7.

53 "Who Will Do the Dirty Work?" *Cotton's Weekly*, 30 Sept., 1909, 8.

54 D. Pedersen, "The Scientific Training of Mothers," and Riley, "Six Saucepans to One."

55 M.M.A. Ward, "Socialism and the New Domestic Economy" (as reprinted from the English *Labour Leader*), *Cotton's Weekly*, 5 Aug. 1909, 7.

56 "Co-operative Housekeeping," *Cotton's Weekly*, 13 May 1909, 7.

57 Julia Dawson, "Why Woman Want [sic] Socialism," *Cotton's Weekly*, 22 July 1909, 7.

58 Hayden discusses some of the contemporary schemes for domestic reform that did not alter class relations, in *The Grand Domestic Revolution*.

59 M.M.A. Ward, "Socialism and the New Domestic Economy." See also *Cotton's Weekly*, 7 Jan. 1909, 7.

60 "Work and the Race," *Cotton's Weekly*, 18 March 1909, 7.

61 Dora F. Kerr, "Should Women Work?" *Cotton's Weekly*, 15 April 1909, 7.

62 *Cotton's Weekly*, 13 May 1909, 4.

63 Mary Cotton Wisdom, "Motherhood and Socialism," *Cotton's Weekly*, 11 Nov. 1909, 4.

64 Mary Cotton Wisdom, "Tea on the Pantry Shelf," *Cotton's Weekly*, 15 July 1909, 7.

65 Mary Cotton Wisdom, "The Pantry Shelf Again," *Cotton's Weekly*, 22 July 1909, 7.

66 "The Woman's Page," *Cotton's Weekly*, 28 Oct. 1909, 7.

67 *Cotton's Weekly*, 4 Nov. 1909, 3.

68 "The Woman's Page" ended in Nov. 1909, but *Cotton's Weekly* carried a women's column in subsequent issues: 11 Nov. 1909, 4; 18 Nov. 1909, 2; 25 Nov. 1909, 2; and 2 Dec. 1909, 2.

69 "In the Ideal Commonwealth," *Cotton's Weekly*, 11 Sept. 1913, 3.

70 For examples of these arguments, see "Acquiring Homes," *Cotton's Weekly*, 7 July 1910, 3, and "Woman under Socialism," ibid., 20 Nov. 1913, 1.

71 Bertha Merrill Burns, "Women and Socialism," *B.C. Federationist*, 31 Oct. 1913, 5.

72 "Would Women Have to Earn Their Living under Socialism?" *Cotton's Weekly*, 19 May 1910, 3.

73   Josephine A. Meyer, "Motherhood," *Cotton's Weekly*, 7 Aug.
     1913, 4. For a discussion of the development of the mother's
     allowance in Canada, see Strong-Boag, "Wages for Housework"
     and "Canada's Early Experience with Income Supplements." For
     the American experience, see Sarvasy, "Beyond the Difference
     versus Equality Policy Debate." For the British experience, see S.
     Pedersen, "The Failure of Feminism."
74   "Woman under Socialism," *Cotton's Weekly*, 13 Nov. 1913, 1.
75   "The Status of Women," *Cotton's Weekly*, 4 May 1911, 2.
76   "What Will Happen under Socialism: The Status of Women," *Cotton's Weekly*, 19 Jan. 1911, 4.
77   "Foolish Questions," *Cotton's Weekly*, 2 Sept. 1910, 4; "Homes
     for the People," ibid., 15 Dec. 1910, 4; and "Who Shall Do the
     Dirty Work?" ibid., 22 Dec. 1910, 3.
78   "A Childless Wage Slave: Race Suicide," *Cotton's Weekly*, 29 Sept.
     1910, 3.
79   "Comrade Miss Brennan at Vancouver," *Cotton's Weekly*, 16 Jan.
     1913, 4.
80   *Cotton's Weekly*, 29 Sept. 1910, 3, and 26 May 1910, 3; Robert
     Hunter, "Will Socialism Destroy the Home?" 11 Aug. 1910, 3;
     25 May 1911, 3; and 29 May 1913, 1.

CHAPTER FIVE

1   The terms "working girl" and "working woman" were com-
    monly used in the socialist press to refer to women who earned
    wages outside the home. I have tried to avoid these terms
    because of the implication that women who did not earn wages,
    but who did domestic labour, were not working. Such was
    clearly not the case. Therefore, instead of the term "working
    woman" I refer to "women in the paid labour force" or "wage-
    earning women."
2   In 1901, 14 per cent of women in Canada were in the paid labour
    force; by 1921 this had increased to 17 per cent (Leacy, *Historical
    Statistics of Canada*). Sources on women and employment include
    Acton, ed., *Women at Work*; Brandt, "Weaving It Together";
    Cohen, *Women's Work*; Frager, "No Proper Deal"; Heron, "Work-
    ing Class Hamilton, 1895–1930," ch. 5; Latham and Pazdro, *Not
    Just Pin Money*; Latham and Kess, *In Her Own Right*; Lavigne
    and Stoddart, "Women's Work in Montreal"; Parr, *Gender of
    Breadwinners*, "Women Workers," and "Rethinking Work and Kin-
    ship"; Roberts, *Honest Womanhood*; Rosenthal, "Union Maids";
    Sangster, "Canadian Working Women" and "Women and Unions";

H. Smith, "Women Workers and Industrialization"; White, *Women and Unions.*

3 Parr, "Work and Kinship"; Steedman, "Skill and Gender"; Frager, "Sewing Solidarity"; McCallum, "Separate Spheres"; Ferland, "In Search of the Unbound Prometheia"; Brandt, "Weaving It Together."

4 For discussions of teaching, see A. Prentice, "Bluestockings" and "The Feminization of Teaching"; Danylewycz and A. Prentice, "Teacher's Work"; and E. Graham, "Schoolmarms." For research on women in the medical professions, see Strong-Boag, "Canada's Women Doctors"; Coburn, "Nursing in Ontario"; Buckley, "Ladies or Midwives"; Fingard, *Dark Side of Victorian Halifax,* 34; Whittaker, "Search for Legitimacy"; Biggs, "The Case of the Missing Midwives"; and Laforce, "Elimination of Midwives in Quebec."

5 Tillotson discusses the gendering of skill in the telegraph industry in "First-Class Men" and "Operators along the Coast."

6 The importance of gender, class, ethnicity, and religion in the Nova Scotia labour force is discussed by Muise in "Industrial Context of Inequality." Muszinski discusses gender and race in "British Columbia's Salmon Cannery Labour Force"; Hamilton looks at aspects of black women's work in Nova Scotia, including the exclusion of black women from professions such as nursing until well into the twentieth century, in "Our Mothers Grand and Great." Frager's "Class and Ethnic Barriers" and *Sweatshop Strife* show that ethnicity served to undermine support for women's issues in the Jewish labour movement. Lindstrom-Best offers extensive research on women in the Finnish community. There are several useful sources on women from other ethnic or racial groups: Burnet, *Looking into My Sister's Eyes*; Juteau-Lee and B. Roberts, "Ethnicity and Feminism"; Indra, "Invisible Mosaic"; Woywitka, "Pioneer Woman"; Pivato, "Italian Canadian Women"; Adilman, "Chinese Women and Work"; Doman, "Asian Indian Women in B.C."; and a special issue of *Polyphony* 8 (1986) devoted to women and ethnicity.

7 Lacelle, *Urban Domestic Servants*; Barber, "The Women Ontario Welcomed," "The Servant Problem in Manitoba," "Sunny Ontario for British Girls," and "In Search of a Better Life"; Leslie, "Domestic Service in Canada."

8 Leacy, *Historical Statistics*; Synge, "Young Working Class Women."

9 Marvin McInnis argues that the labour market in Ontario provided few opportunities for women's paid employment compared with the numbers of women available to work; see his "Women,

Work and Childbearing." Parr describes the survival strategies of single women in her book *The Gender of Breadwinners*. Chambers, in "Living Standards of Toronto Blue Collar Workers," discusses the changing living standards in Toronto without recognizing the gendered implications of his findings; working women would have been devastated by the increased cost of living and the relative decline in wages for unskilled workers. D. Pedersen discusses the problems single women had in finding accommodation; see her "Building Today," 228. See also Creese, "Politics of Dependence."

10 Acton, *Women at Work in Ontario*, 8–12, 38–9; Sangster, "Canadian Working Women," 60–1; and Cohen, *Women's Work* and "The Decline of Women in Canadian Dairying."

11 For a discussion of the struggle over the census treatment of women's domestic labour, see Folbre, "The Unproductive Housewife." For Canadian sources on women's financial contribution to households, see Strong-Boag, "Keeping House in God's Country"; Bullen, "Hidden Workers"; Bradbury, "Pigs, Cows and Boarders"; Lavigne and Stoddart, "Women's Work in Montreal"; Forestall, "Times Were Hard"; and R. Pierson, "History of Women and Paid Work." Children's labour also contributed needed income to the household. See Sutherland, "We Always Had Things to Do" and "I Can't Recall When I Didn't Help."

12 White, *Women and Unions*, 1; and Russell, "A Fair or Minimum Wage?"

13 G. Kealey and Palmer, *Dreaming of What Might Be*, and Levine, "The Best Men in the Order" and "Labour's True Woman."

14 *Platform of the Socialist Labour Party* (adopted at the Chicago Convention, Oct. 12, 1889), box 52:19, and *Platform and Constitution of the Socialist Labour Party of the Dominion of Canada* (amended Sept. 2, 1901), box 31A-18, Angus MacInnis Collection, UBC.

15 Hobbs, "Dead Horses and Muffled Voices," 34.

16 *Butler's Journal*, June 1903, 2; Sam Landers, *Weekly Bulletin of the Clothing Trades* (New York), 14 Oct. 1910, 6 (reference courtesy of Ruth Frager); *Citizen and Country*, 12 July 1902, 3. See also Russell, "A Fair or Minimum Wage," 75–6; Frager, "Class and Ethnic Barriers," 150; Creese, "Politics of Dependence"; Naylor, *The New Democracy*, ch. 5; L. Kealey, "Women and Labour"; and Derry and Douglas, "The Minimum Wage."

17 Klein and Roberts, "Besieged Innocence," 219–20; Labour Commission Proceedings, British Columbia. There are no published studies that assess whether the perception that working women

drove down men's wages was accurate for this period in Canada, or, if so, in which sectors. In teaching and clerical work, women began to take jobs which gave the appearance that they were displacing men. In fact, a gender hierarchy was emerging, as men were displaced to higher-paying more powerful positions as inspectors or managers. In other sectors, such as cigar making and bookbinding, mechanization eliminated the skilled labour traditionally performed by men. See Abbott, "Accomplishing a Man's Task"; Creese, "Politics of Dependence"; Lowe, *Women in the Administrative Revolution*. Ruth Frager's unpublished paper, "Deluded Assumptions about Diluted Labour," provides an excellent assessment of this issue during the war years.

18   One unemployed single woman was against hiring married women who worked for "spare money" because she felt they undercut the wage demands of women who supported themselves. See *The Garment Worker*, New York, 163D (reference courtesy of Ruth Frager).

19   Cobble finds that the craft union structure was not inherently detrimental to women. The craft-based American waitresses' union supported women's struggles, but similar evidence for the Canadian context is limited. See Cobble, "Craft Unionism and Female Activism"; see also L. Kealey, "Women and Labour."

20   Klein and Roberts, "Besieged Innocence," 215; Backhouse, *Petticoats and Prejudice*, 265–92; L. Kealey, "Women and Labour"; Derry and Douglas, "The Minimum Wage."

21   Strong-Boag, *The Parliament of Women*, 257–8; R. Pierson, "Gender and the Unemployment Insurance Debates," 82; Hobbs, "Dead Horses and Muffled Voices," 22–33; and Forbes, "Battles in Another War."

22   Bacchi, *Liberation Deferred*, 117–21.

23   For a discussion of the family wage debate, see Humphries, "Class Struggle and the Working Class Family," "The Working Class Family, Women's Liberation, and Class Struggle," and "The Working Class Family: A Marxist Perspective"; Barrett and McIntosh, "The 'Family Wage'"; Barrett, *Women's Oppression Today*; and Land, "The Family Wage." For Canadian sources on the family wage, see Connelly, "Women Workers and the Family Wage in Canada"; L. Kealey, "Canadian Socialism and the Woman Question"; Naylor, *The New Democracy*; and Bradbury, "Women's History and Working Class History." Preliminary research on the working class in other countries indicates that the ideal of a family wage was not necessarily shared by other cultures. See Valverde, "Catalan and British Cotton Mill Workers" and "Giving the Female a Domestic Turn."

24 Kautsky's work was reprinted by both the SPC and the SDPC. See
    "The Dissolution of the Proletarian Family," *Western Clarion*,
    9 Dec. 1911, 3, and the following articles in *Cotton's Weekly*:
    "Breaking Up the Home," 10 April 1913, 3; "A New Middle
    Class," 29 May 1913, 2; "Wages," 13 Nov. 1913, 3; "The Prole-
    tariat," 20 Nov. 1913, 2; and "The Expropriation of the Expropri-
    ators," 16 July 1914, 1.

25 "Wages," *Western Clarion*, 20 Jan. 1912, 4.

26 "Wages," *Cotton's Weekly*, 13 Nov. 1913, 2.

27 See *Cotton's Weekly*, 26 Dec. 1912, 2; "May Day," 1 May, 1913,
    1; 28 Aug. 1913, 4; "The Socialization of Society," 11 Dec. 1913,
    2. See also *Western Clarion*, 1 Dec. 1906, 2, and ibid., "Treat
    Them as Pariahs," 3; "Women and Socialism," 8 Dec. 1906, 4;
    letter to Eugene Debs, 6 July 1907, 2.

28 Bebel, *Western Clarion*, 1 Dec. 1906, 3.

29 *Western Clarion*, 17 Oct. 1908, 4.

30 *Cotton's Weekly*, 12 Aug. 1909, 7, and 11 March 1909, 7. The
    SPC press often ridiculed these papers even while drawing on their
    work. See, for example, *Western Clarion*, 16 Jan. 1909, 4.

31 See *Cotton's Weekly* as follows: "We, as Women," 18 Feb. 1909,
    7; "The Poor Ye Have Always with You," 20 May 1909, 7; "The
    Wolf at the Door," 27 May, 1909, 7, and 21 July 1910, 2; "A
    Hope," 10 June 1909, 7; "To Labour," 28 July 1910, 2; and
    7 Nov. 1912, 4; see also *Canadian Forward* as follows: "It Takes
    Strength," 27 Dec. 1916, 7; 10 May 1917, 1; and excerpt from
    Women and Economics, 10 June 1918, 3; and see *Western Clar-
    ion* as follows: "To the Workers," 27 Oct. 1906, 4; and 8 Dec
    1906, 4.

32 Lacelle, *Urban Domestic Servants*; Barber, "The Women Ontario
    Welcomed," "Sunny Ontario for British Girls, 1900–30," "The Ser-
    vant Problem in Manitoba," and "In Search of a Better Life";
    Strong-Boag, "Keeping House in God's Country"; Lindstrom-Best,
    "I Won't Be a Slave" and "Going to Work in America."

33 *Western Clarion*, 28 July 1906, 1; 27 July 1907, 3; and 3 Nov.
    1906, 3.

34 Ibid., 24 Feb. 1906, 1.

35 Lindstrom-Best, *Defiant Sisters* and "Going to Work in America,"
    18.

36 "Servants and Regular Hours," *Hamilton Times* as cited in *Citizen
    and Country*, 2 Sept. 1899, 2; 4 May 1900, 2; 20 June 1900, 4.
    See also Ben Hanford, "Under Socialism There Ain't Goin' to Be
    No Servant Girls," *Cotton's Weekly*, 15 April 1909, 7.

37 *Cotton's Weekly*, 26 June 1913, 4. See also "A Fairy Story Revised," ibid., 28 Jan. 1909, 3.

38 *Citizen and Country*, 9 March 1900, 1.

39 "Unsheaths Her Sword in the Cause of Freedom," *Western Clarion*, 31 Aug. 1907, 1.

40 Ibid.

41 Gustav Prager, "Odd Thoughts of an Odd Fellow," *Cotton's Weekly*, 9 Sept. 1909, 7. The labour press was not above joking about the sexual abuse of servants. One article, "A Little Management," suggested how to get one's wife to fire the servant: pretend to kiss the servant girl when kissing your wife (*Independent*, 19 Oct. 1901, 3).

42 "Woman and the Social Problem," *Western Clarion*, 13 Aug. 1904, 4.

43 Ibid.

44 For the labour perspective of the impact of immigration on domestic service, see *Independent*, 22 June 1901, 1. In British Columbia, the Conservative Party campaigned on a platform "To aid in the immigration of female domestic servants" (*Ferguson Eagle* 28 March 1900, 1). See also *Independent*, 28 April 1900, 5; *Western Clarion*, 14 Sept. 1907, 2; 30 Nov. 1907, 1; 14 March 1908, 2; July 1911, 29–30; and 1 March 1913, 4; *Cotton's Weekly*, 21 Dec. 1911, 1.

45 The immigration of non-white women was also opposed for fear that fertile women would reproduce and increase the size of the non-white community. See Adilman, "Chinese Women and Work."

46 *Cotton's Weekly*, 13 Feb. 1913, 2.

47 *Western Clarion*, 23 Feb. 1907, 1, and 27 April 1907, 1.

48 Ibid., 1 March 1913, 4.

49 Ibid., 8 June 1907, 1. For a discussion of the YWCA's response to working-women's housing needs, see Mitchinson, "Early Women's Organizations."

50 *Cotton's Weekly*, 24 June 1909, 8. For a discussion of Mrs Sanford's activities, see Barber, "The Servant Problem in Manitoba."

51 *Independent*, 29 June 1901, 1.

52 It is not clear whether these articles assume this because the Chinese servant was thought to be male or because Chinese women were thought to be unattractive to white men. The scarcity of Chinese women suggests the former. See *Independent*, 28 Dec. 1901, 4; *Lardeau Eagle*, 11 July 1900, 3.

53 *Western Clarion*, 18 Aug. 1906, 4.

54 *Cotton's Weekly*, 3 Aug. 1911, 1; 27 Nov. 1913, 2; and 21 Dec. 1911, 1.
55 *Western Clarion*, 18 March 1905, 4; 6 Jan. 1906, 4; and 24 May 1913, 2; *Citizen and Country*, 30 Sept. 1899, 4, and 27 April 1900, 12.
56 Rev. George Lunn, *Cotton's Weekly*, 25 Nov. 1909, 2.
57 *Western Clarion*, 24 Nov. 1906, 1.
58 M. Campbell, "Sexism in British Columbia Trade Unions," 170; *Independent*, 4 May 1901, 4; 17 Aug. 1901, 3; 12 Oct. 1901, 2; and 26 Oct. 1901, 3; *Citizen and Country*, 11 May 1900, 2; Rosenthal, "Union Maids," 49–53; Vancouver Trades and Labor Council, Minutes, July 17 1913 to 5 Aug. 1915.
59 R.B. Kerr, *Western Clarion*, 1 Feb. 1908, 3.
60 *Cotton's Weekly*, 15 June 1911, 3.
61 *Citizen and Country*, 2 Dec. 1899, 2; 2 March 1900, 4; and 4 May 1900, 7.
62 *Western Socialist*, 13 Dec. 1902, 1; "The Worker's Parliament," *Western Clarion*, 6 June 1903, 1.
63 "Organization Committee," *Citizen and Country*, 29 July 1899, 2.
64 *Citizen and Country*, 8 July 1899, 2.
65 Landers sold subscriptions for the *Citizen and Country* (27 July, 1900, 4).
66 *Independent*, 27 Oct. 1900, 1.
67 *Canadian Socialist*, 12 July 1902, 3.
68 *Western Socialist*, 6 Dec. 1902, 2.
69 *Citizen and Country*, 7 Dec. 1900, 2.
70 *Western Clarion*, 11 June 1903, 4.
71 "Made in B.C. by Organized Labour," *Western Socialist*, 24 Jan. 1903, 3.
72 *Western Socialist*, 17 Jan. 1903, 3.
73 "We Women," *Western Socialist*, 1 Nov. 1902, 3.
74 *Canadian Socialist*, 2 Aug. 1902, 3.
75 *Western Clarion*, 22 Oct. 1903, 3.
76 *Western Socialist*, 29 Nov. 1902, 3.
77 *Canadian Socialist*, 16 Aug. 1902, 3.
78 *Western Socialist*, 27 Sept. 1902, 3.
79 Letter from L.G.C., *Canadian Socialist*, 13 Sept. 1902, 3; A.M. Simon, "Who are the Union Wreckers?" ibid., 30 Aug. 1902, 1.
80 *Western Clarion*, 24 June 1905, 2; 31 March 1906, 4; and 19 May 1906, 4.
81 Mainly through the efforts of Helena Gutteridge, a Women's Employment League was established in Vancouver to aid women who were unemployed and seeking work during this depression.

According to one report, 882 women registered: 132 of them were married and were sent to the relief office; 150 were employed in doll making; 140 were engaged as domestics; which left 495 women who also needed help. See "Work of the Women's Employment League," Minutes, Vancouver Trades and Labor Council, book 3, 23a, and I. Howard, *Social Justice*, ch. 6.

82 *Western Clarion*, 6 Jan. 1906, 1, 4; 14 Nov. 1908, 3; and 18 March, 1905, 4.

83 Ibid., 1 Jan. 1910, 4.

84 Ibid., 15 Feb. 1908, 1, 4, and "Women in Mines," ibid., 8 March 1913, 3.

85 Contrary to the argument put forward by P. Campbell, in "Making Socialists," that the SPC did not aspire to tell the workers "how the socialist society would actually be created, and what character it would take," leaving it to workers and farmers to develop their own analysis of capitalism, the SPC certainly told women what their place was in the socialist revolution.

86 See *Western Clarion* as follows: "Work Women Like Beasts in Iron Plant," 24 Feb. 1912, 3; 23 June 1906, 1; 21 July 1906, 1; and 29 June 1912, 1.

87 *Western Clarion*, 20 April 1912, 1.

88 J.K. Mergler, "What Then Shall They Do?" *Western Clarion*, 27 Sept. 1913, 2.

89 Eve, "How Working Girls 'Throw' Their Money Away," *Western Clarion*, 31 Jan. 1914, 2.

90 See *Western Clarion* as follows: Gourock, "The Woman's Invasion," 26 Dec. 1908, 4; "Mudder Still Workin," 27 May 1905, 3; 2 Feb. 1907, 3; Stonehenge, 5 Oct. 1907, 4; William Haywood, 7 Sept. 1907, 1; 4 July 1908, 4; and 2 Jan. 1909, 2.

91 Kaneko, "The Modern Priscilla," *Western Clarion*, 11 May 1912, 3.

92 Moses Baritz, "Infantile Mortality," *Western Clarion*, 30 July 1910, 1. See also Gourock, ibid., 12 Dec. 1908, 1, and Arnup, "Education for Motherhood: Government Health Publications, Mothers and the State," 3–4.

93 This point is made by Lewis in "Motherhood Issues," 7.

94 W.E. Hardenburg, "What is Socialism? A Short Study of its Aims and Clauses: Breaking up the Home," *Western Clarion*, 20 July 1912, 4.

95 A. Budden, "The Woman's Place: From a Proletarian Rather than Sex Standpoint," *Western Clarion*, 10 Dec. 1910, 1; see also 24 March 1906, 4.

96 A.C.B., "Women and Wages in New York City," *Western Clarion*, 8 Oct. 1910, 4, as reprinted from *New York Call*.

97   *Western Clarion*, 18 July 1908, 4.
98   "Two Letters," *Western Clarion*, 18 Aug. 1906, 4.
99   *Cotton's Weekly*, 2 Dec. 1909, 1; 3 Nov. 1910, 2; Nov. 30, 1911, 1; 7 Dec. 1911, 4; and 21 Dec. 1911, 3.
100 See the following in *Cotton's Weekly*: "Wolf at the Door," 27 May 1909, 7; "The Toll of the System," 24 March 1910, 2; "Girl Workers in Montreal," 25 Feb. 1909, 1; "Vicious Fining System in Factories," 26 March 1914, 1; "The Dangers from Dust," 10 June 1909, 7; and "Sacrificing Young Girls," 22 April 1909, 7.
101 "Why Do Children Die?" *Cotton's Weekly*, 8 Sept. 1910, 1; see also 23 July 1914, 2.
102 Dora F. Kerr, "Should Women Work?" *Cotton's Weekly*, 15 April 1909, 7.
103 See the following articles in *Cotton's Weekly*: "To Keep My Job," 9 Oct. 1913, 2; "Unemployed Female Labour," 3 July 1913, 2; and J.W. Eastwood, "A Socialist Challenges a Parson," 20 Oct. 1910, 3, as reprinted from the Saint John *Standard*.
104 *Cotton's Weekly*, 24 April 1913, 1.
105 Ibid., 29 May 1913, 4.
106 Ibid., 12 June 1913, 3.
107 Theresa S. Malkiel, "The to [sic] Working Women," *Cotton's Weekly*, 4 Dec. 1913, 3.
108 *Cotton's Weekly*, 2 Sept. 1909, 1.
109 M. Wisdom, "Woman's Suffrage," *Cotton's Weekly*, 8 April 1909, 7.
110 Dora F. Kerr, "Should Women Work?" *Cotton's Weekly*, 15 April 1909, 7.
111 "Women," *Cotton's Weekly*, 11 Feb. 1909, 7.
112 "Would Women Have to Earn Their Living under Socialism?" *Cotton's Weekly*, 19 May 1910, 3.
113 John M. Work, "Shall Women Work?" *Cotton's Weekly*, 16 Nov. 1911, 4.
114 See *Cotton's Weekly* as follows: "Women's Rights," 5 Dec. 1912, 1; William Shier, "About Women," 9 Sept. 1909, 7; "Women Should be Socialists," 18 March 1909, 7; and 12 May 1910, 2.
115 *Cotton's Weekly*, 26 May 1910, 3.
116 Ibid., 27 Oct. 1910, 3; 21 Jan. 1909, 5; and 9 April 1910, 1.
117 See *Cotton's Weekly* as follows: "A Toronto Minister Worth While," 30 Jan. 1913, 2; 6 Feb. 1913, 2; 13 March 1913, 4; 12 June 1913, 4; "Departmental Stores," 15 May 1913, 1.
118 *Cotton's Weekly*, 4 March 1909, 3.
119 See *Cotton's Weekly* as follows: "Early Closing Laws," 29 July 1909, 1; 16 Dec. 1909, 4; 7 April 1910, 1; 19 May 1910, 2; 28 July 1910, 2; 26 Jan. 1911, 1; "Why a Working Man Should be a

Socialist," 25 May 1911, 3; 13 April 1911, 1; 20 Feb. 1913, 1; 10 April 1913, 1; 22 May 1913, 1; and 31 July 1913, 4.

120 *Cotton's Weekly* 17 Aug. 1911, 4.

121 Ibid., 17 Aug. 1911, 4, and 14 Sept. 1911, 1.

122 In one rare instance, *Cotton's* published a working woman's letter that explained she had little time to read because she worked so hard (5 Feb. 1914, 4).

CHAPTER SIX

1 For a discussion of the prevailing concepts of sexuality, see Valverde, *Age of Light, Soap and Water*; DuBois and Gordon, "Seeking Ecstasy on the Battlefield"; Herman, "Loving Courtship or the Marriage Market?"; and Bliss, "Pure Books." Jefferis's *Safe Counsel: Light on Dark Corners* and Drake's *What a Young Wife Ought to Know* provide marvellous overviews of contemporary mores on love, courtship, marriage, and sexuality. They include detailed instructions and advice on birth control, masturbation, marital sex, sexual diseases, and child rearing.

2 Dodd, "Dissemination of Contraceptive Technology," "Canadian Birth Control Movement on Trial," and "The Hamilton Clinic"; McLaren and McLaren, *Bedroom and the State*; and Bishop, "The Early Birth Controllers of B.C."

3 For a discussion of the sex radicals, see L. Gordon, *Woman's Body, Woman's Right*; Schwantes, "Free Love and Free Speech"; Hayden, *The Grand Domestic Revolution*, 90–113; Marsh, *Anarchist Women*; and Fishbein, *Rebels in Bohemia*.

4 Bebel, *Woman under Socialism*, 79–86; 343–4.

5 DeLeon's, introduction to Bebel's *Woman under Socialism*, xviii.

6 The free love group of Victoria Woodhull was expelled from the International Workingmen's Association branch of the First International for its feminist causes of "free love and suffrage" (Hayden, *The Grand Domestic Revolution*, 101–3).

7 "In the Ideal Commonwealth," *Cotton's Weekly*, 11 Sept. 1913, 3.

8 *Western Clarion*, 21 April 1906, 1, and 23 Nov. 1907, 1–2. For a more extensive discussion of the utopian socialist communities in Canada, see Newton, "Enough of Exclusive Masculine Thinking."

9 Lindstrom-Best, *Defiant Sisters*; Seager, "Finnish Canadians"; Sangster, "Finnish Women in Ontario."

10 "A Russian Spy in Canada," *Western Clarion*, 5 Sept. 1908, 1, and W.J. Curry, "Socialism Booms in Vancouver," ibid., 19 June 1913, 3; see also "Free Love Denied at Adv. Rates," *Cotton's Weekly*, 20 Feb. 1913, 3.

11 *Lucifer,* 21 July 1904, 129; 4 Aug. 1904, 140–1; and 16 Feb. 1905, 252. Press censorship was exercised through the postmaster general. *Cotton's Weekly* was denied the reduced postal rates that were provided to similar papers from the United States. See *Cotton's Weekly,* 7 April 1910, 2.

12 "We Women," *Western Socialist,* 29 Nov. 1902, 3.

13 Ibid., 8 Nov. 1902, 3.

14 "Economics or Esoterics," *Western Clarion,* 13 Oct. 1906, 2.

15 "Socialist Movement Defined," *Western Clarion,* 17 June 1905, 1.

16 *Cotton's Weekly,* 26 March 1914, 2.

17 Gerald O. Desmond, "Free Love and the Home," *Cotton's Weekly,* 1 July 1909, 3.

18 According to Drake, the advice of "mothers, mothers-in-law, sisters, aunts, 'friends,' young matrons" makes the majority of young brides "far better informed in the methods of preventing conception, or producing abortion after conception has really taken place, than of any proper preparation for motherhood" (*What a Young Wife Ought to Know,* 89–90). McInnis, in "Women, Work and Childbearing," discusses the decline of fertility in Ontario. Dodd, "Canadian Birth Control Movement on Trial," and McLaren and McLaren, *Bedroom and the State,* discuss the variety of early birth control methods available for use before 1920. Jefferis, in *Safe Counsel,* discusses birth control in the section "Prevention and Its Follies." He advises against avoiding pregnancy (except in cases of "unfit" parents); recommends moderation in sexual activity (preferably once a month); reviews the laws regarding birth control; advises against withdrawal or patent medicines; and recommends "the physiological method," rhythm, as absolutely safe, natural, and legal (243–8). Backhouse discusses the social and legal implications of infanticide and abortion in nineteenth-century Canada. She argues that women accused of infanticide received lenient sentences, whereas abortion was punished more severely by the courts. See her *Petticoats and Prejudice,* chs. 4 and 5, and "Desperate Women and Compassionate Courts."

19 Drake, *What a Young Wife Ought to Know,* 133.

20 We must not assume that the anxiety about "race suicide" was restricted to the right wing. J.S. Woodsworth expressed his concern about this issue in *Strangers within Our Gates* and *My Neighbour.* See also Valverde, *Age of Light, Soap and Water*; Angus McLaren, "Birth Control and the Canadian Left," "Birth Control and Abortion in Canada," and *Our Own Master Race*; McLaren and McLaren, *Bedroom and the State*; Chapman, "The Early

Eugenics Movement in Western Canada"; and Gamble, "Race Suicide in France."

21   Dodd discusses the tensions between the feminists and eugenists in the birth control movement of the 1920s and 1930s. See her "Canadian Birth Control Movement" and "The Hamilton Birth Control Clinic."

22   John Spargo, "The Great Problem," *Cotton's Weekly*, 25 March 1909, 2. For articles on race suicide, see, in *Citizen and Country*, "Female Labour," 7 Oct. 1899, 2, and "The Birthrate in Ontario," 7 Dec. 1900, 1; in *Western Clarion*, "Race Suicide," 12 May 1903, 2; N.M.T., "Socialism Would Destroy the Home," 24 July 1909, 3; J. Stewart, "Causes of Race Suicide," 21 May 1910, 1; and "Birth Rate Decreases," 21 Jan. 1911, 2; and see *Cotton's Weekly* as follows: 13 May 1909, 8; 21 Jan. 1909, 2; Robert Spendler, "The Fit and the Unfit," 18 March 1909, 8; "Recorder Wier on the Family," 4 Oct. 1909, 1; 13 July 1911, 4; 24 April 1913, 3; "Race Suicide," 29 Sept. 1910, 3. For articles on infant mortality, see the following in *Cotton's Weekly*: "Infant Mortality," 8 Sept. 1910, 3; "Infant Mortality," 22 June 1911, 1; Wm. U. Cotton, "Why Do Children Die?" 23 July 1914, 2; 28 Aug. 1913, 2; 31 July 1913, 2; and "Infant Mortality," 17 April 1913, 2.

23   *Cotton's Weekly*, 5 June 1913, 4; *Western Clarion*, 9 Nov. 1907, 4; 24 Sept. 1910, 4; 8 March 1913, 1; and "Causes of Race Suicide," 21 May 1910, 1.

24   For a discussion of Finnish methods of birth control, see Lindstrom-Best, *Defiant Sisters*. It is possible that one device advertised in the *Western Clarion*, a "Vacuum Hand Massager," was intended to be used for abortions. It promised "an increased blood circulation" to "whatever part of the body applied to" (*Western Clarion*, 17 Jan. 1914, 4). The paper also contained ads for pharmaceutical products, such as "Gillets Lye," which were used at the time in recipes for pessaries (17 Dec. 1908, 3). None of the ads made direct reference to the possible use of these products for abortion or birth control.

25   See *Cotton's Weekly* as follows: Justice, "Increase of Population," 16 March 1911, 2; "Race Suicide," 8 June 1911, 2; and 7 Aug. 1913, 1. See also B.M. Burns, "Why Women Should Be Socialists," *Canadian Socialist*, 20 June 1902, 2.

26   Justice, "Increase of Population."

27   Between 1900 and 1908, *Lucifer* had less than ten identifiable Canadian subscribers. Of these, few could be identified with the Canadian left. Several of them complained of the isolation they felt in Canada, lacking other comrades who shared their views.

See, for example, Rudolph Kurtzhals, *Lucifer*, 3 Nov. 1903, 335, and A.B.C., *Western Clarion*, 7 Dec. 1905.

28 "To Protect Virtue," *Citizen and Country*, 13 May 1899, 3.

29 For a discussion of prostitution in Canada, see Lindstrom-Best, *Defiant Sisters*; Cooper, "Red Lights of Winnipeg"; Rotenberg, "The Wayward Worker"; Gray, *Red Lights on the Prairies*; Nilsen, "Prostitution in Vancouver"; Adilman, "A Preliminary Sketch of Chinese Women"; and Backhouse, "Canadian Prostitution Law." Useful sources outside Canada include Rosen, *The Lost Sisterhood*, Gorham, "The Maiden Tribute of Modern Babylon," and Walkowitz, "Politics of Prostitution."

30 See *Cotton's Weekly* as follows: "The White Slave Traffic," 1 May 1909, 7; "Vice," 8 Dec. 1910, 1; "Calgary Worse than Chicago," 20 Feb. 1913, 1; and 3 July 1913, 2. See also *Western Clarion*, 29 Oct. 1903, 2; "Strain at a Gnat," 27 Aug. 1904, 2; 2 July 1904, 4; 16 Dec. 1905, 3; 3 Feb. 1906, 4; 4 Aug. 1906, 3; 17 Nov. 1906, 1; 24 Aug. 1907, 2; 2 Jan. 1908, 2; 9 May 1908, 3; 15 Aug. 1908, 3; 18 Nov. 1911, 1; 16 Aug. 1913, 1; and 11 Oct. 1913, 2.

31 See *Citizen and Country* as follows: "Immorality in Toronto," 3 June 1899, 3; 10 June 1899, 1; "A Subject that is Tabooed," 28 Oct. 1899, 1; 4 Nov. 1899, 2; and 7 Dec. 1900, 2. See also, in *Cotton's Weekly*, "The White Slave Traffic," 1 May 1909, 7, and "Futile Attack," 26 June 1913, 4.

32 See *Cotton's Weekly* as follows: 21 Jan. 1909, 1, 2; "Girl Workers in Montreal," 25 Feb. 1909, 1; Rosa Gabriel, "Recorder Dupuis' Speech," 4 March 1909, 1, 3; "The Servants of the People" and "Recorder Dupuis and the Girl in Blue," 6 May 1909, 1; "Vice," 8 Dec. 1910, 1; 2 Nov. 1911, 4; 19 June 1913, 4; 7 May 1914, 1; and 14 May 1914, 1. See also *Western Clarion*, 26 Aug. 1905, 2, and 13 Jan. 1906, 3; and Bell, *Traffic in Young Girls*, 308.

33 "The Slaves of Sensuality," *Citizen and Country*, 27 April 1900, 4; *Western Clarion*, 11 Sept. 1903, 1, and 8 March 1913, 4. See also *Cotton's Weekly* as follows: 20 May 1909, 7; Edwin Sims, "Betraying and Selling Girls for Profit One Aspect of the Capitalist System," 24 June 1909, 3; "White Slave Traffic," 26 Dec. 1909, 2; Elizabeth Gurly Flynn, 13 Jan. 1910, 1, 2; and "The Pembroke Standard Attacks Socialism," 24 April 1913, 4.

34 J. Eastwood, "Socialist Challenges a Parson," *Cotton's Weekly*, 27 Oct. 1910, 3.

35 Rosen, *The Lost Sisterhood*, 116. Considerable publicity was given to this matter, for government commissions were struck in Canada and the United States to investigate the existence of the white slave trade in North America. Sources on prostitution in

Canada, cited above, note cases where women prostitutes were held as slaves. For an excellent discussion of the white slave trade in the United States, see Rosen, "White Slavery: Myth or Reality," in *The Lost Sisterhood*, 112–36.

36 Bell, 291 and 14.

37 See the following articles in *Cotton's Weekly*: Edwin Sims, "Betraying and Selling Girls for Profit: One Aspect of Capitalist System," 24 June 1909, 3; "A Socialist Woman in the Colorado Legislature," 10 April 1913, 4; "Profits Create Slavers," 6 Jan. 1910, 4; "Profit Causes Immorality," 17 Aug. 1911, 2; and in *Western Clarion* see "One Women's [*sic*] Shame Another's Fortune," 11 Sept. 1903, 1, and "The Reign of Business," 28 Oct. 1905, 3.

38 *Cotton's Weekly*, 7 May 1914, 1. See also the earlier discussion of prostitution in British Columbia.

39 Few contemporaries have addressed the racist element in the furore over white slavery. One notable exception is Emma Goldman's "Traffic in Women," in *The Traffic in Women and Other Essays on Feminism*.

40 *Western Clarion*, 29 Feb. 1908, 1, and 23 June 1910, 4.

41 For a discussion of the condition of black prostitutes in Halifax, see Fingard, *Dark Side of Victorian Halifax*, ch. 4; for a discussion of Chinese prostitutes in British Columbia, see Adilman, "Chinese Women." Muszynski briefly mentions native women prostitutes in "B.C.'s Salmon Cannery Labour Force," 112.

42 *Cotton's Weekly*, 6 July 1911, 4, and 13 July 1911, 1; *Western Clarion*, 16 Dec. 1911, 2–3; and Dubinsky and Iacovetta, "Murder, Womanly Virtue and Womanhood," 523.

43 W. Laurence, "Reform, Social and Moral," *Western Clarion*, 25 Feb. 1911, 1.

44 See *Cotton's Weekly* as follows: 24 Dec. 1908, 2; Roscoe A. Fillmore, "The Social Evil," 9 Sept. 1909, 8; 14 Oct. 1909, 1; 11 Nov. 1909, 1; 16 June 1910, 1; 20 Feb. 1913, 1; and 17 April 1913, 1.

45 In 1909 and 1910 the Canadian Trades and Labor Congress cooperated with the Social and Moral Reform Association on the issues of gambling and white slavery (*Eastern Labour News*, 2 Oct. 1909, 1, and Agnes Downing, *Vancouver World*, 19 Feb. 1910, 8). The Winnipeg Trades and Labor Council showed less cooperation when it refused to send delegates to the local Social and Moral Reform Council (*Cotton's Weekly*, 20 Feb. 1913, 3).

46 "Reform or Revolution: Edmonton Unionists Expose the Inefficiency of Reform Measures," *Western Clarion*, 16 Aug. 1913, 1; "A Crushing Reply," *Cotton's Weekly*, 4 Sept., 1913, 3.

47 *Cotton's Weekly*, 10 July 1913, 1.

48   "Sweat Shop Slavery: Low Wages the Means of Increasing Immorality," *Citizen and Country*, 2 Sept. 1899, 2; "Why Working Women Sell Their Honor," *Western Clarion*, 27 July 1912, 4; "What Can a Girl Live On," *Cotton's Weekly*, 1 July 1909, 7.

49   "Punishment," *Cotton's Weekly*, 21 Jan. 1909, 1; and 9 Dec. 1909, 1.

50   "Perfect Nonsense," *Cotton's Weekly*, 3 July 1913, 1; and 20 April 1911, 2. See also "Economic Discontent: Father Haggerty on War and Prostitution," *Western Socialist*, 13 March 1903, 1, and "Profit and Human Depravity," ibid., 8 Nov. 1902, 1.

51   *Western Socialist*, 27 Sept. 1902, 3; Will R. Hubberd, "Be True to Class," *Cotton's Weekly*, 1 April 1909, 8.

52   Valverde, "Love of Finery."

53   "The White Slave Trade of Today," *Western Clarion*, 14 Nov. 1908, 4.

54   See the following in *Western Clarion*: "A Fine Sense of Decency," 18 July 1908, 1; "Home-Making under Capitalism," 15 Dec. 1906, 4; 15 June 1907, 1; "One of Mary's Sons," 14 Dec. 1907, 4; Eugene Debs, "Prohibition, Stockings and Garters," 21 May 1914, 3; "Moral Leprosy," 22 Dec. 1906, 2; 6 Oct. 1906, 3; "Capitalist Morality," 23 Nov. 1907, 2.

55   "Depravity of the Rich," *Western Clarion*, 7 July 1906, 1.

56   May Walden Kerr, "Socialism and the Home," *Western Socialist*, 11 Oct. 1902, 3; *Cotton's Weekly*, 7 Oct. 1909, 1; *Western Clarion*, 23 May 1903, 1.

57   Ben Hanford, "Under Socialism There Ain't Goin' to Be No Servant Girls," *Cotton's Weekly*, 15 April 1909, 7.

58   *Cotton's Weekly*, 14 July 1910, 2, and 19 June 1913, 1.

59   Roscoe A. Fillmore, "The Social Evil," *Cotton's Weekly*, 9 Sept. 1909, 8.

60   Gerald Desmond, "To the Social and Moral Reformers," *Cotton's Weekly*, 13 May 1909, 2.

61   "Socialists and the Sexual Relations," *Western Clarion*, 11 June 1903, 2; "Immorality," ibid., 11 March 1909, 1; "Love, Courtship, Marriage and Divorce," *Cotton's Weekly*, 23 Sept. 1909, 8.

62   Gordon Nye, "Who Destroys the Home?" *Cotton's Weekly*, 7 Sept. 1911, 1.

63   "Depravity of the Rich," *Western Clarion*, 7 July 1906, 1; Alf Budden, "Calgary Local," ibid., 23 March 1912, 3; W.W.L., "Morality," ibid., July 1911, 40–5.

64   Wilhelmina Rees, "Dominant Man," *Western Clarion*, 3 Aug. 1912, 2.

65 Alf Budden, "In Reply to Comrade Rees," *Western Clarion*, 21 Sept. 1912, 2.

66 "Wouldn't It Make You Sick," *Western Clarion*, 11 Dec. 1909, 2; Wm. Scott, "Socialists and the Sexual Relations," ibid., 11 June 1903, 2.

67 "The Church and the Social Evil," *Western Clarion*, 14 Aug. 1903, 1.

68 Gerald Desmond, "Prostitution," *Western Clarion*, 30 April 1910, 1.

69 Wilfred Gribble, "The White Slave Traffic," *Western Clarion*, 14 Feb. 1914, 2.

70 In contrast, social purity reformers saw women as the primary victims in contracting venereal disease, either as prostitutes or as unsuspecting wives infected by their husbands, and even children (Bell, *Traffic in Young Girls*, 292–3).

71 Gerald Desmond, "Free Love and the Home," *Cotton's Weekly*, 1 July 1909, 3.

72 Interview with Martin Baker, David Miller, National Archives of Canada, MG31 B6 v. 1. See also interview with Bill Brown, ibid.

73 "Punishment," *Cotton's Weekly*, 21 Jan. 1909, 1; "A Letter from Mr French," ibid., 28 Jan. 1909, 1.

74 Mary Cotton Wisdom, "Women Judged by Men," *Cotton's Weekly*, 28 Jan. 1909, 7.

75 Rosa Gabriel, "Recorder Dupuis' Speech," *Cotton's Weekly*, 4 March 1909, 3.

76 Kate Richards O'Hare, "Wimmin Ain't Got No Kick," *Cotton's Weekly*, 7 Nov. 1912, 2.

77 Social purity reformers believed that men using prostitutes became depraved, both physically and mentally, and were a threat to "good" women: "A 'sporty' man associating with harlots loses his respect for good women, and may murder them if they resist his wicked will" (Bell, *Traffic in Young Girls*, 268).

78 Married women successfully sued their husbands for divorce in England on the grounds that their husbands gave them venereal disease (Savage, "Wilful Communication of a Loathsome Disease"). For a history of the development of the treatment of VD in Canada, see McGinnis, "From Salvarsan to Penicillin," and McLaren, *Master Race*, 72–4.

79 Mrs Jane V. Brown, "The Woman Who Knows," *Cotton's Weekly*, 2 July 1914, 1.

80 "What Will Happen to Women under Socialism?" *Cotton's Weekly*, 19 Jan. 1911, 4.

81 Stonehenge, "Economics or Esoterics," *Western Clarion*, 13 Oct. 1906, 2.

82 Mitchinson, "Women and Childbirth"; Bliss, "Pure Books on Avoided Subjects"; and Jefferis, *Safe Counsel*, 204–11.
83 Mary Nicolseff, "Women under Socialism," *Cotton's Weekly*, 4 June 1914, 1.
84 See the following in *Western Clarion*: "One Way Out," 26 Nov. 1910, 3; Gorouck, "Simply Socialism," 10 June 1911, 1; and "Why Working Women Sell Their 'Honor,'" 27 July 1912, 4. In *Cotton's Weekly*, see Mary Cotton Wisdom, "Time to Wake," 11 Feb. 1909, 7; 5 Aug. 1909, 4; and 5 Aug. 1909, 4.
85 "We Women," *Western Socialist*, 27 Sept. 1902, 3.
86 Medicus, "We Women," ibid., 18 Oct. 1902, 3.
87 May Darwin, "We Women," ibid., 18 Oct. 1902, 3.
88 Dorothy Drew, "We Women," ibid., 4 Oct. 1902, 3.
89 "We Women," ibid., 13 Dec. 1902, 3. See also *Cotton's Weekly* as follows: "Betrayed," 11 Feb. 1909, 8; Mary Cotton Wisdom, "The Facts of a Case," 18 March 1909, 7; Julia Dawson, "Why Women Want Socialism," 22 July 1909, 7; and Rosa Gabriel, "Woman's Honour," 18 Feb. 1909, 7.
90 Rosa Gabriel, ibid.
91 "Socialism and Christianity," *Western Clarion*, 30 May 1903, 1; and the following articles in *Cotton's Weekly*: "A Little Child Shall Lead Them," 28 Oct. 1909, 7; "The Status of Women," 4 May, 1911, 2; "Woman Ware," 26 March 1910, 2; and Dora F. Kerr, "The Woman Question," 11 March 1909, 7.
92 "The Socialists and the Sexual Relations," *Western Clarion*, 11 June 1903, 2.
93 F.J. Flatman, "The Question of Free Love," *Cotton's Weekly*, 28 Aug. 1913, 4. See also "Socialism and Sex: The New Woman," *Western Clarion*, 14 Dec. 1907, 4.
94 Articles by J.K. Mergler are one exception to this. He writes of a "woman's passion" and "gnawing desire for vicious recreation." See "What Then Shall They Do?" *Western Clarion*, 27 Sept. 1913, 2.
95 Two articles in the *Western Clarion* discuss monogamy as "unnatural": "Economics or Esoterics," 13 Oct. 1906, 2, and "Letter from Mr French," 28 Jan. 1909, 1.
96 *Cotton's Weekly*, 17 Feb. 1910, 4.
97 "Girl Workers in Montreal," *Cotton's Weekly*, 25 Feb. 1909, 1.

CHAPTER SEVEN

1 Key sources on the suffrage movement across Canada include A. Prentice, et al., eds., *Canadian Women*, chs. 5–8; Cleverdon, *Woman Suffrage Movement in Canada*; Bacchi, *Liberation*

Deferred; L. Kealey, ed., *A Not Unreasonable Claim*; Hale, "The British Columbia Woman Suffrage Movement"; Cramer, "Woman's Suffrage Campaign in British Columbia"; Clarke, "The St John Women's Enfranchisement Association"; Forbes, "Edith Archibald" and "The Suffragists of Halifax"; Gorham, "Singing Up the Hill," "The Canadian Suffragists," "English Militancy," and "Flora MacDonald Denison"; Kinnear, *First Days, Fighting Days*; Arendt, "Why So Late?"; Holt, "Woman's Suffrage in Alberta;" and Strong-Boag, "Canadian Feminism in the 1920s."

2 Clarke, "The St John Women's Enfranchisement Association," 75–93. The Hatheway family was prominent in the Saint John suffrage movement and was active in this early socialist movement. Ella Hatheway wrote to *Citizen and Country* to commend it for being free of vulgarity (16 May 1902, 1).

3 It is unclear whether the speaker was Emily Stowe or her daughter Augusta Stowe-Gullen, though it is likely the latter, since this was shortly before Emily Stowe's death in 1903. See Fryer, *Emily Stowe*, and Joanne Thompson, "Influence of Dr. Emily Howard Stowe." Dr Margaret Gordon, president of the Canadian Suffrage Association 1914–25, was invited to share the platform, but the paper does not report her appearance.

4 See *Ontario Socialist Platform* (adopted by the Ontario Socialist League by referendum vote, Jan. 1902), National Archives of Canada; see also *Citizen and Country*, 16 May 1902, 1, and 30 May 1902, 2.

5 Hale's excellent thesis, "British Columbia Woman Suffrage Movement," briefly mentions the role of socialists. Unfortunately, she relies on a misleading article, which causes her to overemphasize the platform of the short-lived Socialist Party of British Columbia, which fleetingly supported suffrage (108). Hale does not acknowledge the rise of the Socialist Party of Canada, which supplanted the SP of BC in 1904 and rejected its support of suffrage. Her otherwise excellent thesis on the suffrage movement is thus not reliable in its comments on the socialists.

6 See SPC platform, p. 23 above.

7 *Western Socialist*, 25 Oct. 1902, 3; 11 Oct. 1902, 1–4; and 8 Nov. 1902, 1.

8 *Western Clarion*, 4 July 1914, 1.

9 Ibid., 26 June 1909, 4.

10 *Cotton's Weekly*, 1 April 1909, 8; *Western Clarion*, O'Brien, 31 March 1906, 3. See also Campbell, "Making Socialists."

11 Mrs R.M. Mendelson, "Woman Suffrage and Socialism," *Cotton's Weekly*, 9 Jan. 1913, 3.

12 Dorothy Steeves argues that, at best, the socialists and labourites
    in British Columbia paid mere lip service to feminism. It was only
    the constant efforts of women such as Helena Gutteridge that kept
    them in line. See Steeves, *The Compassionate Rebel*, 32–3.
13 *Western Clarion*, Aug. 1911, 18. His argument bears a striking
    resemblance to the views expressed by Matti Kurikka, Finnish
    leader at Sointula. See Wilson, "Never Believe What You Have
    Never Doubted," 143–4.
14 For an example of antisuffragist arguments, see: Stuart Cameron
    McLeod, "Woman Voters in Canadian Cities," *National Municipal
    Review* 5 (July 1916): 456–60; and Goldwin Smith, as reported in
    Canadian Annual Review (1904): 567–8. See also Hale, British
    Columbia Woman Suffrage Movement," 34, 96–104, and Clarke,
    "The St John Women's Enfranchisement Association," ch. 4.
15 *Western Clarion*, 10 Oct. 1908, 4.
16 Ibid., 3 Oct. 1908, 4.
17 Ibid., 22 Sept. 1906, 3; 22 Dec. 1906, 4; 5 Dec. 1908, 1; and
    10 Aug. 1912, 1.
18 Ibid., 12 Sept. 1908, 2; 27 March 1909, 3; 10 July 1909, 1; and
    27 May 1911, 3.
19 F.J. Webb, *Western Clarion*, 23 July 1910, 1; 8 Oct. 1910, 4;
    20 May 1911, 4; 27 Sept. 1913, 1–4; and 4 July 1908, 2. For a
    brief account of the convention, see *International Socialist Review*
    8, no. 2 (June 1908): 782–3.
20 *Western Clarion*, 19 June 1909, 3.
21 Ibid., 17 Oct. 1908, 3; 25 Sept. 1909, 1; and 18 Nov. 1911, 1.
    For a further account of the tensions between the Socialist Party
    and the WCTU, see letter by L. Thorpe, *Western Clarion*, Aug.
    1915, 12.
22 *Western Clarion*, 2 Dec. 1911, 1.
23 Ibid., 22 April 1911, 2.
24 Ibid., 20 Dec. 1913, 4.
25 Bertha Merrill Burns, letter to Mrs Ramsay MacDonald,
    29 April 1907, Ramsay MacDonald Collection, National
    Archives of Canada. See also *Western Socialist*, 15 Nov. 1902, 4;
    22 Nov. 1902, 4; 29 Nov. 1902, 3; and 17 Jan. 1903, 4; *Cotton's Weekly*, 11 March 1909, 7; "Should Women Work,"
    15 April 1909, 7; and "The Value of the Franchise," 22 April
    1909, 7; *Western Clarion*, 1 Feb. 1908, 3; *Champion*, 12 Nov.
    1912, 12; 13 Jan. 1913, 3; and 13 Feb. 1915; Clipping File,
    Women's Suffrage, Public Archives of British Columbia; and
    McLaren, *Bedroom and the State*, 73–5.
26 *Western Clarion*, 10 Feb. 1906, 1.

27 Ibid., 7 July 1906, 4.
28 Ibid., 27 Jan. 1906, 1; 10 Feb. 1906, 1; 12 May 1906, 4; 30 June 1906, 4; 7 July 1906, 4. The government refused to debate the 1909 bill, which thus went down to defeat. See *Western Clarion*, 13 Feb. 1909, 4; 20 Feb. 1909, 1; 20 March 1909, 4; and 13 Nov. 1909, 1.
29 Ibid., 26 Sept. 1908, 1; 3 Feb. 1906, 4; and 22 Nov. 1913, 2.
30 Ibid., 21 Sept. 1912, 2; 27 Sept. 1913, 1, 4; 4 July 1914, 1; 1 Aug. 1914, 1; Aug 1915, 12; Dec. 1915, 4; May 1916, 8; June 1917, 12; and Jan. 1918, 4.
31 Robin, *Radical Politics*, 104–18; Penner, *Canadian Left*, 46–55; McCormack, *Reformers, Rebels and Revolutionaries*, 74–6.
32 *B.C. Federationist*, 20 May 1912, 3.
33 *Western Clarion*, 26 Sept. 1908, 1, 4.
34 Ibid., 24 April 1909, 3.
35 Ibid., 3 April 1909, 3; *Cotton's Weekly*, 29 Dec. 1910, 3, and 6 March, 1913, 1.
36 *Cotton's Weekly*, 3 April 1913, 3, and 4 May 1911, 1, 7–8.
37 *Western Clarion*, 22 Jan. 1910, 1. N. Fillmore's biography, *Maritime Radical*, does not do justice to the full scope of Roscoe's hostility to women's issues.
38 *Cotton's Weekly*, 9 Jan. 1913, 4.
39 Ibid., 24 Nov. 1910, 4; 11 Feb. 1909, 7; and 24 Dec. 1908, 1.
40 Ibid., 9 Jan. 1913, 2.
41 Ibid., 12 Jan. 1911, 1.
42 For a discussion of a woman's legal status in Canada, see Backhouse, *Petticoats and Prejudice*; MacGill, *Daughters, Wives and Mothers, Supplement*, and *Laws for Women and Children in British Columbia*; and National Council of Women, *Women of Canada*, ch. 3.
43 *Observer*, 19 Nov. 1908, 1; *Cotton's Weekly*, 4 May 1911, 2; 21 Sept. 1911, 4; 24 Dec. 1908, 1; 26 June 1913, 3; 29 Jan. 1909, 6; and 15 Jan. 1914, 1.
44 *Cotton's Weekly*, 3 Dec. 1908, 4; 30 Sept. 1909, 7; 10 July 1913, 3; and 16 April 1914, 1. Interview with Mary Ford, Jan. 1983. Mrs Miles Beech, letter to author, Aug. 30, 1983.
45 Hale, "British Columbia Woman Suffrage Movement," 59; Naylor, *The New Democracy*, 139; Forbes, "Battles in Another War" and "Ideas of Carol Bacchi"; Clarke, "The St John Women's Enfranchisement Association," 108.
46 *Cotton's Weekly*, 18 Feb. 1909, 7.
47 Meta L. Stern, "Votes for Working Women," *Cotton's Weekly*, 2 July 1914, 2; and 27 March 1913, 2.

48 "Women and the Vote," *Eastern Labour News*, 25 Sept. 1909, 3; and Winnie E. Bransetter, "Woman's Fight for Equality Is World-wide," *B.C. Federationist*, 19 Oct. 1912, 4.

49 See *Cotton's Weekly* as follows: 9 Jan. 1913, 2; 18 Feb. 1909, 7; 27 March 1913, 2; Dora F. Kerr, "The Value of the Franchise," 22 April 1909, 7; E.M. Epplett, "Sit Up and Take Notice," 8 April 1909, 7; and 18 March 1909, 7.

50 *Cotton's Weekly*, 25 Feb. 1909, 7.

51 "Gow Ganda Camps," *Cotton's Weekly*, 23 Sept. 1909, 7.

52 "Our Legislators," ibid., 30 Sept. 1909, 7.

53 "The Suffragists," ibid., 22 July 1909, 1.

54 *Canadian Forward*, 24 June 1918, 6. See also the column "Of Interest to Women," edited by Margaret Allen, in: *Cotton's Weekly*, 28 Sept. 1911, 4; 7 Sept. 1911, 2; and 14 Sept. 1911, 4.

55 *Cotton's Weekly*, 20 May 1909, 7.

56 For rejoinders to the antisuffragist arguments, see *Cotton's Weekly*, 14 Jan. 1909, 6; 4 Feb. 1909, 4; 25 March 1909, 7; 22 April 1909, 7; 6 May 1909, 5; 17 June 1909, 1; 5 Aug. 1909, 7; 10 April 1913, 4; and 12 Feb. 1914, 1.

57 By mid-1914, Jack Place had left the socialist ranks and joined the Liberals (*B.C. Federationist*, 7 March 1913, 3–4). See also *Champion*, Feb. 1914, 2; *Cotton's Weekly*, 13 Feb. 1913, 2; 12 June 1913, 2; and 20 March 1913, 4; and B.C. Legislative Assembly, Sessional Clipping Books, section 1, 1890–1920.

58 Dorothy Davis to premier of British Columbia, 13 Feb. 1913, McBride Papers, file 97, as cited in Hale, "British Columbia Woman Suffrage Movement," 79.

59 *Cotton's Weekly*, 5 Feb. 1914, 3; 14 Nov. 1912, 3; 13 Feb. 1913, 2; and 3 April 1913, 3.

60 Ibid., 3 April 1913, 3.

61 Ibid., 13 Feb. 1913, 3.

62 Ibid., 31 Aug. 1911, 4, and 13 Feb. 1913, 2. Unmarried propertied women had the municipal and school franchise in Montreal at this time (Cleverdon, *Woman Suffrage Movement*, 218–20).

CHAPTER EIGHT

1 Developments in the Canadian left during the war years are discussed in the following sources: Penner, *The Canadian Left*, 56–76; Angus, *Canadian Bolsheviks*, 1–48; McCormack, *Reformers, Rebels and Revolutionaries*, 117–64; Avery, *Dangerous Foreigners*, 65–89; Read, ed., *The Great War*; John Thompson, "The Beginnings of Our Regeneration"; Socknat, *Witness against War*;

G. Kealey, "The State, the Foreign-Language Press and the Canadian Labour Revolt."

2 *Western Clarion*, 15 Aug., 1915, 1.

3 See order-in-council, 27 Sept. 1918. For a discussion of censorship and state repression of radicals during the war, see Drystek, "Deportation from Canada before World War II"; B. Roberts, "Shovelling out the 'Mutinous'" and "Doctors and Deports."

4 Angus, *Canadian Bolsheviks*, 14–30; Laine, "Finnish Canadian Radicalism"; Pilla, "Finnish-Canadian Radicalism"; Swyripa and Thompson, *Loyalties in Conflict*.

5 Interview with William Pritchard, David Millar Papers, vol. 2, National Archives of Canada.

6 *Western Clarion*, 10 April 1915, 16.

7 For SPC opposition to suffragists, see *Western Clarion* as follows: W.W. Lefeaux, "Socialism, Feminism and War," June 1915, 9; Budden, "Our Bookshelf," May 1916, 8–9; 1 Aug. 1914, 1; Aug. 1915, 12; and Dec. 1915, 9. In "Nellie McClung and Peace," Warne argues that although McClung came to support the war effort, "she did so late and reluctantly"(36). See also B. Roberts, "Women against War" and "Why Do Women Do Nothing?"; and Socknat, "For Peace and Freedom."

8 For a discussion of the activities of women's groups and the war years, see Geller, "Wartimes Elections Act"; Strong-Boag, "Ever a Crusader"; R. Pierson, *Women and Peace* and "Ellen Key"; Marshall, Ogden and Florence, *Militarism versus Feminism*; J. Thompson, "The Beginnings of Our Regeneration"; Tennyson, "Premier Hearst"; Cook, "Francis Marion Beynon"; Ramkhalawansingh, "Women during the Great War"; Costin, "Feminism, Pacifism, Internationalism"; Hale, "British Columbia Woman Suffrage Movement," 85–6; B. Roberts, "Women against War" and "Why Do Women Do Nothing?"

9 C.M. Christiansen, "The Suffragettes," *Western Clarion*, June 1917, 13.

10 W.A.P., "The Election," *Western Clarion*, Jan. 1918, 4.

11 Interview with William Pritchard, David Millar Papers, National Archives of Canada.

12 Wade argues that the fear of women taking men's jobs led the labour movement in British Columbia to withdraw its support of suffrage ("Helena Gutteridge," 193–5). Hale contends that the suffragists' support of the Liberal Party accounted for the withdrawal of labour's support for suffrage ("Woman Suffrage Movement in British Columbia," 114). Doubtless both facts contributed to labour and SPC indifference, if not outright hostility, to suffrage in

British Columbia. Similar hostility to women taking men's jobs is discussed in Naylor, *The New Democracy*, ch. 5. See also Frager, "Deluded Assumptions."

13 Manifesto of the SPC, *Western Clarion*, Feb. 1916, 1.

14 W.B. "What of the Women?" *Western Clarion*, March 1916, 6.

15 J. Harrington, "Woman's Rights," *Western Clarion*, March 1917, 8–9.

16 P. Campbell stresses the shift to industrial unionism but ignores the party's view on working women ("Making Socialists").

17 For a discussion of these developments, see Davin, "Imperialism and Motherhood."

18 W.A.P., "Tommy's Love Fruit," *Western Clarion*, July 1915, 6–7.

19 *Western Clarion*, 18 Aug. 1914, 1.

20 W.A. Pritchard, "Woman and Motherhood," *Western Clarion*, May 1918, 8–9.

21 Sonya Levien, "Girls for Sacrifice," *Western Clarion*, Aug. 1915, 8–9.

22 *Western Clarion*, Sept. 1915, 4.

23 Moses Baritz, "Oppose Malthus," *Western Clarion*, Dec. 1916, 2–3.

24 Pritchard, "After the War Problems: The Remedy," *Western Clarion*, Sept. 1918, 4–5; "The Nightmare of Universal Syphillis [*sic*]," ibid., June 1918, 8; and "The Backwash of War," ibid., Jan. 1918, 8–11.

25 *Cotton's Weekly*, 6 Nov. 1913, 3.

26 *Canadian Forward*, 28 Oct. 1916, 2; Nov. 1916, 4; 10 Sept. 1917, 8; and 24 Aug. 1917, 8.

27 *Industrial Banner*, 28 Aug. 1914.

28 Angus, *Canadian Bolsheviks*, 9–16.

29 *Cotton's Weekly*, 17 April 1913, 3; 15 Oct. 1914, 3; and "Secretarial Notes," 12 Nov. 1914, 3. See also the following in *Canadian Forward*: "The Twin Stamp," 18 Oct. 1916, 8; 11 Nov. 1916, 8; "Big Undertaking by Toronto Women's Social Democratic League," 2 Dec. 1916, 6; "New Idea Bazaar was a Great Success," 27 Dec. 1916, 3; 10 April 1917, 8; 24 Sept. 1917, 8; 10 Oct. 1917, 8; and 24 Dec. 1917, 1.

30 Rev. W.E.S. James, "Socialist Women Needed," *Cotton's Weekly*, 15 Oct. 1914, 2.

31 *Canadian Forward*, 13 Jan 1917, 3; 2 April 1917, 2; 24 May 1917, 2, 6; 25 June 1917, 8; 10 Aug. 1917, 3; 10 Jan. 1918, 3; and 10 June 1918, 7. In "Women against War" and "Why Do Women Do Nothing," B. Roberts discusses the role of several socialist women in the pacifist movement.

32 John Bruce Papers, Manuscript Collection, National Archives of Canada; see also interview with John Walter, Paul Fox Collection, ibid.

33 *Canadian Forward*, 24 April 1917, 1; 3 June 1917; 12 June 1917, 4; 10 Aug. 1917, 8; 24 Aug. 1917, 8; and 24 Aug. 1918, 7; *Western Clarion*, 15 Nov. 1918, 7; *Manitoba Free Press*, 3 Oct. 1918; *Winnipeg Tribune*, 3 Oct. 1918; *Western Labour News*, 18 Oct. 1918, 7.

34 "Martyrdom in Canada," *Canadian Forward*, 25 Jan. 1918, 2.

35 *Western Clarion*, Oct. 1916, 3.

36 *Canadian Forward*, 24 Sept. 1918, 5; 24 July, 1918, 7; 24 April 1918, 5; and 10 March 1918, 5. The left-wing papers typically conflated the term suffrage with feminism.

37 *Canadian Forward*, 12 Nov. 1914, 4; 10 Aug. 1916, 3; 28 Oct. 1916, 2; 24 Feb. 1917, 7; 24 March 1917, 7; 10 April 1917, 3, 8; 10 May 1917, 4; 10 Aug. 1917, 5; 10 April 1918, 3; and 24 June 1918, 6.

38 *Cotton's Weekly*, 29 Oct. 1914, 4, and 12 Nov. 1914, 4.

39 *Canadian Forward*, 27 Dec. 1916, 6.

40 G. Stafford Whitby, "Capitalist Militalist," *Canadian Forward*, 24 Oct. 1917, 1; "Prostitution and War," ibid. 10 Oct. 1917, 3; ibid. 10 March 1917, 6.

41 "Economic Basis of Prostitution," *Canadian Forward*, 13 Jan. 1917, 7.

42 B. Roberts argues that "her appeal to women was based on a maternalist perspective: it was as mothers that she spoke to them. But her view of the causes of the present anguish was based on a socialist and feminist perspective" ("Why Do Women Do Nothing?" 22). The "but" seems to suggest that her maternalism was not feminist; I argue that it was.

43 The main source of biographical information on Richardson is a biography, "Her Life and Labor," published in *Canadian Forward*, 10 Sept. 1917, 6, and 10 April 1918, 5; and her Women's Peace Crusade columns in the *Canadian Forward*.

44 "Motherhood and War," *Canadian Forward*, 24 Nov. 1917, 5.

45 "Unto This Last the Mother Cry Is Supreme," *Canadian Forward*, 24 Aug. 1917, 1–2.

46 Richardson, "Militant Women," *Canadian Forward*, 24 Oct. 1917, 3.

47 McIlvina K. Hall, "Woman's Relation to War," *Cotton's Weekly*, 15 Oct. 1914, 1.

48 For a discussion of maternal mortality, see Buckley, "Ladies or Midwives?"; Leavitt, "Under the Shadow of Maternity"; and McLaren and McLaren, *Bedroom and the State*.

49 See *Canadian Forward* as follows: 10 April 1917, 5; "German Women Issue Manifesto," 24 July 1917, 3; Gertrude Richardson, "What Others Are Thinking," 10 July 1917, 3; Grace Isabel Col-

bron, "Militarism the Foe of Women's Progress," 10 July 1917, 6; 24 Oct. 1917, 7; 10 June 1918, 7; "To Women: Your Country Needs You: Preserve Your Children's Freedom," 13 Jan. 1917, 5–6; 10 March 1917, 7; 2 April 1917, 8; Adela Pankhurst, "The Women's Revolution," 24 Oct. 1917, 7.

50 Socknat, "For Peace and Freedom," 68–9; B. Roberts, "Why Do Women Do Nothing?"

51 Richardson, "Unto This Last," *Canadian Forward*, 24 Aug. 1917, 1–2. This version appears to be in error, since it does not correspond with the later version published in the *Canadian Forward*, nor does it correspond with a copy of a leaflet published by the crusade. See Gertrude Richardson, "The Women's Crusade." It is nonetheless worthwhile noting that this version calls for "equality" while the other versions call for "purity."

52 *Canadian Forward*, 24 June 1918, 1.

53 See the following articles in *Canadian Forward*: "To the Women Crusaders," 24 Oct. 1917, 1; "What Others Are Thinking," 10 July 1917, 3; "An Appeal to Women," 25 Jan. 1918, 4; "To Women," 10 June 1918, 7; "Woman's Column," 10 April 1918, 5; "The Hand of Militarism," 10 March 1918, 3. See also letters by Richardson and Frances Marion Beynon in *Western Labour News*, 9 Aug. 1918, 8, and 20 Sept. 1918, 8.

54 Bliss discusses how the Methodist Church's support of the war reflected pressures inherent in its own theology and its general sympathy for government regulation and exercise of state power ("The Methodist Church and World War I").

55 See the following articles in *Canadian Forward*: Gertrude Richardson, "To the Women Crusaders," 24 Oct. 1917, 3; letter from Mrs R. C. Maxwell, 24 Nov. 1917, 2; Harriet Dunlop Prentor, "The Kingdom of Self Respect," 10 Aug. 1918, 6; Gertrude Richardson, "The Justice of Jesus," 24 Aug. 1917, 2; Gertrude Richardson, "Within the Shadow," 10 July 1918, 4.

56 For accounts of Buhay's activities and speeches in the SDPC press, see *Canadian Forward* as follows: 27 Dec. 1916, 3; "The Tragedy of War," 10 April 1917, 3; 24 May 1917, 6; 10 June 1917, 3; 25 June 1917, 3, 8; 10 Aug. 1917, 8; 24 Aug. 1917, 8; 10 Sept. 1917, 8; "Labour Party," 10 Nov. 1917, 8.

57 Laura Hughes, central organizer for the Women's International League for Peace and Freedom, may be exceptional. She claimed that the war was kept alive by the drive for profits, but there is no record of her using maternalist rhetoric in the socialist press (see *Canadian Forward*, 12 June 1917, 6). Unfortunately, neither Socknat, in "For Peace or Freedom," nor B. Roberts in "Why Do

Women Do Nothing?" addresses this absence, which is striking in contrast to the other articles published by maternal pacifists.

58   In "Ellen Key," Pierson argues convincingly that maternalism provided an unsound basis for Ellen Key's pacifism. Socknat, in "For Peace or Freedom," contends that many of the feminist pacifists who opposed the war were socialists.

59   William Cotton, "Biographical Memo," June 26, 1942, 2, in author's private collection.

60   Letter from Mary Cotton Wisdom to William Cotton, 27 Feb. 1922, in author's private collection.

61   Ibid.

62   Letter from Mary Cotton Wisdom to William Cotton, n.d., in author's private collection.

63   She was also a devout Anglican, a philanthropist, and a supporter of the Salvation Army. In later years, Wisdom developed an interest in her family history and wrote a biography of Rev. Charles Cotton. Surviving her husband and two children, she died at the age of 84 in 1961.

64   References to her in Canadian sources indicate that she spoke in Canada and that her activities and writing were known in Canada. See *Western Socialist*, 20 Sept., 1902, 3; *Western Clarion*, 1 July 1905, 4; 30 Sept. 1905, 1; 10 Aug. 1907, 4; 28 Sept. 1907, 1; and 5 Oct. 1907, 2; see also, in *Cotton's Weekly*, "The Homeless," 10 Feb. 1910, 2, and "The Working Girl," 3 March 1910, 2; and in *Canadian Forward*, "The Real Sex Revolt," 24 Sept. 1917, 7.

65   Hazlett, "The Real Sex Revolt," ibid.

66   R. Pierson, "Ellen Key."

CHAPTER NINE

1   Strong-Boag, "Ever a Crusader," 188, and "Canadian Feminism in the 1920's." Strong-Boag may have overstated the case, for organized feminism did survive in the women's peace movement. See Socknat, "For Peace and Freedom."

2   Sangster, *Dreams of Equality.*

3   Naylor, *The New Democracy.*

4   Strong-Boag, "Girl of the New Day."

Bibliography

PRIMARY SOURCES

Manuscripts

AUTHOR'S PRIVATE COLLECTION
Correspondence of Harriet Beech
Correspondence of Mary Cotton Wisdom
Interview Transcript, Mary Ford, 1983
Manuscript of William Cotton

DALHOUSIE UNIVERSITY ARCHIVES
Autobiography of Roscoe Fillmore

METROPOLITAN TORONTO LIBRARY
James Simpson Papers

NATIONAL ARCHIVES OF CANADA
John Bruce Papers
Federal Records, RCMP Papers
W.C. Good Papers
Department of Justice Records
Kovalevitch Papers
Ramsay MacDonald Papers
David Millar Papers
Secretary of State, Chief Press Censor
Phillips Thompson Papers
Woodsworth Collection
A.W. Wright Papers

PUBLIC ARCHIVES OF BRITISH COLUMBIA
Women's Labour History Project
Women's Suffrage Clipping File

UNIVERSITY OF BRITISH COLUMBIA ARCHIVES
O. Lee Charlton Family Papers
Angus MacInnis Collection
Dorothy Gretchen Steeves Papers
E.E. Winch Papers

VANCOUVER CITY ARCHIVES
Helena Gutteridge, Clipping File

Newspapers

B.C. Federationist, Vancouver, British Columbia
Butler's Journal, Fredericton, New Brunswick
Canadian Forward, Toronto, Ontario
Canadian Socialist, Vancouver, British Columbia
Champion, Victoria, British Columbia
Citizen and Country, Toronto, Ontario
Cotton's Weekly, Cowansville, Quebec
Eastern Labour News, Moncton, New Brunswick
Ferguson Eagle, Ferguson, British Columbia
Globe, Toronto, Ontario
Hamilton Times, Hamilton, Ontario
Independent, Vancouver, British Columbia
International Socialist Review, Chicago, Illinois
Lance, Toronto, Ontario
Lardeau Eagle, Lardeau, British Columbia
Lucifer, Chicago, Illinois
Manitoba Free Press, Winnipeg, Manitoba
Vancouver World, Vancouver, British Columbia
Western Clarion, Vancouver, British Columbia
Western Labour News, Winnipeg, Manitoba
Western Socialist, Vancouver, British Columbia
Winnipeg Tribune, Winnipeg, Manitoba
Winnipeg Voice, Winnipeg, Manitoba

SECONDARY SOURCES

Abbott, John. "Accomplishing 'a Man's Task': Rural Women Teachers, Male Culture and the School Inspectorate in Turn-of-the-Century Ontario." *Ontario History* 78 (Dec. 1986): 313–30.

Acton, Janice, et al. *Women at Work: Ontario, 1850–1930.* Toronto: Canadian Women's Educational Press, 1974.

Adams, Audrey. "A Study of the Use of Plebiscites and Referendums by the Province of British Columbia." Master's thesis, University of British Columbia, 1958.

Adilman, Tamara. "A Preliminary Sketch of Chinese Women and Work in British Columbia, 1858–1950." In *Not Just Pin Money*, ed. Barbara Latham and Roberta Pazdro, 53–78. Victoria, B.C.: Camosun College, 1984.

Ahlquist, J. B. "The Socialist Movement in Canada before the War." *Worker*, 27 February 1926.

Akers, David. "Rebel or Revolutionary? Jack Kavanagh and the Early Years of the Communist Movement in Vancouver, 1920–1925." *Labour/ Le Travail* 30 (Fall 1992): 9–44.

Allen, Richard. *The Social Passion: Religion and Social Reform in Canada, 1914–1928.* Toronto: University of Toronto Press, 1971.

Angus, Ian. *Canadian Bolsheviks: The Early Years of the Communist Party of Canada.* Montreal: Vanguard Publications, 1981.

Arendt, Sylvie D'Augerot. "Why So Late? Cultural and Institutional Factors in the Granting of Quebec and French Women's Political Rights." *Journal of Canadian Studies* 26 (Spring 1991): 138–65.

Arnup, Katherine. "Educating Mothers: Government Advice for Women in the Inter-War Years." In *Delivering Motherhood*, ed. Katherine Arnup, Andrée Lévesque, and Ruth Pierson, 190–201. London: Routledge, 1990.

– "Education for Motherhood: Government Health Publications, Mothers and the State." Paper presented to the CSAA meetings, Winnipeg, Man., 6 June 1986.

– Arnup, Katherine, Andrée Lévesque and Ruth Roach Pierson, eds. *Delivering Motherhood: Maternal Ideologies and Practices in the 19th and 20th Centuries.* London: Routledge, 1990.

Avakumovic, Ivan. *The Communist Party of Canada: A History.* Toronto: McClelland and Stewart, 1975.

Avery, Donald. *'Dangerous Foreigners': European Immigrant Workers and Labour Radicalism in Canada, 1896–1932.* Toronto: McClelland and Stewart, 1979.

Bacchi, Carol Lee. "Divided Allegiances: The Response of Farm and Labour Women to Suffrage." In *A Not Unreasonable Claim*, ed. Linda Kealey, 89–107. Toronto: Women's Press, 1979.

– "'First Wave' Feminism in Canada: The Ideas of the English-Canadian Suffragists, 1877–1918." *Women's Studies International Journal* 5, no. 6 (1982): 575–83.

– "Liberation Deferred: The Ideas of the English Canadian Suffragists, 1877–1918." Ph.D. diss., McGill University, 1976.

- "Liberation Deferred: The Ideas of the English Canadian Suffragists, 1877–1918." *Histoire Sociale/Social History* 20 (November 1977): 433–4.
- *Liberation Deferred? The Ideas of the English Canadian Suffragists, 1877–1918.* Toronto: University of Toronto Press, 1983.
- "Race Regeneration and Social Purity: A Study of the Social Attitude of Canada's English Speaking Suffragists." *Histoire Sociale/Social History* 22 (November 1978): 460–73.

Backhouse, Constance. "Desperate Women and Compassionate Courts: Infanticide in Nineteenth Century Canada." *University of Toronto Law Journal* 34 (1984): 447–78.
- "Nineteenth-Century Canadian Prostitution Law: Reflection of a Discriminatory Society." *Histoire Sociale/Social History* 18 (November 1985): 387–423.
- *Petticoats and Prejudice: Women and Law in Nineteenth Century Canada.* Toronto: Women's Press for Osgoode Society, 1991.

Baines, Carol. *Women's Reform Organizations in Canada, 1870–1930.* Toronto: Faculty of Social Work, University of Toronto, 1988.

Barber, Marilyn. "Help for Farm Homes: The Campaign to End Housework Drudgery in Rural Saskatchewan in the 1920's." In *Science, Technology and Medicine from Canada's Past: Selections from Scientia Canadensis*, ed. Richard Jarrell and James Hull. Thornhill: Scientia Press, 1991.
- "In Search of a Better Life: A Scottish Domestic in Rural Ontario." *Polyphony* 8 (1986): 13–16.
- "The Servant Problem in Manitoba, 1896–1930." In *First Days, Fighting Days*, ed. Mary Kinnear, 100–19. Regina: Canadian Plains Research Centre, 1987.
- "Sunny Ontario for British Girls, 1900–1930." In *Looking into My Sister's Eyes*, ed. Jean Burnet, 55–73. Toronto: Multicultural History Society, 1986.
- "The Women Ontario Welcomed: Immigrant Domestics for Ontario Homes, 1870–1930." In *Neglected Majority*, vol. 2, ed. Alison Prentice and Susan Trofimenkoff, 102–21. Toronto: McClelland and Stewart, 1985.

Barman, Jean. *The West beyond the West.* Toronto: University of Toronto Press, 1991.

Barrett, Michele. *Women's Oppression Today: Some Problems in Marxist Feminist Analysis.* London: Verso, 1980.

Barrett, Michele, and Mary McIntosh. "The 'Family Wage': Some Problems for Socialists and Feminists." *Capital and Class* 11 (Summer 1980): 51–72.

Basen, Neil K. "Kate Richards O'Hare: First Lady of American Socialism, 1901–1917." *Labour History* 21 (Spring 1980): 165–99.

- "Radical Women in Grass-Roots America: Kate Richards O'Hare and the 'Jennie Higginses' of the Socialist Party of America, 1901–1917." Paper presented to the Organization of American Historians, St Louis, Mo., 10 April 1976.

Bator, Paul Adolphus. "The Struggle to Raise the Lower Classes: Public Health Reform and the Problem of Poverty in Toronto, 1910 to 1921." *Journal of Canadian Studies* 14 (Spring 1979): 43–9.

Bebel, August. *Women under Socialism.* New York, 1904.

Bell, Ernest A. *Fighting the Traffic in Young Girls, or the War on the White Slave Trade.* G.S. Ball, 1910.

Bellamy, Edward. *Looking Backward, 2000–1887.* Boston: Houghton Mifflin, 1917.

Bennett, Yvonne A. "Vera Brittain: Feminism, Pacifism and the Problem of Class, 1900–1953." *Atlantis* 12 (Spring 1987): 18–23.

Benoit, Cecilia. "Mothering in a Newfoundland Community, 1900–1940." In *Delivering Motherhood*, ed. Katherine Arnup, Andrée Lévesque, and Ruth Pierson, 173–89. London: Routledge, 1990.

Bercuson, David J. *Fools and Wise Men: The Rise and Fall of the One Big Union.* Toronto: McGraw-Hill Ryerson, 1978.

Berger, Carl, and Ramsay Cook, eds. *The West and the Nation.* Toronto: McClelland and Stewart, 1976.

Bick, A. "Socialism and the Woman Question." *New Age*, 17 Dec. 1908, 162–3.

Biggs, Lesley C. "The Case of the Missing Midwives: A History of Midwifery in Ontario from 1795–1900." In *Delivering Motherhood*, ed. Katherine Arnup, Andrée Lévesque, and Ruth Pierson, 20–35. London: Routledge, 1990.

Bishop, Mary F. "The Early Birth Controllers of B.C." *B.C. Studies* 61 (Spring 1984): 64–84.

- "Vivian Dowding: Birth Control Activist, 1892–." In *Not Just Pin Money*, ed. Barbara Latham and Roberta Pazdro, 327–35. Victoria, B.C.: Camosun College, 1984.

Bliss, Michael. "The Methodist Church and World War One." *Canadian Historical Review* 49 (September 1968): 213–33.

- "Neglected Radicals: A Sober Second Look." *Canadian Forum*, April-May 1970, 16–17.

- "Pure Books on Avoided Subjects: Pre-Freudian Sexual Ideas in Canada." Canadian Historical Association, *Papers*, 1970, 89–108.

Bohachevsky-Chomoak, Martha. "Feminism in Ukrainian History." *Journal of Ukrainian History* 7 (Spring 1982): 16–30.

Bourne, Paula, ed. *Women's Paid and Unpaid Work: Historical and Contemporary Perspectives.* Toronto: New Hogtown Press, 1985.

Boxer, Marilyn. "'First Wave' Feminism in Nineteenth Century France: Class, Family, and Religion." *Women's Studies International Forum* 5, no. 6 (1982): 551–9.

Boxer, Marilyn, and Jean H. Quataert. *Socialist Women: European Socialist Feminism in the Nineteenth and Early Twentieth Centuries.* New York: Elsevier, 1978.

Bradbury, Bettina. "Pigs, Cows and Boarders: Non-Wage Forms of Survival among Montreal Families." *Labour/Le Travail* 14 (Fall 1984): 9–48.

– "Women's History and Working Class History." *Labour/Le Travail* 19 (Spring 1987): 23–43.

Bradwin, Edwin. *The Bunkhouse Man: A Study of the Work and Pay in the Camps of Canada, 1903–1914.* New York: Columbia University Press, 1928.

Brandt, Gail Cuthbert. "Organizations in Canada: The English Protestant Tradition." In *Women's Paid and Unpaid Work*, ed. Paula Bourne, 79–95. Toronto: New Hogtown Press, 1985.

– "Postmodern Patchwork: Some Recent Trends in the Writing of Women's History." *Canadian Historical Review* 72 (1991): 441–70.

– "Weaving It Together: Life Cycle and the Industrial Experience of Female Cotton Workers in Quebec, 1910–1950." *Labour/Le Travailleur* 7 (Spring 1981): 113–26.

Braude, Anna. *Radical Spirits: Spiritualism and Women's Rights in Nineteenth Century America.* Boston: Beacon Press, 1989.

Bridenthal, Renate, and Claudia Koonz, eds. *Becoming Visible: Women in European History.* Boston: Houghton Mifflin, 1977.

Brigden, Beatrice. "One Woman's Campaign for Social Purity and Social Reform." In *The Social Gospel in Canada*, ed. Richard Allen, 36–62. Ottawa: National Museums of Canada, 1975.

"British Columbia." *International Socialist Review* 4 (October 1903): 249.

Brouwer, Ruth. "Transcending the 'Unacknowledged Quarantine': Putting Religion into English-Canadian Women's History." *Journal of Canadian Studies* 27 (Fall 1992): 47–61.

Brown, R.C., and Ramsay Cook. *Canada: A Nation Transformed: 1896–1920.* Toronto: McClelland and Stewart, 1976.

Buck, Tim. *Canada and the Russian Revolution.* Toronto: Progress Books, 1967.

Buckley, Suzann. "Ladies or Midwives?: Efforts to Reduce Infant and Maternal Mortality." In *A Not Unreasonable Claim*, ed. Linda Kealey, 131–50. Toronto: Women's Press, 1979.

– "The Search for the Decline of Maternal Mortality: The Place of Hospital Records." In *Essays in the History of Canadian Medicine*, ed. Wendy Mitchinson and Janice Dickin McGinnis, 148–67. Toronto: McClelland and Stewart, 1988.

Buckley, Suzann, and Janice Dickin McGinnis. "Venereal Disease and Public Health Reform in Canada." *Canadian Historical Review* 63 (September 1982): 337–54.

Buhle, Mari Jo. "Gender and Labour History." In *Perspectives on American Labour History: The Problems of Synthesis*, ed. J. Carroll Moody and Alice Kessler-Harris, 55–79. DeKalb: Northern Illinois Press, 1989.

– "Politics and Culture." *Feminist Studies* 6 (Spring 1980): 37–42.

– "*Socialist Woman, Progressive Woman* and *Coming Nation*." In *The American Radical Press, 1880–1960*, ed. Joseph R. Conlin, 2:442–9. Westport, Conn.: Greenwood Press, 1974.

– *Women and American Socialism, 1870–1920*. Chicago: University of Illinois Press, 1981.

– *Women and the Socialist Party, 1901–1914*. Massachusetts: New England Free Press, n.d.

Bullen, John. "Hidden Workers: Child Labour and the Family Economy in Late Nineteenth-Century Urban Ontario." *Labour/Le Travail* 18 (Spring 1986): 163–87.

Burnet, Jean, ed. *Looking into My Sister's Eyes: An Exploration in Women's History*. Toronto: Multicultural History Society, 1986.

Cahan, J.F. "A Survey of the Political Attitudes of the Ontario Labour Movement, 1850–1935." Master's thesis, University of Toronto, 1945.

Caine, Barbara. "Feminism, Suffrage and the Nineteenth-Century English Woman's Movement." *Women's Studies International Forum* 5, no. 6 (1982): 537–50.

Campbell, Marie. "Sexism in British Columbia Trade Unions, 1900–1920." In *In Her Own Right*, ed. Barbara Latham and Cathy Kess, 167–86. Victoria, B.C.: Camosun College, 1980.

Campbell, Peter. "'Making Socialists': Bill Pritchard, the Socialist Party and the Third International." *Labour/Le Travail* 30 (Fall 1992): 45–63.

Canada. Department of Labour. *Women at Work in Canada: A Fact Book on the Female Labour Force*. Ottawa: Department of Labour, 1965.

– Royal Commission on the Status of Women. *Cultural Tradition and Political History of Women in Canada*, no. 8. Ottawa: Information Canada, 1971.

Caplan, Jane, et al. "Patrolling the Borders: Feminist Historiography and the New Historicism." *Radical History Review* 43 (1989): 23–43.

Caroli, Betty Boyd, Robert Harney, and Lydio F. Thomasi, eds. *The Italian Immigrant Woman in North America*. Toronto: Multicultural History Society of Ontario, 1978.

Carroll, Berenice A., ed. *Liberating Women's History: Theoretical and Critical Essays*. Urbana, Ill.: University of Chicago Press, 1976.

Chambers, Edward. "New Evidence on the Living Standards of Toronto Blue Collar Workers in the Pre-1914 Era." *Histoire Sociale/Social History* 18 (November 1985): 285–314.

Chapman, Terry L. "The Early Eugenics Movement in Western Canada." *Alberta History* 25 (Autumn 1977): 9–17.

Chisick, Ernie. "The Development of Winnipeg's Socialist Movement, 1900–1915." Master's thesis, University of Manitoba, 1972.

– "The Early Marxist Socialist Movement in Manitoba, 1901–1926." Honours essay, history, University of Winnipeg, 1968.

Chown, Alice. *The Stairway.* Boston: Cornhill, 1921.

Clarke, Mary Eileen. "The St John Women's Enfranchisement Association, 1894–1919." M.A. thesis, Department of History, University of New Brunswick, 1979.

Cleverdon, Catherine L. *The Woman Suffrage Movement in Canada*, 2d ed., with introduction by Ramsay Cook. Toronto: University of Toronto Press, 1974.

Cobble, Dorothy Sue, "Rethinking Troubled Relations between Women and Unions: Craft Unionism and Female Activism." *Feminist Studies* 16 (Fall 1990): 519–48.

Coburn, Judi. "I See and I Am Silent: A Short History of Nursing in Ontario." In *Women at Work in Ontario, 1850–1930*, ed. Janice Acton et al., 127–64. Toronto: Women's Press, 1974.

Cohen, Marjorie Griffin. "The Decline of Women in Canadian Dairying." In *The Neglected Majority*, vol. 2, ed. Alison Prentice and Susan Trofimenkoff, 61–83. Toronto: McClelland and Stewart, 1985.

– *Women's Work, Markets, and Economic Development in Nineteenth Century Ontario.* Toronto: University of Toronto Press, 1988.

Comacchio, Cynthia. "Taking Up the Gauntlet: Historical Writing and Challenges to Class Analysis." *Journal of Canadian Studies* 27 (Spring 1992): 146–56.

Communist Party of Canada. *Canada's Party of Socialism: History of the Communist Party of Canada, 1921–1976.* Toronto: Progress Books, 1982.

Connelly, Patricia. "Women Workers and the Family Wage in Canada." In *Women and the World of Work*, ed. Anne Hoiberg, 223–37. New York: Plenum Press, 1980.

Connelly, Patricia, and Martha MacDonald. "Women's Work: Domestic and Wage Labour in a Nova Scotia Community." *Studies in Political Economy* 10 (1983): 45–72.

Connor, James McArthur. "The Labour and Socialist Movement in Canada." Unpublished manuscript, Woodsworth Collection, University of Toronto, n.d.

Conrad, Margaret. "The Re-Birth of Canada's Past: A Decade of Women's History." *Acadiensis* 12 (Spring 1983): 147–63.

Cook, Ramsay. "Francis Marion Beynon and the Crisis of Christian Reformism." In *The West and the Nation*, ed. Carl Berger and Ramsay Cook, 187–208. Toronto: McClelland and Stewart, 1976.

- "Henry George and the Poverty of Canadian Progress." Canadian Historical Association, *Historical Papers* (1977): 143–56.

- *The Regenerators: Social Criticism in Late Victorian English Canada*. Toronto: University of Toronto Press, 1985.

Cook, Ramsay, and Wendy Mitchinson. *The Proper Sphere: Woman's Place in Canadian Society*. Toronto: Oxford University Press, 1976.

Cooper, Joy. "Red Lights in Winnipeg." Manitoba Historical and Scientific Society, *Transactions* 27 (1971): 61–74.

Copp, Terry. *The Anatomy of Poverty: The Condition of the Working Class in Montreal, 1897–1929*. Toronto: McClelland and Stewart, 1974.

Corrective Collective. *Never Done: Three Centuries of Women's Work in Canada*. Toronto: Canadian Women's Educational Press, 1974.

Costin, Lela B. "Feminism, Pacifism, Internationalism and the 1915 International Congress of Women." *Women's Studies International Forum* 5, no. 2 (1982): 310–15.

Cotton, Chas. S. *Side Lights on the Civil War, 1861–1865: Early Days in Nevada*. Cowansville, Que.: Cotton's Co-operative Publishing Company, 1912 (author's private collection).

Cramer, Michael H. "Public and Political: Documents of the Woman's Suffrage Campaign in British Columbia, 1871–1917: The View from Victoria." In *In Her Own Right*, ed. Barbara Latham and Cathy Kess, 79–100. Victoria, B.C.: Camosun College, 1980.

Creese, Gillian. "The Politics of Dependence: Women, Work, and Unemployment in the Vancouver Labour Movement before World War II." In *Class, Gender and Region: Essays in Canadian Historical Sociology*, ed. Gregory Kealey, 121–42. St John's, Nfld: Committee on Labour History, 1988.

Creese, Gillian, and Veronica Strong-Boag, eds. *British Columbia Reconsidered: Essays on Women*. Vancouver: Press Gang, 1992.

Cross, Michael S., and Gregory S. Kealey. *The Consolidation of Capitalism: 1896–1929*. Readings in Canadian History, vol. 4. Toronto: McClelland and Stewart, 1983.

Crowley, Terry. "Agnes Macphail and Canadian Working Women." *Labour/Le Travail* 8 (Fall 1991): 129–48.

Dahlie, Jorgen. "Socialist and Farmer: Ole Hjelt and the Norwegian Radical Voice in Canada, 1908–1928." *Canadian Ethnic Studies* 10, no. 2 (1978): 55–64.

Dahlie, Jorgen, and Tissa Fernando, eds. *Ethnicity, Power, and Politics*. Agincourt, Ont.: Methuen, 1981.

Dancis, Bruce. "Socialism and Women in the United States, 1900–1917." *Socialist Revolution* 6, no. 1 (1976): 81–144.

Danylewycz, Marta, and Alison Prentice. "Teacher's Work: Changing Patterns and Perceptions in the Emerging School Systems of Nineteenth and Early Twentieth Century Central Canada." *Labour/Le Travail* 17 (Spring 1986): 59–80.

Davies, Margery. "Woman's Place Is at the Typewriter: The Feminization of the Clerical Labour Force." *Radical America* 8 (July–August 1974): 1–28.

Davin, Anna. "Imperialism and Motherhood." *History Workshop* 5 (Spring 1978): 9–66.

Debs, Eugene. "The Socialist Party and the Working Class." In Debs, *Writings and Speeches*, 125–39. New York: Hermitage Press, 1948.

– "Woman: Comrade and Equal." In Debs, *Writings and Speeches*, 453–5. New York: Hermitage Press, 1948.

DeLeon, Daniel. *The Ballot and the Class Struggle.* 1933. Reprint, New York: Labour News Co., 1947.

Derry, Kathleen, and Paul H. Douglas. "The Minimum Wage in Canada." *Journal of Political Economy*, April 1922, 155–86.

Dixler, Elsa. "Women and Socialist Movements: A Review Essay." *Feminist Studies* 10 (Summer 1984): 315–22.

Dobie, Edith. "Party History in British Columbia, 1903–1933." *Pacific Northwest Quarterly* 28 (April 1936): 153–66.

– "Some Aspects of Party History in British Columbia: 1871–1903." *Pacific Historical Review* 1 (1932): 235–51.

Dodd, Dianne. "The Canadian Birth Control Movement: Two Approaches to the Dissemination of Contraceptive Technology." In *Science, Technology and Medicine in Canada's Past: Selections from Scientia Canadensis*, ed. Richard A. Jarrell and James P. Hull, 309–22. Thornhill, Ont.: Scientia Press, 1991.

– "The Canadian Birth Control Movement on Trial, 1936–1937." *Histoire Sociale/Social History* 16 (November 1983): 411–28.

– "Women's Involvement in the Canadian Birth Control Movement of the 1930s: The Hamilton Birth Control Clinic." In *Delivering Motherhood*, ed. Katherine Arnup, Andrée Lévesque, and Ruth Pierson, 150–72. London: Routledge, 1990.

Doman, Mahinder. "A Note on Asia Indian Women in British Columbia, 1900–1935." In *Not Just Pin Money*, ed. Barbara Latham and Roberta Pazdro, 99–104. Victoria, B.C.: Camosun College, 1984.

Drake, Emma F. Angell. *What a Young Wife Ought to Know.* Philadelphia, 1901.

Draper, Paula J., and Janice B. Karlinsky. "Abraham's Daughters: Women, Charity and Power in the Canadian Jewish Community." In *Looking into My Sister's Eyes*, ed. Jean Burnet, 75–90. Toronto: Multicultural History Society, 1986.

Drystek, Henry F. "'The Simplest and Cheapest Mode of Dealing with Them': Deportation from Canada before World War II." *Histoire Sociale/Social History* 15 (November 1982): 407–41.

Dubinsky, Karen. "Love among the Historians." *Labour/Le Travail* 30 (Fall 1992): 223–31.

Dubinsky, Karen, and Franca Iacovetta. "Murder, Womanly Virtue and Womanhood: The Case of Mrs Napolitano, 1911–1921." *Canadian Historical Review* 72 (1991): 505–31.

DuBois, Ellen. *Feminism and Suffrage: The Emergence of an Independent Woman's Movement in America, 1848–1869.* Ithica: Cornell, 1978.

– "Making Women's History: Activist Historians of Women's Rights, 1880–1940." *Radical History Review* 49 (1991): 61–84.

– ed. *Unequal Sisters: A Multicultural Reader in U.S. Women's History.* New York: Routledge, 1990.

DuBois, Ellen, and Linda Gordon. "Seeking Ecstasy on the Battlefield: Danger and Pleasure in Nineteenth Century Feminist Thought." *Feminist Studies* 9 (Spring 1983): 7–25.

DuBois, Ellen, et al. "Politics and Culture in Women's History." *Feminist Studies* 6 (Spring 1980): 26–70.

– "The Radicalism of the Woman Suffrage Movement: Notes toward the Reconstruction of Nineteenth Century Feminism." *Feminist Studies* 3 (Fall 1975): 63–71.

Dye, Nancy Schrom. "Creating a Feminist Alliance: Sisterhood and Class Conflict in the New York Women's Trade Union League, 1903–1914." *Feminist Studies* 2 (1975): 24–38.

Edgard, Milhaud. "Socialist Propaganda among Women in Germany." *International Socialist Review* 1 (May 1901): 713–18.

Eisenstein, Sarah. *Give Us Bread but Give Us Roses: Working Women's Consciousness in the United States, 1890 to the First World War.* London: Routledge and Kegan Paul, 1983.

Engel, Barbara Alpern. "The Emergence of Women Revolutionaries in Russia." *Frontiers* 2 (Spring 1977): 92–105.

Engels, Friedrich. *The Origin of the Family, Private Property and the State.* 1884. Reprint, with introduction by Evelyn Reed. New York: Pathfinder Press, 1973.

England, H. E. "Will Socialism Break Up the Family?" *International Socialist Review* 8 (January 1908): 431–2.

Fay, C. R. "Women as Wage-earners and the Significance Thereof in the Development of Economic Theory." *University of Toronto Quarterly* 2 (April 1933): 263–84.

Feaver, George. "Self-Respect and Hopefulness: The Webbs in the Canadian West." *B.C. Studies* 43 (Autumn 1979): 45–64.

– "The Webbs as Pilgrims." *Encounter* 50 (March 1978): 23–32.

– "The Webbs in Canada: Fabian Pilgrims on the Canadian Frontier." *Canadian Historical Review* 58 (September 1977): 263–76.

Ferland, Jacques. "'In Search of the Unbound Prometheia': A Comparative View of Women's Activism in Two Quebec Industries, 1869–1908." *Labour/Le Travail* 24 (Fall 1989): 11–44.

Ferns, Henry, and Bernard Ostry. *The Age of Mackenzie King*, introd. John Meisel. Toronto: James Lorimer, 1976.

Fillmore, Nicholas. *Maritime Radical: The Life and Times of Roscoe Fillmore*. Toronto: Between the Lines, 1992.

Fillmore, Roscoe. "Strikes and Socialism in Eastern Canada." *International Socialist Review* 10 (April 1910): 890–3.

– "The Strike Situation in Eastern Canada." *International Socialist Review* 10 (May 1910): 1007–9.

Fingard, Judith. *The Dark Side of Victorian Halifax*. Potters Lake, N.S.: Pottersfield Press, 1989.

Fishbein, Leslie. "The Failure of Feminism in Greenwich Village before World War I." *Women's Studies* 9 (1982): 275–89.

– "Freud and the Radicals: The Sexual Revolution Comes to Greenwich Village." *Canadian Review of American Studies* 12 (Fall 1981): 173–89.

– "Harlot or Heroine? Changing Views of Prostitution." *Historian* 43 (November 1980): 23–35.

– "Radicals and Religion Before the Great War." *Journal of Religious Thought* 37 (Fall/Winter 1980–81): 45–58.

– *Rebels in Bohemia: The Radicals of 'The Masses,' 1911–1917*. Chapel Hill: University of North Carolina Press, 1982.

Flynn, Elizabeth Gurley. "The Golden Jubilee of International Women's Day." *Political Affairs* 39 (March 1960): 25–32.

– *The Rebel Girl: An Autobiography, My First Life, 1906–1926*. New York: International Publishers, 1973.

– "Women in American Socialist Struggles." *Political Affairs* 39 (April 1960): 33–9.

Folbre, Nancy. "The Unproductive Housewife: Her Evolution in Nineteenth Century Economic Thought." *Signs* 16 (1991): 463–83.

Foner, Philip S., ed. *Mother Jones Speaks: Collected Speeches and Writings*. New York: Monad Press, 1983.

Foner, Philip S., and Sally Miller, eds. *Kate Richards O'Hare: Selected Writings and Speeches*. Baton Rouge: Louisanna State University Press, 1982.

Forbes, E. "Battles in Another War: Edith Archibald and the Halifax Feminist Movement." In *Challenging the Regional Stereotype: Essays on the Twentieth Century Maritimes*, 67–90. Fredericton: Acadiensis Press, 1989.

– "The Ideas of Carol Bacchi and the Suffragists of Halifax." *Atlantis* 10 (Spring 1985): 119–26.

– "Prohibition and the Social Gospel in Nova Scotia." *Acadiensis* 1 (Autumn 1971): 11–36.

Forestall, Nancy. "Times Were Hard: The Pattern of Women's Paid Labour in St. John's Between the Two World Wars." *Labour/Le Travail* 24 (Fall 1989): 147–66.

Forsey, Eugene. *Trade Unions in Canada, 1812–1902*. Toronto: University of Toronto Press, 1982.

Fox, Paul. "Early Socialism in Canada." In *The Political Process in Canada*, ed. J. H. Aitcheson. Toronto: University of Toronto Press, 1963.

Frager, Ruth. "Class and Ethnic Barriers to Feminist Perspectives in Toronto's Jewish Labour Movement, 1919–1939." *Studies in Political Economy* 30 (Autumn 1989): 143–65.

– "Deluded Assumptions about Diluted Labour." Unpublished paper, 1977.

– "No Proper Deal: Women Workers and the Canadian Labour Movement, 1870–1940." In *Union Sisters*, ed. Linda Briskin and Linda Yanz, 44–64. Toronto: Women's Educational Press, 1983.

– "Politicized Housewives in the Jewish Communist Movement of Toronto, 1923–33." In *Beyond the Vote*, ed. Linda Kealey and Joan Sangster, 258–75. Toronto: University of Toronto Press, 1989.

– "Sewing Solidarity: The Eaton Strike of 1912." *Canadian Women's Studies* 7 (Fall 1986): 96–8.

– *Sweatshop Strife: Class, Ethnicity, and Gender in the Jewish Labour Movement of Toronto, 1900–39*. Toronto: University of Toronto Press, 1992.

– "Uncloaking Vested Interests: Class, Ethnicity and Gender in the Jewish Labour Movement of Toronto, 1900–1939." Ph.D. diss., Department of History, York University, 1986.

Frank, Dana. "Housewives, Socialists, and the Politics of Food: The 1917 New York Cost of Living Protests." *Feminist Studies* 11 (Summer 1985): 255–86.

Frank, David, and Nolan Reilly. "The Emergence of the Socialist Movement in the Maritimes, 1899–1916." In *Underdevelopment and Social Movements in Atlantic Canada*, ed. Robert Brym and R. J. Sacouman, 81–106. Toronto: New Hogtown Press, 1979.

Freedman, Estelle. "Separatism as Strategy: Female Institution Building and American Feminism, 1870–1930." *Feminist Studies* 5 (Fall 1979): 512–29.

Friesen, Gerald. "'Yours in Revolt': The Socialist Party of Canada and the Western Canadian Labour Movement." *Labour/Le Travailleur* 1 (1976): 136–57.

Fryer, Mary Beacock. *Emily Stowe: Doctor and Suffragist.* Toronto: Dundurn Press, 1990.

Gamble, Eliza Burt. "Race Suicide in France." *International Socialist Review* 9 (January 1909): 511–13.

Geller, Gloria. "Wartimes Elections Act of 1917 and the Canadian Women's Movement." *Atlantis* 2 (Autumn 1976): 88–106.

George, Margaret. "From 'Goodwife' to 'Mistress': The Transformation of the Female in Bourgeois Culture." *Science and Society* 37 (Summer 1973): 152–75.

Gilman, Charlotte Perkins. *Herland*, with introduction by Ann J. Lane. New York: Pantheon Books, 1979.

– *Women and Economics: A Study of the Economic Relation between Men and Women as a Factor in Social Evolution*, ed. with introduction by Carl Degler. Boston: Small Maynard and Co., 1898. Reprint, New York: Harper and Row, 1966.

– *The Yellow Wallpaper*, with afterword by Elaine R. Hedges. Boston: Small Maynard, 1899. Reprint, New York: Feminist Press, 1973.

Gilstead, Frances. "Helena Gutteridge Story." *Pacific Tribune*, 8 March 1957.

Goldman, Emma. *Anarchism and Other Essays.* 3d rev. ed. New York: Mother Earth Publishing Association, 1917.

– *Living My Life.* Vols. 1 and 2. New York: Alfred Knopf, 1931. Reprint, New York: Dover, 1970.

– "Mary Wollstonecraft: Her Tragic Life and Passionate Struggle for Freedom." 1911. Reprinted in *Feminist Studies* 7 (Spring 1981): 113–21.

– *The Traffic in Women and Other Essays on Feminism.* New York: Times Change Press, 1970.

Gordon, D. A., Mari Jo Buhle, and Nancy E. Schrom. *Women in American Society: An Historical Contribution.* Reprint from *Radical America* 4 (July–August 1971).

Gordon, Linda. *Woman's Body, Woman's Right.* New York: Penguin, 1977.

Gorham, Deborah. "The Canadian Suffragists." In *Women in the Canadian Mosaic*, ed. Gwen Matheson, 25–56. Toronto: Peter Martin, 1976.

– "English Militancy and the Canadian Suffrage Movement." *Atlantis* 1 (Fall 1975): 83–112.

– "Flora MacDonald Denison: Canadian Feminist." In *A Not Unreasonable Claim*, ed. Linda Kealey, 47–70. Toronto: Women's Press, 1979.

– "The 'Maiden Tribute of Modern Babylon' Re-examined: Child Prostitution and the Idea of Childhood in Late-Victorian England." *Victorian Studies* 21 (Spring 1978): 353–69.
– "Singing up the Hill." *Canadian Dimension* 10 (June 1975): 26–38.
– "Three Books on the History of Housework: A Review Article." *Atlantis* 10 (Spring 1985): 138–45.
Gosse, Van. "To Organize in Every Neighbourhood." *Radical History Review* 50 (Spring 1991): 109–42.
Graham, Elizabeth. "Schoolmarms and Early Teaching in Ontario." In *Women at Work in Ontario, 1850–1930*, ed. Janice Acton et al., 165–210. Toronto: Women's Press, 1974.
Graham, Ronald. "The Majority Principle in Canadian Socialist Thought." Master's thesis, Carleton University, 1973.
Grantham, Ronald. "Some Aspects of the Socialist Movement in British Columbia, 1898–1933." Master's thesis, University of British Columbia, 1942.
Gray, James H. *Bacchanalia Revisited: Western Canada's Boozy Skid to Social Disaster*. Saskatoon: Western Producer Prairie Books, 1982.
– *Red Lights on the Prairies*. 2d. ed. Saskatoon: Western Producer Prairie Books, 1986.
Green, James R. "The Salesmen Soldiers of the *Appeal* Army: A Profile of Rank and File Socialist Agitators." In *Socialism and the Cities*, ed. Bruce M. Stave, 13–40. Port Washington, N.Y.: Kennikat Press, 1975.
Griffin, Harold. *British Columbia: The People's Early Story*. Vancouver: Tribune Publishing, 1958.
Hackett, Amy. "The German Woman's Movement and Suffrage, 1890–1914: A Study of National Feminism." In *Modern European Social History*, ed. Robert Bezucha. Indianapolis: D.C. Heath, 1972.
Hale, Linda Louise. "British Columbia Woman Suffrage Movement, 1890–1917." Master's thesis, University of British Columbia, 1977.
Hamilton, Sylvia. "Our Mothers Grand and Great." *Canadian Women's Studies* 11 (Spring 1991): 45–53.
Hansen, Barbara. "A Historical Study of Women in Canadian Banking." *Canadian Women's Studies* 1 (Winter 1978–79): 17–22.
Hareven, Tamara K. "Family Time and Industrial Time: Family and Work in a Planned Corporation Town, 1900–1924." In *Family and Kin in Urban Communities, 1700–1930*, ed. Hareven. New York, 1977.
Hart, John Edward. "William Irvine and Radical Politics in Canada." Ph.D. diss., University of Guelph, 1972.
Harzig, Christiane, and Dick Hoerder, eds. *The Press of Labour Migrants in Europe and North America 1880s to 1930s*. Bremen: Publications of the Labour Newspaper Preservation Project, 1985.

Hayden, Dolores. *The Grand Domestic Revolution: A History of Feminist Designs for American Homes, Neighbourhoods, and Cities.* Cambridge, Mass.: MIT Press, 1981.

Herman, Sondra R. "Loving Courtship or the Marriage Market? The Ideal and Its Critics, 1871–1911." *American Quarterly* 25 (May 1973): 235–52.

Heron, Craig. "Working Class Hamilton, 1895–1930." Ph.D. diss., Dalhousie University, 1981.

Heron, Craig, and Bryan Palmer. "Through the Prism of the Strike: Industrial Conflict in Southern Ontario, 1901–1914." *Canadian Historical Review* 58 (December 1977): 423–58.

Heron, Craig, and Robert Storey, eds. *On the Job: Confronting the Labour Process in Canada.* Montreal and Kingston: McGill-Queen's University Press, 1986.

Hertog, Johanna den. "Helena Gutteridge, 1880–1960." B.C. Teachers' Federation, *Labour History* 1 (Fall 1978): 37.

Hobbs, Margaret. "'Dead Horses' and 'Muffled Voices': Protective Legislation, Education and the Minimum Wage for Women in Ontario." M.A. thesis, Department of Education, University of Toronto, 1985.

– "The Perils of 'Unbridled Masculinity': Pacifist Elements in the Feminist and Socialist Thought of Charlotte Perkins Gilman." In *Women and Peace*, ed. Ruth Roach Pierson, 149–69. London: Croom Helm, 1987.

Hobbs, Margaret, and Ruth Roach Pierson. "'A Kitchen that Wastes No Steps': Gender, Class and the Home Improvement Plan, 1936–40." *Histoire Sociale/Social History* 21 (May 1988): 9–37.

Hobsbawm, Eric. "Man and Woman in Socialist Iconography." *History Workshop* 6 (Autumn 1978): 121–38.

Hoiberg, Anne, ed. *Women and the World of Work.* New York: Plenum Press, 1980.

Holt, Faye Reinberg. "Woman's Suffrage in Alberta." *Alberta History* 39 (Autumn 1991): 25–31.

Homel, Gene. "Fading Beams of the Nineteenth Century: Radicalism and Early Socialism in Canada's 1890's." *Labour/Le Travailleur* 5 (Spring 1980): 7–32.

– "James Simpson and the Origins of Canadian Social Democracy." Ph.D. diss., University of Toronto, 1978.

Honeycutt, Karen. "Clara Zetkin: A Socialist Approach to the Problem of Woman's Oppression." *Feminist Studies* 3 (Spring/Summer 1976): 131–44.

Horodski, Mary. "Women and the Winnipeg General Strike of 1919." *Manitoba History* 11 (Spring 1986): 28–37.

Howard, Irene. *The Struggle for Social Justice in British Columbia: Helena Gutteridge the Unknown Reformer.* Vancouver: Univeristy of British Columbia Press, 1992.

Humphries, Jane. "Class Struggle and the Persistence of the Working Class Family." *Cambridge Journal of Economics* 1 (September 1977): 241–58.

– "Women: Scapegoats and Safety Valves in the Great Depression." *Review of Radical Political Economics* 8 (Spring 1976): 98–121.

– "The Working Class Family: A Marxist Perspective." In *The Family in Political Thought*, ed. Jean Bethke Elshtain, 197–22. Amherst: University of Massachusetts Press, 1982.

– "The Working Class Family, Women's Liberation, and Class Struggle: The Case of Nineteenth Century British History." *Review of Radical Political Economics* 9 (Fall 1977): 25–41.

Indra, Doreen. "The Invisible Mosaic: Women, Ethnicity and the Vancouver Press, 1905–1976." *Canadian Ethnic Studies* 13, no. 1 (1981): 63–74.

Jameson, Sheilagh S. "Give Your Other Vote to the Sister." *Alberta Historical Review* 15 (Autumn 1967): 10–16.

– "Women in the Southern Alberta Ranch Community, 1881–1914." Western Canadian Studies Conference, 1976. *Papers*, 63–78.

Jefferis, B.G. *Safe Counsel: Search Lights on Health; Light on Dark Corners.* 18th ed. Toronto: J.L. Nichols, n.d.

Jeffreys, Sarah. "'Free from All Uninvited Touch of Man': Women's Campaigns around Sexuality, 1880–1914." *Women's Studies International Forum* 5, no. 6 (1982): 629–45.

Jenson, Jane, and F. Keyman. "Must We All Be Post-Modern?" *Studies in Political Economy* 31 (Spring 1990): 141–57.

Johnson, Laura C., and Robert E. Johnson. *The Seam Allowance: Industrial Home Sewing in Canada.* Toronto: Women's Press, 1982.

Johnson, Ross A. "No Compromise, No Political Trading: The Marxist Socialist Tradition in B.C." Ph.D. diss., University of British Columbia, 1975.

Jones, David C. "'There Is Some Power about the Land': The Western Agrarian Press and Country Life Ideology." *Journal of Canadian Studies* 17 (Fall 1982): 96–108.

Juteau-Lee, Daniel, and Barbara Roberts. "Ethnicity and Feminism." *Canadian Ethnic Studies* 13 (1981): 1–23.

Karlinsky, Janice. "The Pioneer Women's Organization: A Case Study of Jewish Women in Toronto." Master's thesis, University of Toronto, 1979.

Karni, Michael G., ed. *Finnish Diaspora. I: Canada, South America, Africa, Australia and Sweden.* Papers of the Finn Forum Conference held in Toronto, Ontario, 1–3 November 1979. Toronto: Multicultural History Society of Ontario, 1981.

Karni, Michael G., et al., eds. *The Finnish Experience in the Western Great Lakes Region: New Perspectives.* Turku: Institute for Migration, 1975.

Karvonen, Hilja. "Three Proponents of Women's Rights in the Finnish-American Labour Movement from 1910–1930: Selma Jolela McCone, Maiju Nurmi and Helmi Mattson." In *For the Common Good*, ed. Michael Karni and Douglas Ollila, 195–216. Superior, Wis.: Tyomes Society, 1977.

Kawecki, Tad. "The Origins of the Canadian Communist Party." Master's thesis, McMaster University, 1978.

Kazymyra, Nadia. "The Defiant Pavlo Krat and the Early Socialist Movement in Canada." *Canadian Ethnic Studies* 10 (1978): 38–54.

Kealey, Gregory S. "The State, the Foreign-Language Press and the Canadian Labour Revolt of 1917–1920." In *The Press of Labour Migrants in Europe and North America 1880s to 1930s*, ed. Christiane Harzig and Dick Hoerder, 311–45. Bremen: Publications of the Labour Newspaper Preservation Project, 1985.

– *Toronto Workers Respond to Industrial Capitalism, 1867–1892*. Toronto: University of Toronto Press, 1980.

– *Working Class Toronto at the Turn of the Century*. Toronto: New Hogtown Press, 1974.

Kealey, Gregory S., and Bryan D. Palmer. "The Bonds of Unity: The Knights of Labour in Ontario, 1880–1900." *Histoire Sociale/Social History* 14 (November 1981): 369–411.

– *Dreaming of What Might Be: The Knights of Labour in Ontario, 1880–1900*. Cambridge: Cambridge University Press, 1982.

Kealey, Gregory S., and Peter Warrion, eds. *Essays in Canadian Working Class History*. Toronto: McClelland and Stewart, 1976.

Kealey, Linda. "Canadian Socialism and the Woman Question." *Journal of Canadian Labour Studies* 13 (Spring 1984): 77–100.

– "Introduction: Special Issue on Women's History." *Canadian Historical Review* 72 (1991): 437–40.

– "Sophie." *New Maritimes*, November 1987, 12–13.

– "Women and Labour during World War I: Women Workers and Minimum Wage in Manitoba." In *First Days Fighting Days*, ed. Mary Kinnear, 76–99. Regina: Canadian Plains Research Centre, 1987.

– "Women in the Canadian Socialist Movement." In *Beyond the Vote*, ed. Linda Kealey and Joan Sangster, 171–95. Toronto: University of Toronto Press, 1989.

Kealey, Linda, ed. *A Not Unreasonable Claim: Women and Reform in Canada, 1880's-1920's*. Toronto: Women's Press, 1979.

Kealey, Linda, and Joan Sangster, eds. *Beyond the Vote*. Toronto: University of Toronto Press, 1989.

Kelly-Godal, Joan. "The Social Relations of the Sexes: Methodological Implications of Women's History." *Signs* 1, no. 4 (1976): 809–23.

Kennedy, Susan Estabrook. "'The Want It Satisfies Demonstrates the Need of It': A Study of *Life and Labour* of the Women's Trade Union League." *International Journal of Women's Studies* 3, no. 4 (1980): 391–406.

Kessler-Harris, Alice. "A New Agenda for American Labour History: A Gendered Analysis and the Question of Class." In *Perspectives on American Labour History: The Problem of Synthesis*, 217–34. DeKalb: Northern Illinois Press, 1989.

– "Where Are the Organized Women Workers?" *Feminist Studies* 3 (Fall 1975): 92–110.

Kinnear, Mary, ed. *First Days, Fighting Days: Women in Manitoba History.* Regina: Canadian Plains Research Centre, 1987.

Klein, Alice, and Wayne Roberts. "Besieged Innocence: The Problem and Problems of Working Women – Toronto, 1896–1914." In *Women at Work in Ontario, 1850–1930*, ed. Janice Acton et al., 211–60. Toronto: Women's Press, 1974.

Knight, Andrea. "Educating Working Women for the Vote: The Response of the Toronto Labour Movement to Women Suffrage." Master's thesis, University of Toronto, 1982.

Kolehmainen, John. "Harmony Island: A Finnish Utopian Venture in British Columbia." *B.C. Historical Quarterly* 5 (April 1941): 111–23.

Kollantai, Alexandra. *The Autobiography of a Sexually Emancipated Communist Woman*, ed. I. Fetscher, with foreword by Germaine Greer. New York: Schoken Books, 1975.

– *Sexual Relations and the Class Struggle.* London: Falling Wall Press, 1972.

– *Women Workers Struggle for Their Rights.* London: Falling Wall Press, 1975.

Kotsch, Georgina. "The Mother's Future." *International Socialist Review* 10 (June 1910): 1097–101.

Kouhi, Christine. "Labour and Finnish Immigration to Thunder Bay, 1876–1914." *Lakehead University Review* 9 (Spring 1977): 41–54.

Kovacs, Martin, ed. *Ethnic Canadians: Culture and Education.* Regina: Canadian Plains Research Centre, 1978.

– *Roots and Realities among Eastern and Central Europeans.* Edmonton: Central and East European Studies Association of Canada, 1983.

Krawchuck, Peter. *The Ukrainian Socialist Movement in Canada, 1907–1918.* Toronto: Progress Books, 1979.

Kruks, Sonia, et al. *Promissory Notes: Women in the Transition to Socialism.* New York: Monthly Review Press, 1989.

Kuitunen, A. N. "The Finnish Canadian Socialist Movement." Master's thesis, University of Calgary, 1978.

Lacelle, Claudette. *Urban Domestic Servants in 19th Century Canada.* Studies in Archaeology, Architecture and History. Ottawa: Environment Canada, National Historic Parks and Sites, 1987.

Lacombe, Michele. "Theosophy and the Canadian Idealist Tradition: A Preliminary Exploration." *Journal of Canadian Studies* 17 (Summer 1982): 100–17.

Ladoff, Isador. "Sexual Slavery." *International Socialist Review* 5 (February 1905): 449–59.

Lafargue, Paul. "The Woman Question," trans. Charles H. Kerr. *International Socialist Review* 5 (March 1905): 547–59.

Laforce, Hélène. "The Different Stages of the Elimination of Midwives in Quebec." *Delivering Motherhood,* ed. Katherine Arnup, Andrée Lévesque, and Ruth Pierson, 36–50. London: Routledge, 1990.

Laine, Edward W. "Finnish Canadian Radicalism and Canadian Politics: The First Forty Years, 1900–1940." In *Ethnicity, Power and Politics,* ed. Jorgen Dahlie and Tissa Fernando, 94–112. Agincourt, Ont.: Methuen, 1981.

Land, Hilary. "The Family Wage." *Feminist Review* 6, no. 3 (1980): 55–77.

Landes, Joan B. "Marxism and the 'Woman Question.'" In *Promissory Notes: Women and the Transition to Socialism,* 15–28. New York: Monthly Review Press, 1989.

Latham, Barbara, and Cathy Kess, eds. *In Her Own Right: Selected Essays on Woman's History in British Columbia.* Victoria, B.C.: Camosun College, 1980.

Latham, Barbara, and Roberta Pazdro. "A Simple Matter of Justice: Agnes Dean Cameron and the British Columbia Department of Education, 1906–8." *Atlantis* 10 (Fall 1984): 111–15.

– *Not Just Pin Money: Selected Essays on the History of Women's Work in British Columbia.* Victoria, B.C.: Camosun College, 1984.

Lavigne, Marie, and Jennifer Stoddart. "Women's Work in Montreal at the Turn of the Century." In *Women in Canada,* ed. Marylee Stephenson, 129–47. Rev. ed., Don Mills, Ont.: General Publishing, 1977.

Leacock, Stephen. "The Woman Question." 1915. Reprinted in *The Social Criticism of Stephen Leacock,* ed. A. Bowker, 52–60. Toronto: University of Toronto Press, 1973.

Leacy, F.H., ed. *Historical Statistics of Canada.* 2d ed. Ottawa: Statistics Canada and the Social Science Research Federation, 1983, series D102–122.

Leavitt, Judith. "Under the Shadow of Maternity: American Women's Response to Death and Debility Fears in Nineteenth Century Childbirth." *Feminist Studies* 12 (Spring 1986): 129–54.

Lemons, Stanley. "Socialist Feminism in the 1920's." *Labour History* 14 (Winter 1973): 83–91.

Lenin, V.I. *On the Emancipation of Women*. Moscow: Progress Publishers, 1972.

Lenjskyj, H. "Social Change Affecting Women in Urban Canada, 1890–1930." Master's thesis, University of Toronto, 1979.

Lerner, Gerda. *The Majority Finds Its Past: Placing Women in History*. New York: Oxford University Press, 1979.

Leslie, Genevieve. "Domestic Service in Canada, 1880–1920." In *Women at Work in Ontario, 1850–1930*, ed. Janice Acton et al., 71–126. Toronto: Women's Press, 1974.

Levine, Susan. "The Best Men in the Order: Women in the Knights of Labour." Unpublished paper presented to the Canadian Historical Association, London, Ontario, 1978.

– "Labour's True Woman: Domesticity and Equal Rights in the Knights of Labour." *Journal of American History* 70 (September 1983): 323–39.

Lewis, Jane. "'Motherhood Issues' in the Late Nineteenth and Twentieth Centuries." In *Delivering Motherhood*, ed. Katherine Arnup, Andrée Lévesque, and Ruth Roach Pierson, 1–19. London: Routledge, 1990.

Liddington, Jill. "Rediscovering Suffrage History." *History Workshop* 4 (Autumn 1974): 192–202.

Liddington, Jill, and Jill Norris. *One Hand Tied Behind Us: The Rise of the Women's Suffrage Movement*. London: Virago, 1978.

Light, Beth, and Joy Parr, eds. *Canadian Women on the Move, 1867–1920*. Toronto: New Hogtown Press and Ontario Institute for Studies in Education, 1983.

Light, Beth, and Ruth Roach Pierson, eds. *Not an Easy Road: Women in Canada 1920's to 1960's*. Toronto: New Hogtown Press, 1990.

Light, Beth, and Veronica Strong-Boag. *True Daughters of the North: Canadian Women's History. An Annotated Bibliography*. Toronto: Ontario Institute for Studies in Education, 1980.

Lindstrom-Best, Varpu. *Defiant Sisters: A Social History of the Finnish Immigrant Women in Canada, 1890–1930*. Toronto: Multicultural History Society, 1988.

– "The Finnish Immigrant Community of Toronto, 1887–1913." Occasional Paper Series, no. 79–88. Toronto: Multicultural History Society, October 1979.

– "Finnish Immigrants and the Depression: A Case Study in Montreal." Unpublished paper, 1981.

– "Finns in Canada." *Polyphany* 3 (Fall 1981): 3–15.

– "'Fist Press': A Study of the Finnish Canadian Handwritten Newspapers." In *Roots and Realities among Eastern and Central Europeans*, ed. Martin Kovacs, 129–36. Edmonton: Central and East European Studies Association of Canada, 1983.

- "'Going to Work in America': Finnish Maids, 1911–30." *Polyphony* 8 (1986): 17–20.

- "'I Won't Be a Slave!': Finnish Domestics in Canada, 1911–1930." In *Looking into My Sister's Eyes: An Exploration in Women's History*, ed. Jean Burnet, 33–53. Toronto: Multicultural History Society, 1986.

- "The Socialist Party of Canada and the Finnish Connection, 1905–1911." In *Ethnicity, Power and Politics*, ed. Jorgen Dahlie and Tissa Fernando, 113–22. Agincourt, Ont.: Methuen, 1981.

- "The Unbreachable Gulf: The Division in the Finnish Community of Toronto, 1902–1913." In *Finnish Diaspora. I: Canada, South America, Africa, Australia and Sweden*, ed. Michael G. Karni, 11–18. Toronto: Multicultural History Society of Ontario, 1981.

Lindstrom-Best, Varpu, and Allan Seager. "*Troveritar* and Finnish Canadian Women, 1900–1930." In *The Press of Labour Migrants in Europe and North America 1880s to 1930s*, ed. Christiane Harzig and Dick Hoerder, 243–64. Bremen: Publications of the Labour Newspaper Preservation Project, 1985.

Loosemore, Thomas Robert. "The British Columbia Labour Movement and Political Action, 1879–1933." Master's thesis, University of British Columbia, 1954.

Lowe, Graham. "The Administrative Revolution in the Canadian Office: An Overview." In *Work in the Canadian Context*, ed. Katherine L.P. Lundy and Barbara D. Warme, 153–73. Toronto: Butterworths, 1981.

- "Mechanization, Feminization and Managerial Control in the Early Twentieth Century Canadian Office." In *On the Job*, ed. Craig Heron and Robert Storey, 177–210. Montreal and Kingston: McGill-Queen's University Press, 1986.

- *Women in the Administrative Revolution*. Toronto: University of Toronto Press, 1987.

- "Women, Work and Office: The Feminization of Clerical Occupations in Canada, 1901–1931." *Canadian Journal of Sociology* 5 (1980): 361–81.

Luxton, Meg. *More than a Labour of Love: Three Generations of Women's Work in the Home*. Toronto: Women's Educational Press, 1980.

McCallum, Margaret E. "Keeping Women in Their Place: The Minimum Wage in Canada, 1910–1925." *Labour/Le Travail* 17 (Spring 1986): 29–56.

- "Separate Spheres: The Organization of Work in a Confectionary Factory: Ganong Bros., St. Stephen, New Brunswick." *Labour/Le Travail* 24 (Fall 1989): 69–90.

McCormack, Andrew Ross. "British Working-Class Immigrants and Canadian Radicalism: The Case of Arthur Puttee." *Canadian Ethnic Studies* 10, no. 2 (1978): 22–37.

– "The Emergence of the Socialist Movement in British Columbia." *B.C. Studies* 21 (Spring 1974): 3–27.

– "The Industrial Workers of the World in Western Canada, 1905–1914." Canadian Historical Association, *Historical Papers* (1975): 167–90.

– *Reformers, Rebels and Revolutionaries: The Western Canadian Radical Movement, 1899–1919.* Toronto: University of Toronto Press, 1977.

MacDonald, Christine. "How Saskatchewan Women Got the Vote." *Saskatchewan History* 1 (October 1948): 1–9.

MacDonald, Joe. "The Roots of Radical Politics in Nova Scotia: The Provincial Workmen's Association and Political Activity, 1879–1906." Unpublished paper, Carleton University.

MacDonald, Martha, and Patricia Connelly. "Class and Gender in Fishing Communities in Nova Scotia." *Studies in Political Economy* 30 (Autumn 1989): 61–85.

McDonald, Robert A. "Working Class Vancouver, 1886–1914: Urbanism and Class in B.C." *B.C. Studies* 69–70 (Spring 1986): 33–69.

MacGill, Helen Gregory. *Daughters, Wives, and Mothers in British Columbia: Some Laws Regarding Them.* 3d ed. Vancouver: Moore Printing, 1914.

– *Laws for Women and Children in British Columbia.* Vancouver, 1925.

– *Supplement to Daughters, Wives and Mothers in British Columbia,* [1915].

McGinnis, Janice Dickin. "From Salvarsan to Penicillin: Medical Science and Venereal Disease Control in Canada." In *Essays in the History of Canadian Medicine,* ed. Wendy Mitchinson and Janice Dickin McGinnis, 126–95. Toronto: McClelland and Stewart, 1986.

McInnis, Marvin. "Women, Work and Childbearing: Ontario in the Second Half of the Nineteenth Century." *Histoire Sociale/Social History* 48 (November 1991): 237–62.

McIvor, William John. "Revolutionary Socialism." Master's thesis, University of Manitoba, 1912.

McLaren, Angus. "Birth Control and Abortion in Canada, 1870–1920." *Canadian Historical Review* 59, no. 3 (1978): 319–40.

– "The First Campaigns for Birth Control Clinics in British Columbia." *Journal of Canadian Studies* 19 (Autumn 1984): 50–64.

– *Our Own Master Race: Eugenics in Canada, 1885–1945.* Toronto: McClelland and Stewart, 1990.

– "Sex Radicalism and the Canadian Pacific Northwest, 1890–1920." *Journal of the History of Sexuality* 2 (April 1992): 527–46.

- "What Has This to Do with Working Class Women? Birth Control and the Canadian Left, 1900–1939." *Histoire Sociale/Social History* 14 (November 1981): 435–54.
- "Women's Work and the Regulation of Family Size: The Question of Abortion in the Nineteenth Century." *History Workshop* 4 (Autumn 1977): 70–81.

McLaren, Angus, and Arlene Tigar McLaren. *The Bedroom and the State: The Changing Practices and Politics of Contraception and Abortion in Canada, 1880–1980.* Toronto: McClelland and Stewart, 1986.
- "Discoveries and Dissimilations: The Impact of Abortion Deaths on Maternal Mortality in British Columbia." In *Delivering Motherhood*, ed. Katherine Arnup, Andrée Lévesque, and Ruth Pierson, 126–49. London: Routledge, 1990.

MacMurchy, Marjory. "Women and the Nation." In *The New Era in Canada*, ed. J.O. Miller. Toronto: J.M. Dent and Sons, 1917.

Makahonuk, Glen. "Class Conflict in a Prairie City: The Saskatoon Working-Class Response to Prairie Capitalism, 1906–1919." *Labour/Le Travail* 19 (Spring 1987): 89–124.

Makuch, Neston. "The Influence of the Ukrainian Revolution on Ukrainians in Canada, 1917–1922." *Journal of Ukrainian Graduate Studies* 4 (Spring 1979): 42–61.

Malkiel, Theresa. "Where Do We Stand on the Woman Question?" *International Socialist Review* 10 (August 1909): 159–62.

Manley, John. "Preaching the Red Stuff: J.B. McLachlan, Communism and the Cape Breton Miners, 1922–1935." *Labour/Le Travail* 30 (Fall 1992): 65–114.

Mann, Susan. "Family, Class and State in Women's Access to Abortion and Day Care: The Case of the United States." *Family, State and Economy*, ed. James Dickinson and Bob Russell. London: Croom Helm, 1986.

Marks, Lynn. "'The Hallelujah Lasses': Working-Class Women in the Salvation Army in English Canada, 1882–92." *Gender Conflicts*, ed. M. Valverde and F. Iacovetta, 67–117. Toronto: University of Toronto Press, 1992.
- "The Knights of Labour and the Salvation Army: Religion and Working-Class Culture in Ontario, 1882–1890." *Labour/Le Travail* 28 (Fall 1991): 89–127.

Marks, Lynn, and Chad Gaffield. "Women at Queen's University, 1895–1905: A 'Little Sphere' All Their Own?" *Ontario History* 78 (December 1986): 331–50.

Marsh, Margaret S. *Anarchist Women, 1870–1920.* Philadelphia, Pa.: Temple University Press, 1981.

Marshall, Catherine, C.K. Ogden, and Mary Sargeant Florence. *Militarism versus Feminism: Writings on Women and War*, ed. Margaret Kamester and Jo Vellacott. Allen and Unwin, 1915. Reprint, London: Virago, 1987.

Martynowych, Orest T. "The Ukrainian Socialist Movement in Canada, 1900–1918, Part I." *Journal of Ukrainian Graduate Studies* 1 (Fall 1976): 27–44.

– "The Ukrainian Socialist Movement in Canada, 1900–1918, Part II." *Journal of Ukrainian Graduate Studies* 2 (Spring 1977): 22–31.

Marx, Karl, et al. *The Woman Question*. New York: International Publishers, 1951.

Matters, Dianne L. "Public Welfare Vancouver Style, 1910–1920." *Journal of Canadian Studies* 14, no. 1 (1979): 3–15.

Meltz, Noah M. *Manpower in Canada, 1921–1961*. Ottawa: Department of Manpower and Immigration, 1969, table A-4.

Menzies, June. "Votes for Saskatchewan Women." In *Politics in Saskatchewan*, ed. Norman Ward and D. Spafford, 78–92. Toronto: Longmans, 1968.

Mernitz, Susan Curtis. "The Religious Foundations of America's Oldest Socialist Press: A Centennial Note on the Charles H. Kerr Publishing Company." *Labour/Le Travail* 19 (Spring 1987): 133–6.

Miller, Sally M. "From Sweatshop Worker to Labour Leader: Theresa Malkiel, a Case Study." *American Jewish History* 68 (December 1978): 189–205.

– "Women Activists in a Male Bureaucracy: The Socialist Party to 1920." Paper presented to the Organization of American Historians, 10 April 1976, St Louis, Mo.

Mills, Allen. "Single Tax, Socialism and the Independent Labour Party of Manitoba: The Political Ideas of F.J. Dixon and S.J. Farmer." *Labour/Le Travail* 5 (Spring 1980): 33–56.

Mitchinson, Wendy. "Early Women's Organizations and Social Reform: Prelude to the Welfare State." In *The Benevolent State: The Growth of Welfare in Canada*, ed. A. Moscovitch and J. Alberts, 77–92. Toronto: Garamond Press, 1987.

– "Historical Attitudes towards Women and Childbirth." *Atlantis* 4 (Spring 1979): 13–34.

Moller, Jessie M. "The National Convention and the Woman's Movement." *International Socialist Review* 8 (May 1908): 688–90.

Morgan, Wayne H. "American Socialism: A Review Article." *Business History Review* 56 (Winter 1982): 577–84.

Morrison, T.R. "Their 'Proper Sphere': Feminism, the Family and Child-Centered Social Reform in Ontario, 1875–1900, Part I." *Ontario History* 68 (March 1976a): 43–64.

– "Their 'Proper Sphere': Feminism, the Family, and Child Centered Social Reform in Ontario, 1875–1900, Part II." *Ontario History* 68 (June 1976b): 65–74.

Moscovitch, Alan, and Jim Alberts. *The Benevolent State: The Growth of Welfare in Canada.* Toronto: Garamond, 1987.

Muise, D.A. "The Industrial Context of Inequality: Female Participation in Nova Scotia's Paid Labour Force, 1871–1921." *Acadiensis* 20 (Spring 1991): 3–31.

Muncy, Raymond. *Sex and Marriage in Utopian Communities.* Bloomington: Indiana University Press, 1973.

Muszynski, Alicja. "Race and Gender: Structural Determinants in the Formation of British Columbia's Salmon Cannery Labour Forces." In *Class, Gender and Region,* ed. Gregory Kealey, 103–20. St John's: Committee on Canadian Labour History, 1988.

National Council of Women. *Women of Canada: Their Life and Work.* Ottawa: National Council of Women, 1900.

Naylor, James. *The New Democracy: Challenging the Social Order in Industrial Ontario, 1914–25.* Toronto: University of Toronto Press, 1991.

Newton, Janice. "The Alchemy of Politicization: Socialist Women and the Early Canadian Left." In *Gender Conflicts,* ed. Franca Iacovetta and Mariana Valverde, 118–48. Toronto: University of Toronto Press, 1992.

– "'Enough of Exclusive Masculine Thinking': The Feminist Challenge to the Early Canadian Left." Ph.D. diss., York University, 1988.

– "'From Wage Slave to White Slave': The Prostitution Controversy and the Early Canadian Left." In *Beyond the Vote,* ed. Linda Kealey and Joan Sangster, 217–36. Toronto: University of Toronto Press, 1989.

– "Women and *Cotton's Weekly*: A Study of Women and Socialism in Canada, 1909." *Resources for Feminist Research* 8 (Fall 1980): 58–60.

Nilsen, Deborah. "The 'Social Evil': Prostitution in Vancouver, 1900–1920." In *In Her Own Right,* ed. Barbara Latham and Cathy Kess, 205–28. Victoria, B.C.: Camosun College, 1980.

O'Brien, Gary. "Maurice Spector and the Origins of Canadian Trotskyism." Master's thesis, Carleton University, 1974.

– "Towards the Roots of Canadian Radicalism: An Analysis of the Social Democratic Party of Canada." Unpublished paper, Carleton University, 1973.

Olender, Vivian. "The Canadian Methodist Church and the Gospel of Assimilation, 1900–1925." *Journal of Ukrainian Studies* 7 (Fall 1982): 61–74.

Oppenheimer, Jo. "Childbirth in Ontario: The Transition from Home to Hospital in the Early Twentieth Century." In *Delivering Motherhood,* ed. Katherine Arnup, Andrée Lévesque, and Ruth Pierson, 51–74. London: Routledge, 1990.

Oppenheimer, Mary S. "The Suffrage Movement and the Socialist Party." *New Review* 3 (1915): 359–60.

Orlikow, Lionel. "A Survey of the Reform Movement in Manitoba, 1910–1920." Master's thesis, University of Manitoba, 1955.

Palmer, Bryan. *A Culture in Conflict: Skilled Workers and Industrial Capitalism in Hamilton, Ontario 1860–1914.* Montreal: McGill-Queen's University Press, 1979.

– *Working Class Experience: The Rise and Reconstruction of Canadian Labour, 1800–1980.* Toronto: Butterworths, 1983.

Palmer, Howard. *Patterns of Prejudice: A History of Nativism in Alberta.* Toronto: McClelland and Stewart, 1982.

Pankhurst, Sylvia. *The Suffragette Movement.* Longmans, 1931. Reprint, London: Virago, 1977.

Parce, Lida. "Woman and Socialist Philosophy: A Reply to Joseph E. Cohen." *International Socialist Review* 10 (November 1909): 125–8.

Parker, Gilbert, and May Wright Sewall. "The International Council of Women." *North American Review* 513 (August 1899): 154–64.

Parr, Joy. *The Gender of Breadwinners: Women, Men and Change in Two Industrial Towns, 1880–1950.* Toronto: University of Toronto Press, 1990.

– "Rethinking Work and Kinship in a Canadian Hosiery Town, 1910–1950." *Feminist Studies* 13 (Spring 1987): 137–62.

– "Women Workers in the Twentieth Century." In *Lectures in Canadian Labour and Working Class History,* ed. W.J.C. Cherwinski and G.S. Kealey, 79–85. Toronto: New Hogtown Press and Committee on Canadian Labour History, 1985.

Patrias, Carmela. "Passages from the Life: An Italian Woman in Welland, Ontario." *Canadian Women's Studies* 8 (Summer 1987): 69–73.

Pedersen, Diana. "'Building Today for the Womanhood of Tomorrow': Businessmen, Boosters and the YWCA, 1890–1930." *Urban History Review* 15, no. 3 (1987): 225–42.

– "'The Scientific Training of Mothers': The Campaign for Domestic Science in Ontario Schools, 1890–1913." In *Critical Issues in the History of Canadian Science, Technology and Medicine,* ed. Richard A. Jarrell and Arnold E. Roos, 178–94. Ottawa and Thornhill: HSTC Publications, 1983.

Pedersen, Susan. "The Failure of Feminism in the Making of the British Welfare State." *Radical History Review* 43 (Winter 1989): 86–111.

Pelton, Guy Cathcart. "Women's Rights in British Columbia." *British Columbia Magazine* 10 (April 1914): 202.

– "Women's Rights in British Columbia." *Society and Club Magazine* 2 (May 1914): 12.

Penner, Norman. *The Canadian Left: A Critical Analysis.* Scarborough, Ont.: Prentice-Hall, 1977.

– "Jacob Penner's Recollections of the Early Socialist Movement in Winnipeg." *Histoire Sociale/Social History* 7 (November 1974): 366–78.

Penton, Edward M. "The Ideas of William Cotton: A Marxist View of Canadian Society, 1908–1914." Master's thesis, University of Ottawa, 1981.

Philips, Paul. *No Power Greater: A Century of Labour in British Columbia.* Vancouver, B.C.: B.C. Federation of Labour and the Boag Foundation, 1967.

– "The National Policy and the Development of the Western Canadian Labour Movement." Western Canadian Studies Conference, 1970–71. *Papers* (1973): 41–62.

Pierson, Stanley. *British Socialists: The Journey from Fantasy to Politics.* Cambridge: Harvard University Press, 1979.

– *Marxism and the Origins of British Socialism.* Ithaca: Cornell University Press, 1973.

Pierson, Ruth. "Ellen Key: Maternalism and Pacifism." In *Delivering Motherhood*, ed. Katherine Arnup, Andrée Lévesque, and Ruth Roach Pierson, 270–83. London, Routledge, 1990.

– "Gender and the Unemployment Insurance Debates in Canada, 1934–1940." *Labour/Le Travail* 25 (Spring 1990): 77–103.

– "The History of Women and Paid Work." In *Women's Paid and Unpaid Work: Historical and Contemporary Perspectives*, 17–34. Toronto: New Hogtown Press, 1985.

– "Women's History: The State of the Art in Atlantic Canada." *Acadiensis* 7 (Autumn 1977): 121–31.

– ed. *Women and Peace: Theoretical, Historical and Practical Perspectives.* London: Croom Helm, 1987.

Pilla, Arja. "Finnish-Canadian Radicalism and the Government of Canada from the First World War to the Depression." In *Finnish Diaspora. I: Canada, South America, Africa, Australia and Sweden*, ed. Michael G. Karni, 19–32. Toronto: Multicultural History Society of Ontario, 1981.

Pivato, Joseph. "Italian Canadian Women Writers Recall History." *Canadian Ethnic Studies* 18 no. 1 (1986): 79–88.

Porter, Marilyn. "Peripheral Women: Towards a Feminist Analysis of the Atlantic Region." *Studies in Political Economy* 23 (Summer 1987): 41–72.

Prentice, Alison. "Bluestockings, Feminists or Women Workers: A Preliminary Look at Women's Early Employment at the University of Toronto." *Journal of the Canadian Historical Association* 2 (1991): 231–61.

– "The Feminization of Teaching." In *The Neglected Majority*, vol. 1, ed. Susan Trofimenkoff and Alison Prentice, 49–65. Toronto: McClelland and Stewart, 1977.

Prentice, Alison, and Susan E. Houston, eds. *Family, School and Society in Nineteenth Century Canada*. Toronto: Oxford University Press, 1975.

Prentice, Alison, and Susan Mann Trofimenkoff, eds. *The Neglected Majority: Essays in Canadian Women's History*. Vol. 2. Toronto: McClelland and Stewart, 1985.

Prentice, Alison, et al. *Canadian Women: A History*. Toronto: Harcourt Brace International, 1988.

Prentice, Susan. "Workers, Mothers, Reds: Toronto's Postwar Daycare Fight." *Studies in Political Economy* 30 (Autumn 1989): 115–41.

Pucci, Antonio. "At the Forefront of Militancy: Italians in Canada at the Turn of the Century." *Polyphony* 7 (Fall–Winter 1982): 37–42.

Quataert, Jean. *Reluctant Feminists in German Social Democracy, 1885–1917*. Princeton, N.J.: Princeton University Press, 1979.

Rainboth, Mabel. "Socialism and Its Trend in Canada." Master's thesis, University of Ottawa, 1938.

Ramkhalawansingh, Ceta. "Women during the Great War." In *Women at Work in Ontario*, ed. Janice Acton et al., 261–307. Toronto: Women's Press, 1974.

Rasmussen, Linda, et al., eds. *A Harvest Yet to Reap*. Toronto: Women's Press, 1976.

Read, Daphne, ed. *The Great War and Canadian Society*, with introduction by Russell Hann. Toronto: New Hogtown Press, 1978.

Reilly, Sharon. "Material History and the History of Women." In *First Days, Fighting Days*, ed. Mary Kinnear, 1–18. Regina: Canadian Plains Research Centre, 1987.

Richardson, Gertrude. "The Woman's Crusade." *Atlantis* 12 (Spring 1987): 75.

Riley, Barbara. "Six Saucepans to One: Domestic Science vs. the Home in British Columbia, 1900–1930." In *Not Just Pin Money*, ed. Barbara Latham and Roberta Pazdro 159–81. Victoria, B.C.: Camosun College, 1984.

Roberts, Barbara. "Doctors and Deports: The Role of the Medical Profession in Canadian Deportation, 1900–20." *Canadian Ethnic Studies* 18, no. 3 (1986): 17–36.

– "Shovelling Out the 'Mutinous': Political Deportation from Canada before 1936." *Labour/Le Travail* 18 (Fall 1986): 77–110.

– "Why Do Women Do Nothing to Stop the War? Canadian Feminist Pacifists and the Great War." Special Publication no. 13. Ottawa: Canadian Research Institute for the Advancement of Women, December 1985.

– "Women against War, 1914–18: Francis Beynon and Laura Hughes." In *Up and Doing*, ed. Janice Williamson and Deborah Gorham, 48–65. Toronto: Women's Press, 1989.

- "'A Work of Empire': Canadian Reformers and British Female Immigration." In *A Not Unreasonable Claim*, ed. Linda Kealey, 185–210. Toronto: Women's Press, 1979.

Roberts, Wayne. *Honest Womanhood: Feminism, Femininity, and Class Consciousness among Toronto Working Women, 1893 to 1914*. Toronto: New Hogtown Press, 1976.

- "Rocking the Cradle for the World: The New Woman and Maternal Feminism, Toronto, 1877–1914." In *A Not Unreasonable Claim*, ed. Linda Kealey, 15–46. Toronto: Women's Press, 1979.

- "Six New Women: A Guide to the Mental Map of Women Reformers in Toronto." *Atlantis* 3 (Fall 1977): 145–64.

Robin, Martin. "Determinants of Radical Labour and Socialist Politics in English-Speaking Canada between 1880 and 1930." *Journal of Canadian Studies* 2, no. 2 (1967): 27–39.

- *Radical Politics and Canadian Labour*. Kingston, Ont.: Industrial Relations Centre, 1968.

- "Registration, Conscription and Independent Labour Politics, 1916–1917." *Canadian Historical Review* 47, no. 2 (1966): 101–18.

- *The Rush for Spoils: The Company Province, 1871–1933*. Toronto: McClelland and Stewart, 1972.

- "The Trades and Labor Congress of Canada and Political Action, 1889–1908." *Relations Industrielles* 22 (April 1967): 187–214.

Rosen, Ruth. *The Lost Sisterhood: Prostitution in America, 1900–1918*. Baltimore: Johns Hopkins University Press, 1982.

Rosenthal, Star. "Union Maids: Organized Women Workers in Vancouver, 1900–1915." *B.C. Studies* 41 (Spring 1979): 36–55.

Ross, Aileen. "Control and Leadership in Women's Groups: An Analysis of Philanthropic Money-Raising Activity." *Social Forces* 37 (1958): 124–31.

Ross, Steven. "Struggles for the Screen: Workers, Radicals and the Political Uses of Silent Film." *American Historical Review* 96 (April 1991): 333–67.

Rotenberg, Lori. "The Wayward Worker: Toronto's Prostitute at the Turn of the Century." In *Women at Work in Ontario, 1850–1930*, ed. Janice Acton et al., 33–70. Toronto: Women's Educational Press, 1974.

Russell, Bob. "A Fair or Minimum Wage? Women Workers, the State, and the Origins of Wage Regulation in Western Canada." *Labour/Le Travail* 28 (Fall 1991): 59–88.

Salo, A.H. "Kalevan Kansan Colonization Company: Finnish Millenarian Activity in B.C." Master's thesis, University of British Columbia, 1978.

Sangster, Joan. "Canadian Working Women in the Twentieth Century." In *Lectures in Canadian Labour and Working Class History*, ed. W.J.C. Cherwinski and G.S. Kealey, 59–78. Toronto: New Hogtown Press and Committee on Labour History, 1985.

- "The Communist Party and the Woman Question, 1922–1929." *Labour/Le Travail* 15 (Spring 1985): 25–56.
- *Dreams of Equality: Women on the Canadian Left, 1920–1950*. Toronto: McClelland and Stewart, 1984.
- "Finnish Women in Ontario, 1890–1930." *Polyphony* 3 (Fall 1981): 46–54.
- "The Making of a Socialist-Feminist: The Early Career of Beatrice Brigden, 1888–1941." *Atlantis* 13 (Fall 1987): 14–28.
- "The 1907 Bell Telephone Strike: Organizing Women Workers." *Journal of Canadian Labour Studies* 3 (1978): 109–30.
- "Women and Unions in Canada: A Review of Historical Research." *Resources for Feminist Research* 10 (July 1981): 2–6.
Sarvasy, Wendy. "Beyond the Difference versus Equality Policy Debate: Post-Suffrage Feminism, Citizenship and the Quest for a Feminist Welfare State." *Signs* 17 (1992): 329–62.
Savage, Gail. "'The Wilful Communication of a Loathsome Disease': Martial Conflict and Venereal Disease in Victorian England." *Victorian Studies* 34 (Autumn 1990): 36–54.
Saywell, John Tupper. "Labour and Socialism in British Columbia: A Survey of Historical Development before 1903." *British Columbia Historical Quarterly* 15 (July – October 1951): 129–50.
Schofield, Ann. "Feminism and Labour Activism." Paper presented to the 7th Berkshire Conference on Women's History, Wellesley, Mass., June 1987.
- "Rebel Girls and Union Maids: The Woman Question in the Journals of the A.F.L. and I.W.W., 1905–1920." *Feminist Studies* 9 (Summer 1983): 335–58.
Schultz, David. "The Industrial Workers of the World and the Unemployed in Edmonton and Calgary in the Depression of 1913–1915." *Labour/ Le Travail* 24 (Spring 1990): 47–75.
Schwantes, Carlos Arnaldo. "Free Love and Free Speech on the Pacific Northwest Frontier." *Oregon Historical Quarterly* 82 (Fall 1981): 271–93.
- *Radical Heritage, Labour, Socialism and Reform in Washington and British Columbia, 1885–1917*. Vancouver: Douglas and McIntyre, 1979.
Scott, Jack. *Plunderbund and Proletariat*. Vancouver: New Star Books, 1975.
Scott, Joan. "Gender: A Useful Category of Historical Analysis." *American Historical Review* 91 (December 1986): 1053–75.
- "History and Difference." *Daedalus, Journal of the American Academy of Arts and Sciences* 16 (Fall 1987): 93–118.
- "On Language, Gender and Working-Class History." *International Labour and Working-Class History* 31 (Spring 1987): 1–13.

Scott, Joan, and Louise A. Tilly. "Women's Work and the Family in Nineteenth Century Europe." *Comparative Studies in Society and History* 17 (January 1975): 36–64.

Seager, Allen. "Finnish Canadians and the Ontario Miners' Movement." *Polyphany* 3 (Fall 1981): 35–45.

– "Socialists and Workers: The Western Canadian Coal Miners, 1900–21." *Labour/Le Travail* 16 (Fall 1985): 23–60.

Seretan, L. Glen. "Daniel DeLeon and the 'Woman Question.'" Paper presented to the Organization of American Historians, St Louis, Mo., 1976.

Sheehan, Nancy M. "Women Helping Women: The WCTU and the Foreign Population in the West, 1905–1930." *International Journal of Women's Studies* 6, no. 5 (1983): 395–411.

Slaughter, Jane, and Robert Kern, eds. *European Women on the Left: Socialism, Feminism, and the Problems Faced by Political Women, 1880 to the Present*. Westport, Conn.: Greenwood Press, 1981.

Smart, John. "Populist and Socialist Movements in Canadian History." In *Canada Ltd.*, ed. Robert Laxer. Toronto: McClelland and Stewart, 1973.

Smith, Dorothy. "Feminist Reflections on Political Economy." *Studies in Political Economy* 30 (Autumn 1989): 37–59.

Smith, Goldwyn. "The Female Suffrage." *Canadian Monthly and National Review* 6 (July 1874): 68–78.

Smith, Helen. "Women Workers and Industrialization in Canada, 1870–1910." Master's thesis, University of Ottawa, 1980.

Smith, Matthew Eliot. "The Development of Socialist Opposition: The Case of British Columbia, 1880–1945." Ph.D. diss., University of North Carolina, Chapel Hill, 1978.

Smith-Rosenberg, Carroll. "Beauty, the Beast and the Militant Woman: A Case Study of Sex Roles and Social Stress in America." *American Quarterly* 23 (October 1971): 562–84.

– "The Female World of Love and Ritual: Relations Between Women in Nineteenth Century America." *Signs* 1 (Autumn 1975): 1–29.

Socknat, Thomas P. "For Peace and Freedom: Canadian Feminists and the Interwar Peace Campaign." *Up and Doing*, ed. Janice Williamson and Deborah Gorham, 66–87. Toronto: Women's Press, 1989.

– *Witness against War: Pacifism in Canada, 1900–1945*. Toronto: University of Toronto Press, 1987.

Sowerwine, Charles. *Sisters or Citizens? Women and Socialism in France Since 1876*. Cambridge: Cambridge University Press, 1982.

Spargo, John. "Woman and the Socialist Movement." *International Socialist Review* 8 (February 1908): 449–55.

Sproul, Dan. "The Situation in British Columbia." *International Socialist Review* 10 (February 1910): 741–4.

Steedman, Mercedes. "Skill and Gender in the Canadian Clothing Industry, 1890–1940." In *On the Job*, ed. Craig Heron and Robert Storey, 152–76. Montreal and Kingston: McGill-Queen's University Press, 1986.

Steeves, Dorothy G. *The Compassionate Rebel: Ernest Winch and the Growth of Socialism in Western Canada*, with introduction by Tommy Douglas. Boag Foundation, 1960. Reprint, Vancouver: J.J. Douglas, 1977.

Stoddart, Jennifer, and Veronica Strong-Boag. "...And Things Were Going Wrong at Home." *Atlantis* 1 (Fall 1975): 38–44.

Strasser, Susan. *Never Done: A History of American Housework*. New York: Pantheon Books, 1982.

Strom, Sharon Hartman. "Challenging 'Woman's Place': Feminism, the Left and Industrial Unionism in the 1930's." *Feminist Studies* 9 (Summer 1983): 359–86.

Strong-Boag, Veronica. "Canada's Early Experience with Income Supplements: The Introduction of Mother's Allowances." *Atlantis* 4 (Spring 1979): 35–43.

– "Canada's Women Doctors: Feminism Constrained." In *A Not Unreasonable Claim*, ed. Linda Kealey, 109–30. Toronto: Women's Press, 1979.

– "Canadian Feminism in the 1920s: The Case of Nellie McClung." *Journal of Canadian Studies* 12 (Summer 1977): 58–68.

– "Discovering the Home: The Last 150 Years of Domestic Work in Canada." In *Women's Paid and Unpaid Work*, ed. Paula Bourne, 35–60. Toronto: New Hogtown Press, 1985.

– "Ever a Crusader: Nellie McClung First Wave Feminist." In *Re-thinking Canada*, ed. Veronica Strong-Boag and Anita Clair Fellman, 178–90. Toronto: Copp Clark, 1986.

– "The Girl of the New Day: Canadian Working Women in the 1920's." *Labour/Le Travailleur* 4 (1979): 131–64.

– "Home Dreams: Women and the Suburban Experiment in Canada, 1945–60." *Canadian Historical Review* 72 (1991): 471–504.

– Introduction to *In Times Like These*, by Nellie McClung. 1915. Reprint, Toronto: University of Toronto Press, 1972.

– "Keeping House in God's Country: Canadian Women at Work in the Home." In *On the Job*, ed. Craig Heron and Robert Storey, 124–51. Montreal and Kingston: McGill-Queen's University Press, 1986.

– *The New Day Recalled: The Lives of Girls and Women in English Canada, 1919–1939*. Toronto: Copp Clark Pitman, 1988.

– *The Parliament of Women: The National Council of Women of Canada, 1893–1929*. National Museum of Man Series no. 18. Ottawa: National Museum of Man, 1976.

- "Peace-Making Women: Canada 1919–1939." In *Women and Peace*, ed. Ruth Roach Pierson, 170–91. London: Croom Helm, 1987.
- "Pulling in Double Harness or Hauling a Double Load: Women, Work and Feminism on the Canadian Prairie." *Journal of Canadian Studies* 21 (Fall 1986): 32–52.
- "'Setting the Stage': National Organization and the Women's Movement in the Late Nineteenth Century." In *The Neglected Majority*, ed. Susan Mann Trofimenkoff and Alison Prentice, 87–103. Toronto: McClelland and Stewart, 1977.
- "'Wages for Housework': Mothers' Allowance and the Beginnings of Social Security in Canada." *Journal of Canadian Studies* 14 (Spring 1979): 24–34.
Strong-Boag, Veronica, and Anita Clair Fellman, eds. *Re-thinking Canada: The Promise of Women's History.* 2d. ed. Toronto: Copp Clark Pitman, 1991.
Strong-Boag, Veronica, and Katheryn McPherson. "The Confinement of Women: Childbirth and Hospitalization in Vancouver, 1919–1939." In *Delivering Motherhood*, ed. Katherine Arnup, Andrée Lévesque and Ruth Pierson, 75–107. London: Routledge, 1990.
Stuart, H.H. "Socialism in Eastern Canada." *Weekly People*, 24 February 1906.
Stuart, Richard Grey. "The Early Political Career of Angus MacInnis." Master's thesis, University of British Columbia, 1970.
Sutherland, Neil. "'I Can't Recall When I Didn't Help': The Working Lives of Pioneering Children in Twentieth-Century British Columbia." *Histoire Sociale/Social History* 48 (November 1981): 263–88.
- "'We Always Had Things to Do': The Paid and Unpaid Work of Anglophone Children between the 1920s and the 1960s." *Labour/Le Travail* 25 (Spring 1990): 105–41.
Swyripa, Frances. *Ukrainian Canadians: A Survey of Their Portrayal in English-Language Works.* Edmonton, Alta: University of Alberta Press, 1978.
- "The Ukrainian Image: Loyal Citizen or Disloyal Alien." In *Loyalties in Conflict*, ed. Frances Swyripa and John Herd Thompson, 47–68. Edmonton: Canadian Institute of Ukrainian Studies, 1983.
Swyripa, Frances, and John Herd Thompson, eds. *Loyalties in Conflict: Ukrainians in Canada during the Great War.* Edmonton: Canadian Institute of Ukrainian Studies, 1983.
Synge, J. "Young Working Class Women in Early 20th Century Hamilton: Their Work and Family Lives." In *Proceedings*, Workshop Conference on Blue Collar Workers and Their Communities, ed. A.H. Turritin. York University, 10–11 April 1975.

Tadeusz, Adam K. "Canadian Socialism and the Origin of the CPC, 1900–1922." Master's thesis, McMaster University, 1980.

Tax, Meridith. *The Rising of the Women: Feminist Solidarity and Class Conflict, 1880–1917.* New York: Monthly Review Press, 1980.

Taylor, Barbara. *Eve and the New Jerusalem: Socialism and Feminism in the Nineteenth Century.* London: Virago Press, 1983.

Taylor, Georgina. "Gender and the History of the Left: Review Article." *Saskatchewan History* 44 (Winter 1992): 31–4.

Tennyson, B. "Premier Hearst, the War and Votes for Women." *Ontario History* 57, no. 3 (1965): 115–22.

Thomas, John D. "Servants of the Church: Canadian Methodist Deaconess Work, 1890–1926." *Canadian Historical Review* 65, no. 3 (1984): 371–95.

Thompson, Dorothy. "Women and Nineteenth Century Radical Politics: A Left Dimension." In *The Rights and Wrongs of Women*, ed. Juliet Mitchell and Anne Oakley, 112–38. Harmondsworth, U.K.: Penguin Books, 1976.

Thompson, Joanne Emily. "The Influence of Dr. Emily Howard Stowe on the Woman Suffrage Movement in Canada." *Ontario History* 54 (December 1962): 253–66.

Thompson, John Herd. "The Beginnings of Our Regeneration: The Great War and Western Canadian Reform Movements." Canadian Historical Association, *Historical Papers* (1972): 227–45.

– "The Enemy Alien and the Canadian General Election of 1917." In *Loyalties in Conflict*, ed. Frances Swyripa and John Herd Thompson, 25–46. Edmonton: Canadian Institute of Ukrainian Studies, 1983.

Thompson, John Herd, and Allan Seager. *Canada 1922–1939: Decades of Discord.* Toronto: McClelland and Stewart, 1985.

Thompson, Maud. "The Value of Woman's Work." *International Socialist Review* 10 (December 1909): 513–23.

Tillotson, Shirley. "The Operators along the Coast: A Case Study of the Link between Gender, Skilled Labour and Social Power, 1900–1930." *Acadiensis* 20 (Autumn 1990): 72–88.

– "We May All Soon Be 'First-Class Men': Gender and Skill in Canada's Early Twentieth-Century Urban Telegraph Industry." *Labour/Le Travail* 27 (Spring 1991): 97–125.

Trimberger, Ellen Kay. "Women in the Old and New Left: The Evolution of a Politics of Personal Life." *Feminist Studies* 5 (Fall 1979): 432–50.

Trofimenkoff, Susan Mann. "Feminist Biography." *Atlantis* 10 (Spring 1985): 1–10."

– "Henri Bourassa and 'The Woman Question.'" In *The Neglected Majority*, ed. Susan Mann Trofimenkoff and Alison Prentice, 104–15. Toronto: McClelland and Stewart, 1977.

– "One Hundred and Two Muffled Voices: Canada's Industrial Women in the 1880's." In *Canada's Age of Industry, 1849–1896*, ed. Michael Cross and G. Kealey, 212–29. Toronto: McClelland and Stewart, 1982.

Trofimenkoff, Susan Mann, and Alison Prentice, eds. *The Neglected Majority: Essays in Canadian Women's History*. Toronto: McClelland and Stewart, 1977.

Troop, G.R.F. "Socialism in Canada." Master's thesis, McGill University, 1922.

Tupper, Mila Maynard. "Woman Suffrage as Observed by a Socialist." *International Socialist Review* 5 (January 1905): 385–8.

Tyler, Robert L. "I.W.W. in the Pacific North West: Rebels of the Woods." *Oregon Historical Quarterly* 55 (1954): 3–44.

Tyrell, Ian. *Woman's World, Woman's Empire: The WCTU in International Perspective, 1880–1930*. Chapel Hill: University of North Carolina Press, 1991.

Usiskin, Rosaline. "Continuity and Change: The Jewish Experience in Winnipeg's North End, 1900–1914." *Canadian Jewish Historical Society Journal* 4 (Spring 1980): 71–94.

Valverde, Mariana. *The Age of Light, Soap and Water: Moral Reform in English Canada, 1885–1925*. Toronto: McClelland and Stewart, 1991.

– "Catalan and British Cotton Mill Workers: A Comparative Study of Gender, Skill and Mechanization." Unpublished paper presented to the Social Science History Association, New Orleans, 1 November 1987.

– "'Giving the Female a Domestic Turn': The Social, Legal and Moral Regulation of Women's Work in British Cotton Mills, 1820–1950." *Journal of Social History* 21 (June 1988): 619–34.

– "Love of Finery: Fashion and the Fallen Woman in Nineteenth Century Social Discourse." *Victorian Studies* 32 (Winter 1989): 169–88.

– "Poststructuralist Gender Historians: Are We Those Names?" *Labour/Le Travail* 25 (Spring 1990): 227–36.

Vickers, Jill. "The Intellectual Origins of the Women's Movements in Canada." In *Challenging Times*, ed. Constance Backhouse and David Flaherty, 39–60. Montreal: McGill-Queen's University Press, 1992.

Voisey, Paul. "The 'Votes for Women' Movement." *Alberta History* 23 (Summer 1975): 10–23.

Wade, Susan. "Helena Gutteridge: Votes for Women and Trade Unions." In *In Her Own Right*, ed. Barbara Latham and Cathy Kess, 187–203. Victoria, B.C.: Camosun College, 1980.

Walkowitz, Judith. "Patrolling the Borders: Feminist Historiography and the New Historian." *Radical History Review* 43 (Winter 1989): 23–43.

– "The Politics of Prostitution." *Signs* 6 (1980): 123–35.

Walling, William English, ed. *The Socialists and the War.* New York: Garland Publications, 1972.

Walsh, Susan. "The Peacock and the Guinea Hen: Political Profiles of Dorothy Gretchen Steeves and Grace McInnis." In *Not Just Pin Money,* ed. Barbara Latham and Roberta Pazdro, 365–77. Victoria, B.C.: Camosun College, 1984.

Warne, R.R. "Nellie McClung and Peace." In *Up and Doing,* ed. Janice Williamson and Deborah Gorham, 35–47. Toronto: Women's Press, 1989.

Webster, Daisy. *Growth of the N.D.P. in B.C., 1900–1970: Eighty-one Political Biographies.* N.p., n.d.

Weinrich, Peter. *Social Protest from the Left in Canada, 1870–1970.* Toronto: University of Toronto, 1982.

Wells, H.G. *Socialism and the Family.* London, 1906.

Weppler, Doreen Madge. "Early Forms of Political Activity among White Women in British Columbia, 1880–1925." Master's thesis, Simon Fraser University, 1971.

White, Julie. *Women and Unions.* Ottawa: Canadian Advisory Council on the Status of Women, 1980.

Whittaker, Jo Ann. "The Search for Legitimacy: Nurses Registration in British Columbia, 1915–1935." In *Not Just Pin Money,* ed. Barbara Latham and Roberta Pazdro, 314–26. Victoria, B.C.: Camosun College, 1984.

Williamson, Janice, and Deborah Gorham, ed. *Up and Doing: Canadian Women and Peace.* Toronto: Women's Press, 1989.

Wilson, Donald J., and Jorgen Dahlie. "Introduction: Ethnic Radicals." *Canadian Ethnic Studies* 10, no. 2 (1978): 1–8.

Wilson, Donald J., "The Canadian Sojourn of a Finnish-American Radical." *Canadian Ethnic Studies* 16, no. 2 (1984): 102–15.

– "The Finnish Organization of Canada, the 'Language Barrier' and the Assimilation Process." *Canadian Ethnic Studies* 9, no. 2 (1977): 105–16.

– "Finns in British Columbia before the First World War." *Polyphany* 3 (Fall 1981): 55–64.

– "Matti Kurikka and A.B. Makela: Socialist Thought among the Finns in Canada, 1900–1932." *Canadian Ethnic Studies* 10, no. 2 (1978): 9–21.

– "'Never Believe What You Have Never Doubted': Matti Kurikka's Dream for a New World Utopia." In *Finnish Diaspora. I: Canada, South America, Africa, Australia and Sweden,* ed. Michael G. Karni, 131–53. Toronto: Multicultural History Society of Ontario, 1981.

"Women at the Convention." *International Socialist Review* 8, no. 12 (June 1908): 782–3.

Woodcock, George. "Harmony Island: A Canadian Utopia." In *British Columbia: A Centennial Anthology*, ed. R.E. Watters, 206–13. Toronto: McClelland and Stewart, 1958.

Woodsworth, J.S., *My Neighbour*. 1911. 2d ed., with introduction by Richard Allen. Toronto: University of Toronto Press, 1972.

– *Strangers within Our Gates*. Toronto, 1909.

Woywitka, Anne B. "A Pioneer Woman in the Labour Movement." *Alberta History* 26 (Winter 1978): 10–16.

Wright, Sir Almroth. *Suffrage Fallacies*. Pamphlet of letter reprinted from the *Times*, 28 March 1912. London: John Parkinson Bland, 1912.

Wright, Cynthia. "Feminine Trifles of Vast Importance: Writing Gender into the History of Consumption." *Gender Conflicts*, ed. F. Iacovetta and M. Valverde, 229–60. Toronto: University of Toronto Press, 1992.

Wrigley, G. Weston. "Socialism in Canada." *International Socialist Review* 1 (May 1900): 685–9.

Yee, May. "Chinese Canadian Women: Our Common Struggle." In *British Columbia Reconsidered*, ed. Gillian Creese and Veronica Strong-Boag, 233–43. Vancouver: Press Gang, 1992.

Index

laundry workers, 91–2,
96–7
Lestor, Ruth, 25–7, 139–
40
Levien, Sonya, 154
Lucifer, 113, 199n27

McClung, Nellie, 142,
151–2
MacDonald, Mrs Ramsay,
31
MacGill, Mrs, 38
McKenzie, D.G., 44, 138–
9
male domination, 11, 36,
138
Manitoba, 82, 85, 88–9,
117, 157, 158
Manley, John, 181n7
Maritimes, 7, 27–8, 136,
148
marriage, 64–5; destruc-
tion of, 112; women
and, 15–16, 37. *See
also* sexual relations
masculine imagery, 24, 43
maternal feminism, 9–10,
17, 19–20, 169, 171;
domestic labour and, 53–
4; and war, 160–4; and
women's suffrage, 146–
7. *See also* feminism
Merrill, Bertha. *See*
Burns, Bertha Merrill
Methodists, 24–5, 163
minimum wage, 107
monogamy, 111
Montreal, 50
Moral and Social Reform
councils, 121
morality, 82, 93, 98–9,
103–4, 126–7
moral reform. *See* social
purity reformers
mothers: advice to, 59;
dependence of, 105;
under socialism, 67, 71–
2; state support of, 67,
75–6, 154; wage-earning,
26, 99–100, 103, 107;
and war, 153–5

Mushkat, Sophie, 27–9

Napolitano, Mrs, 120
National Committee for
the Suppression of the
White Slave Trade, 121
National Council of
Women, 21, 121; and
suffrage, 151; on wage-
earning women, 82
Norton, Mary, 37–8
Noxon, Mr, 93
nurses, 24, 103

O'Brien, C.M., 97
O'Hare, Kate Richards,
130
Ontario socialists, 45–6,
142–3
Osborne, J.B., 48

pacifism, 156, 160–4
Pankhurst, Mrs, 151, 159
Pettipiece, R.P., 60–1
Place, Jack, 148, 149
political activism: editing
party papers, 49; family
influences on, 37, 39;
fund raising, 29, 47,
50; hospitality, 47, 48–
9; organizing, 46, 49–
50; participation rates,
14–15; public speaking,
28, 50–1; selling party
papers, 49; speaking
tours, 28–9; women's
meetings, 14, 37, 45,
84, 157; writing, 49
Political Equality League,
159
Prager, Gustav, 86–7
Prentice, Alison, 8
Prentor, Mrs, 157
Pritchard, William, 151–
2, 153–4, 155
Progressive Woman, 67,
84, 101
prohibition. *See* temperance
prostitution, 104, 116–31,
153; across Canada,

117–20, 122, 130, 160;
and factory work, 98;
and marriage, 131; and
suffrage, 145; and
wages, 122–3, 125–6,
130; and war, 153, 160
protective legislation, 81,
97, 107
public spaces, 37, 50

Quebec, 47, 50, 89, 91,
103, 118, 119, 121,
122, 130, 149, 157

race suicide, 100–1, 114–
16
racism, 9, 10, 21, 42–3,
89, 92–3, 94, 114–15;
prostitution and, 118–
20; suffrage and, 141;
war and, 166
reproduction: work and,
81–2
Revolutionary Socialist
Party, 136
Roberts, Barbara, 211n42
Roberts, Wayne, 9
Robutchyi Narod, 49
Roman Catholic Church,
24, 74
Russian Revolution, 164

Salvation Army, 24–5, 88
Sanford, Mrs, 88–9
Sanger, Margaret, 111
Saskatchewan, 160
Scott, Mrs, 140–1
"sex question," 110–35
sex radicals, 111–14
sexual autonomy, 111,
116, 134–5, 169
sexuality, 128–34
sexual relations: capitalists and, 124–5, 128,
130; in marriage, 111,
131–2, 134–5; war
and, 153–5, 160;
working-class men and,
125–30
Shier, William, 44,
177n42, 180n72